ABOUT THE EDITORS

Jacob Rader Marcus is the Distinguished Service Professor of American Jewish History at the Hebrew Union College-Jewish Institute of Religion, Cincinnati, Ohio.

Abraham J. Peck is the Administrative Director of the American Jewish Archives on the campus of the Hebrew Union College-Jewish Institute of Religion in Cincinnati, Ohio.

THE AMERICAN RABBINATE

A Century of Continuity and Change;
1883-1983

THE AMERICAN RABBINATE

A Century of Continuity and Change;
1883-1983

Edited by
JACOB RADER MARCUS
and
ABRAHAM J. PECK

With contributions by
JEFFREY S. GUROCK
ABRAHAM J. KARP
DAVID POLISH
JONATHAN D. SARNA

KTAV PUBLISHING HOUSE, INC.
HOBOKEN, NEW JERSEY

BM
652
.A43
1985

Library of Congress Cataloging in Publication Data

Main entry under title:

The American rabbinate.

 "The articles in this volume originally appeared in
the November 1983 issue of American Jewish archives"—
T.p. verso.
  Bibliography: p.
  Includes index.
  1. Rabbis—United States—Office. 2. Orthodox
Judaism—United States—History. 3. Conservative
Judaism—United States—History. 4. Reform Judaism—
United States—History. I. Marcus, Jacob Rader,
1896-   . II. Peck, Abraham J. III. Gurock,
Jeffrey S., 1949-   . IV. American Jewish archives.

BM652.A43   1985   296.6'1'0973   85-5600
ISBN 0-88125-076-7

MANUFACTURED IN THE UNITED STATES OF AMERICA

Contents

Preface

The year 1983 marked the one hundredth anniversary of the first ordination of rabbis from the Hebrew Union College in Cincinnati. Equally important, that special ordination day also marked the beginning of an American-trained rabbinate, one which continues today to provide the spiritual leadership for an American Judaism.

Much has occurred within the American rabbinate since the warm, sultry day of July 11, 1883, when over fifteen hundred people crowded into the Plum Street Temple of K. K. Bnai Yeshurun to witness the ordination of "the first fruits of the American harvest," as the president of the Hebrew Union College's Board of Governors called them.

The editors are pleased to present "the first fruits" of another harvest—that of investigating the historical development of the American rabbinate over the past one hundred years. The three essays as well as the comprehensive introduction in this volume will, we hope, initiate an important new area of scholarly research and publication within the broader field of American Jewish history.

Our authors have approached the study of the American rabbinate during the past century with the critical eye of the historian, seeking to understand change within it as epitomized by the famous remark of Rabbi Solomon Schechter to one of his pupils that "from now on, no one can be a rabbi in America who does not know how to play baseball as well as study Talmud."

At the same time, we have asked our authors to trace the thread of continuity which, after all, also marks the historical process. Indeed, as Rabbi Mordecai Waxman has noted, the American rabbi—whether Orthodox, Conservative, or Reform—still deals with a millennial tradition and with an ancient institution and body of learning, the synagogue and the Torah. And because the major concern of the American rabbinate has been the preservation of American Jewry and Judaism, what emerges from these essays is the hope and the feeling that despite change and challenge the basic ideals which have characterized the American rabbinate for a century will remain constant.

Cincinnati, Ohio   Jacob Rader Marcus
December, 1984   Abraham J. Peck

Introduction

Jonathan D. Sarna

Scholars have, to date, written far more about the history of the rabbinate in ancient and medieval times than about the history of the rabbinate in the United States of America. There are, to be sure, important sociological studies of the American rabbinate, as well as several valuable biographies, sketches of rabbis in individual communities, books and articles written by rabbis based on their own experiences, and some good and bad novels.[1] But no full-scale work detailing the history of the American rabbinate as it changed over time exists. This volume devoted to the history of the American rabbinate thus represents an important first, a pioneering voyage through uncharted historical waters.

Just a century ago, Hebrew Union College began a process that would, in a short while, dramatically change the whole character of the American rabbinate. It made available for the first time a steady supply of American-trained, English-speaking rabbis to serve this country's growing number of pulpits. With this, the era of European-trained rabbis in America drew to a close. Just a few years later, indeed by the turn of the century, America was producing native-trained rabbis of every sort: some ordained at Hebrew Union College, some at the more traditional Jewish Theological Seminary, established in 1887, and some at the even more traditional Rabbi Isaac Elchanan Theological Seminary (later merged into Yeshiva University), incorporated in 1897.

The essays contained in this volume describe the shape of the American rabbinate in the wake of this new era. Jeffrey S. Gurock, tracing the history of the Orthodox rabbinate in America, opens with two significant events of the late 1880's: the establishment of the Jewish Theological Seminary of America, to train rabbis in "a spirit of fidelity and devotion to the Jewish law," and the almost simultaneous establishment of the Association of American Orthodox Hebrew Congregations, "to encourage, foster and promote the observance of the Orthodox Jewish religion . . . [and] to designate, support and maintain a Chief Rabbi." Both developments adumbrated Orthodoxy's increasing presence on the American scene, but as Gurock points out, there the similarity ends. For the Seminary, though Orthodox, was the institutional expression of Westernized Jews already familiar with secular culture, and concerned to steer a middle course between Radical Reform Judaism on the one hand, and East European Orthodox Judaism on the other. The association, by contrast, and more particularly the chief rabbi it selected, Rabbi Jacob Joseph of Vilna, sought to recreate East European Orthodox patterns in America by imposing a centralized rabbinic authority, and by strengthening immigrants' observance of ritual commandments. In a word, the chief rabbi represented *resistance* to America, an unwillingness to succumb to the secular tendencies and modern mores which the surrounding culture sought to impose. The Seminary, meanwhile, represented *accommodation* to America, a desire to be traditional and modern at the same time.

This tension between resisters and accommodators lies at the heart of Gurock's pathbreaking analysis. Stressing diversity within the Orthodox movement—a diversity he associates with different rabbis' divergent backgrounds, training, institutional affiliations, and personal attitudes—he limns the key figures and institutions within the Orthodox rabbinate. As he sees it, resisters have always aimed to reinvigorate rabbinic authority, to lead Jews back toward greater observance of traditional Jewish law, and to counter Americanization. Accommodators have at the same time sought what he describes as simulation of American religious norms, inclusion of as broad a range of Orthodox Jews as possible, and cooperation with non-Orthodox Jews on matters of general Jewish concern. Each side boasts leaders, institutions, and house organs, and each insists that Judaism generally and Orthodoxy in particular can best survive if its particular path is followed.

Gurock realizes that his two categories cover a broad range. One might indeed argue that he is really describing a spectrum of Orthodoxy, with full accommodation on the left, utter resistance on the right, and Orthodox rabbis of various shades ranged along different points of the intervening continuum. The same continuum, with only descriptions changed, could be used to describe the leadership of a great many ethnic and religious groups, for the tension between accommodation and resistance—what in other contexts might be called assimilation and identity—is a pervasive one in America, leaders being no less divided on the subject than their followers.[2]

Abraham J. Karp seeks the roots of Conservative Judaism back before the rise of late-nineteenth-century rabbinical schools. Uncertainties regarding definition, however, emerged equally early. Some rabbis occasionally called "Conservative" in their lifetimes—including Isaac Mayer Wise—would hardly be seen as Conservative today. Others, including many of the founders of the Jewish Theological Seminary, shaped Conservative Judaism, but continued to call themselves Orthodox. In short, from the very beginning, Conservative rabbis suffered from the crisis of identity that Professor Karp finds characteristic of the Conservative rabbinate for the next hundred years: torn between "an ancient tradition and the modern world."

This split between "traditionalists" and "progressives" has a familiar ring given Professor Gurock's essay. But if the basic tension is similar, two critical differences must not be overlooked. First of all, Conservative rabbis were operating from a somewhat different premise than their Orthodox counterparts, for as Karp points out they were institutionally committed to a definition of Judaism that included the words "evolving religious civilization of the Jewish people"—words that rendered change legitimate, and frequently put tradition on the defensive. Second, Conservative rabbis were almost all bound by a common tie to the Jewish Theological Seminary. This gave them an institutional allegiance and a powerful unifying symbol that Orthodox rabbis could not duplicate. Perhaps because the Seminary sent its rabbis out into the world fitted, to use Karp's felicitous metaphor, both with roots and with wings, it was better able to contain within itself the tension which in Orthodoxy came so often into the open. In Conservative Judaism, both traditionalist and progressive rabbis could lay claim to harboring the true spirit of the movement, and Seminary professors would back them up.

Moving beyond ideology, Karp describes in his essay the burgeoning functional problems faced by Conservative rabbis. With increasing demands made upon them from all sources, unending conflicts arose between the various rabbinic roles of preacher, teacher, administrator, pastor, ecclesiastical functionary, participant in communal affairs, participant in national affairs, and sometime lecturer and writer.

Additional problems arose when rabbis sought to pursue scholarship on the side, and when obligations due their congregants clashed with their familial obligations. Not that these problems were necessarily unique to rabbis from the Conservative movement, but as Karp points out, the movement's peculiar situation did accentuate them:

> The Orthodox rabbi preached on Saturday morning, the Reform on Friday, the Conservative on both. . . . The Orthodox dealt with *B'nai Mitzvah*, the Reform with Confirmants, the Conservative with both. The Conservative rabbi would meet his Orthodox colleague at meetings of the Day School and the *Vaad Ha-kashrut*, but not the Reform, whom he would see at meetings of the Ministerial Association and the Committee on Religion and Race, both of which were outside the realm of interest of the Orthodox.

At least in Karp's view, the Conservative rabbi has always had the hardest job of all.

Finally, Karp points in his essay to an ongoing dispute within the Conservative rabbinate (and not there alone!) between the demands of the "calling" and the demands of the "profession". This tension, similar to that described by Ahad Ha'am as between prophet and priest, underscores the dichotomy between the idealism of rabbis eager to strengthen Judaism and improve the spiritual condition of their flock, and the pragmatic demands of the laity who evaluate rabbis on the basis of how well they perform their various occupational functions. An aspiring sense of mission and an ardent desire to do what is Jewishly right pulls rabbis in one direction. A down-to-earth eagerness for job security and a practical need to keep their congregations happy pulls them in the other. Rabbis must try and steer a middle course, a route that can never quite be satisfying. And yet, as Karp concludes from his survey data and long personal association with his fellow Conservative rabbis, even the dissatisfied are not necessarily unhappy, for the rewards of the rabbinical profession remain great.

David Polish, looking at the history of Reform rabbis in America, finds that as was the case in Orthodox and Conservative Judaism, so too in Reform the theme of tradition and change has loomed large, casting its shadow over many issues. But where in Orthodox and Conservative debates tradition always meant classical rabbinic tradition, Reform rabbis have seen tradition also in terms of a Reform Jewish tradition developed in Germany and expressed in nineteenth-century

Reform rabbinical conferences and writings. Both the Pittsburgh Platform of 1885 and the first annual convention of the Central Conference of American Rabbis explicitly linked American developments to those in Germany. Many nineteenth-century Reform rabbis were German-trained, and looked to Germany for guidance much the way their Orthodox counterparts later looked to Eastern Europe.

The issue of Zionism, which Polish examines in detail, represented a deviation from classical Reform tradition. In that sense, it served as a functional equivalent of issues such as mixed seating, which precipitated Conservative and Orthodox debates over tradition and change. At the same time, as Polish realizes, the Zionism debate in the Reform rabbinate was as much a symbolic issue as a substantive one. Zionism, for many, had become a code word, representing far-reaching changes in Reform ideology and practice. The revitalization of various time-honored forms and ceremonies, advocated by some change-minded pro-Zionist rabbis, implied an abandonment of classical Reform traditions. This challenge pitted Reform Judaism's two lines of tradition against one another, creating strains in the Reform rabbinate and laity that continue to the present day.

In discussing how the Reform movement has changed since the Pittsburgh Platform, Polish discusses two themes in the history of the Reform rabbinate that merit special attention. First, he points to the ongoing dialectic between universalism and particularism that has characterized the Reform movement since its founding. Spurred by their reading of the prophets, their belief in Judaism's mission, and their assumption that any improvement in general society would redound to the benefit of the Jew, Reform rabbis have often played a vital role in general movements for social reform, good government, and civil rights. But support for these universalistic causes has never been unanimous; always, there have been those who insist that rabbis should concern themselves first and foremost with matters of Jewish concern, such as Israel and the plight of Jews in distress. In recent years, these latter voices have had a pronounced influence, but the debate continues, as Polish's analysis of Reform rabbinic resolutions amply demonstrates.

Second, Polish notes that Reform rabbis have always been torn between their desire for unity, if not authority, and their simultaneous insistence on rabbinic freedom. On the one hand, Reform rabbis have almost all shared both a common training ground (particularly since the merger of Hebrew Union College with the Jewish Institute of Religion) and a common rabbinic organization (the Central Conference of American Rabbis). On the other hand, as Polish's review of Reform rabbis and the intermarriage question makes clear, they have resolutely refused to accept the dictates of either, be it on matters of congregational policy or of conscience. As in the Conservative movement, shared institutions have by and large managed so far to contain fierce differences between Reform rabbis of divergent persuasions. Indeed, the Centenary Perspective of the Central Conference of American Rabbis, adopted in 1976, makes a virtue of diversity, resolutely declaring that:

> Reform Judaism does more than tolerate diversity; it engenders it. In our uncertain historical situation we must expect to have far greater diversity than previous generations knew. . . . While we may differ in our interpretation and application of the ideas enunciated here, we accept such differences as precious and see in them Judaism's best hope for confronting whatever the future holds for us. Yet in all our diversity we perceive a certain unity and we shall not allow our differences in some particulars to obscure what binds us together.[3]

Such diversity amidst overarching unity, familiar from the secular polity, may not engender harmony. But it does, according to Polish, reflect the needs of the hour, for "in a time of such Jewish upheaval . . . neat and orderly denominational structures are neither feasible nor desirable."

Many common themes run through all three of these essays. Regardless of whether one looks at the history of Orthodox, Conservative, or Reform rabbis, one finds traditionalists locking horns with modernists, rabbinic roles expanding, and everyone expressing great concern about Jewish youth and Judaism's future. Disputes over such things as rabbinic authority, professional standards, and relations with outsiders, Jews and non-Jews, as well as tensions between rabbis and laymen, and more recently between rabbis and Jewish community professionals also feature across the denominational spectrum, affiliational differences notwithstanding. And everywhere, of course, the tacit influence of American religious norms holds sway, and with it the knowledge that rabbis must, at least to some extent, be "Jewish ministers," for that is what their congregants have come to expect. Indeed, for all of the many issues that divide them, practicing rabbis as a group do clearly form a single profession. Functionally speaking, they resemble one another far more than they resemble the traditional *rabbonim* of centuries past.

This fact—the emergence of an American rabbinic profile—is a development of enormous importance that proceeded along, hardly noticed, side by side with the denominational developments discussed in these essays. How this rabbinic profile took shape cannot be detailed here. Certainly, its roots reach far back, at least as far back as Gershom Seixas (1746–1816), who led New York's Congregation Shearith Israel for almost half a century, and Isaac Leeser (1806–1868), whose long rabbinic career in Philadelphia had a far-reaching influence. Both men assumed new and broader rabbinic roles, both introduced vernacular sermons into their synagogues, and both participated actively in their home communities, touching Jews and non-Jews alike.[4] Seixas and Leeser, however, were exceptions, men ahead of their time. The professionalization of the rabbinate in the form that we know it today, complete with selective training schools, formal organizations, standard uniforms, and bureaucratic rules took place later, beginning at the end of the nineteenth century—just at the time when so many other professions in America were first emerging.[5] As the American rabbinate became increasingly native-trained, the prototypical American rabbi began to be seen in more and more communities.

Related to professionalization, another momentous change also worked to transform the American rabbinate. This one took place at the community level, where rabbis began to be perceived in a new way, as men of status. In the nineteenth century, when most rabbis were immigrants and many neither acculturated nor learned English, American Jews grew accustomed, as Marcus Jastrow put it, "to look upon their ministers as those who are good for any service required but otherwise should be as much as possible excluded from active representation in public affairs."[6] Many Jews felt ashamed to display their rabbis in public, fearing that they would suffer by comparison with Christians. Anti-clericalism became quite common in Jewish circles.

With the development of American rabbinical schools (all of which functioned, to some extent, as finishing schools), and the increasing availability of native-trained rabbis, we have seen that a new era be-

gan. Rabbis increasingly became "representative Jews," visible symbols of those values which American Jews held dear.[7] Laymen now
welcomed rabbinic participation in public affairs; indeed, they took
pride in showing their rabbis off. As a result, as Gurock, Polish, and
especially Karp describe, rabbis took on many new roles and responsi-
bilities.

The sands of time have given rise to even more changes in the American rabbinate, many of them also described in these essays.[8] But questions still remain. What, for example, distinguished rabbis who
emerged on the national scene from those who contented themselves
to be active only in their own communities, or in some cases only in
their own congregations? What factors made for success in these various rabbinates? How have congregations gone about choosing rabbis? What regional variations exist in the American rabbinate? And
what can be learned from comparisons between American rabbis and
their counterparts in Europe, or for that matter their counterparts
among the Christian clergy?

Such questions could be multiplied indefinitely, for the more we
learn about the history of the American rabbinate, the more we realize
how little we really know. But an important start has now been made.
While there is plenty of room for more research, all may build on the
foundations laid here.

Notes

1. See the bibliographies in Norman Linzer ed., *Jewish Communal Services in the United States: 1960–1970* (New York, 1972), pp. 128–248; and Elliot L. Stevens ed., *Rabbinic Authori-ty: Papers Presented Before the Ninety-First Annual Convention of the Central Conference of American Rabbis* (New York, 1982), pp. 111–118.

2. I have expanded on this theme in my "The Spectrum of Jewish Leadership in Ante-Bellum America," *Journal of American Ethnic History* 1 (1982): 59–67.

3. On the Centenary Perspective, see Eugene B. Borowitz, *Reform Judaism Today* (New York, 1983); quote is from p. xxi.

4. Jacob R. Marcus, *The Handsome Young Priest in the Black Gown: The Personal World of Gershom Seixas* (Cincinnnati, 1970); on Leeser see the forthcoming Ph.D. dissertation by Rabbi Lance J. Sussman, as well as Bertram W. Korn, "Isaac Leeser: Centennial Reflections," *American Jewish Archives* 19 (1967): 127–141; Maxwell Whiteman, "Isaac Leeser and the Jews of Phila-delphia," *Publications of the American Jewish Historical Society* 48 (1959): 207–244; and Henry Englander, "Isaac Leeser," *Central Conference of American Rabbis Yearbook* 28 (1918): 213–252.

5. Burton J. Bledstein, *The Culture of Professionalism: The Middle Class and the Development of Higher Education in America* (New York, 1976); Thomas L. Haskell, *The Emergence of Professional Social Science: The American Social Science Association and the Nineteenth Century Crisis of Authority* (Urbana, 1977); Donald M. Scott, *From Office to Profession: The New England Ministry 1750–1850* (Philadelphia, 1978).

6. "Organization of the American Jewish Historical Society . . . On Monday the Seventh Day of June 1892." (typescript, American Jewish Historical Society), p. 64; cf. *New Era* 3 (1873): 49.

7. Jacob Bloom, *The Rabbi as Symbolic Exemplar* (New York, 1972); Charles S. Bernheimer, "The American Jewish Minister and His Work," *Godey's Magazine*, February 1898, pp. 211–214; Salo Baron, "The Image of a Rabbi Formerly and Today," *in Steeled by Adversity* (Philadelphia, 1971), pp. 147–157; cf. Milton C. Sernett, "Behold the American Cleric: The Protestant Minister as 'Pattern Man,' 1850–1900," *Winterthur Portfolio* 8 (1973): 1–18.

8. See also Jacob K. Shankman, "The Changing Role of the Rabbi," in Bertram W. Korn ed., *Retrospect and Prospect* (New York, 1965), pp. 230–251; and Arthur Hertzberg, *Being Jewish in America: The Modern Experience* (New York, 1979), pp. 95–124.

Jonathan D. Sarna is Associate Professor of American Jewish History at the Cincinnati campus of the Hebrew Union College—Jewish Institute of Religion. His latest book is *People Walk on Their Heads: Moses Weinberger's Jews and Judaism in New York.*

Resisters and Accommodators: Varieties of Orthodox Rabbis in America, 1886–1983

Jeffrey S. Gurock

Introduction:
Orthodox Rabbis and Institution Building, 1886–1887

On January 31, 1886, Orthodox Rabbis Sabato Morais of Philadelphia, Abraham Pereira Mendes of Newport, Henry Schneeberger of Baltimore, and Bernard Drachman of New York attended a meeting in the vestry rooms of Manhattan's Spanish-Portuguese Synagogue Shearith Israel hosted by Rabbi Henry Pereira Mendes, minister of that oldest Jewish congregation in America. They were brought together to plan an institutional response to the growth of the American Reform movement. Specifically they were concerned with the emergence of Hebrew Union College as a training center for American rabbis and with the liberal denomination's adoption of its 1885 Pittsburgh Platform, "designed," in the words of one contemporary critic, "to deal a mortal blow to Orthodox Judaism."[1] They were joined at this and subsequent deliberations by, among others, New York Rabbis Alexander Kohut, Aaron Wise, and Henry S. Jacobs, Philadelphia's Marcus Jastrow, and Baltimore's Aaron Bettelheim. The latter clerical figures, though possessed of rabbinical training similar in style to that of their Orthodox colleagues, had by the time of these conclaves publicly articulated, and were perceived as supporting, interpretations of Judaism at variance with contemporary Orthodox teachings. These men also served in congregations which deviated liturgically from Orthodox practice.[2] They represented what later denominational leaders and historians would describe as Conservative Judaism in nineteenth century America.[3] The Jewish Theological Seminary of America was the final product of their cooperative labors; a "Jewish Institute of

Rabbi Samuel Belkin
(1911-1976)
Courtesy Yeshiva University Archives

Rabbi Philip Hillel Klein
(1849-1926)
Courtesy Yeshiva University Archives

Rabbi Bernard Drachman
(1861-1945)

Rabbi Bernard Revel
(1885-1940)
Courtesy Yeshiva University Archives

Rabbi Herschel Schacter
(born 1917)
Courtesy Yeshiva University Archives

Rabbi Israel Miller
(born 1918)
Courtesy Yeshiva University Archives

Rabbi Joseph B. Soloveitchik
(born 1903)
Courtesy Yeshiva University Archives

Rabbi Norman Lamm
(born 1927)
president, Yeshiva University
Courtesy Yeshiva University Archives

Rabbi Jacob Joseph
(1848-1902)

Rabbi Moshe Feinstein
(born 1895)
Courtesy Agudath Israel of America Archives

Rabbi Eliezer Silver
(1882-1968)

Rabbi Yakov Yitchak Ruderman
(born 1899)
Courtesy Agudath Israel of America Archives

Rabbi Joseph Breuer (above)
(1882-1980)
Courtesy Agudath Israel of America Archives

Rabbi Eliyahu Meir Bloch (top, l.)
(1894-1955)
Courtesy Agudath Israel of America Archives

Rabbi Aaron Kotler (left)
(1891-1962)
Courtesy Agudath Israel of America Archives

Rabbi Reuven Grozowsky (below)
(1888-1958)
Courtesy Agudath Israel of America Archives

Learning" which its first president, Sabato Morais, prayed would preserve "Historical and Traditional Judaism . . . by educating, training and inspiring teachers–rabbis who would stand for the 'Torah and Testimony.' " Graduates would use "their knowledge of Jewish learning, literature, history, ideals and Jewish Science" to instruct American Jewry how "to live as a power for human uplift and as a factor in the evolution of world civilization in both Americas."[4]

Institution building was also in the air several blocks south on New York's Lower East Side when just a year later, the Association of American Orthodox Hebrew Congregations met at Norfolk Street's Beis Hamedrash Ha-Gadol to search for a chief rabbi for the city. They were desirous of putting an end to the disorganization and lack of discipline which characterized religious life in the ghetto. Perhaps inspired by the publication that same year of immigrant Rabbi Moses Weinberger's lament on contemporary nonobservance and call for an authoritative religious officialdom as a key solution to the dilemma, this group of Orthodox laymen looked to Western and Eastern European seats of learning both for guidance and ultimately for a candidate. They hoped to find a zealous fighter of uncommon ability who would stop "open and flagrant desecration of the Sabbath, the neglect of dietary laws, and the formation of various shades of Orthodoxy and Reform." Most specifically, "his mission" would be "to remove the stumbling blocks from before our people . . . through his scrupulous supervision with an open eye the *shohatim* and all other matters of holiness." After much deliberation and some politicking on both sides of the Atlantic, an agreement was reached in April 1888 between the association and Rabbi Jacob Joseph of Vilna. Three months later, the downtown community rejoiced when the renowned sage and preacher assumed his post in America.[5]

Central figures in each of these institutional initiatives called themselves Orthodox rabbis.[6] But they shared little in common. The most striking difference between the more traditional element in the Seminary coalition and the chief rabbi chosen by the downtown religious association was their respective educational backgrounds. The East European-born Rabbi Jacob Joseph received the traditional *heder* and yeshiva schooling in his hometown of Krohze, Lithuania, where he showed great promise as a scholar and potential religious leader. His quest for advanced training led him to the Volozin Yeshiva, where he became a disciple of Rabbi Hirsch Leib Berlin and Rabbi Israel Salanter. Rabbi Joseph's homiletic and literary skills made him an accomplished speaker and writer in Hebrew and Yiddish. He was not exposed to formal education in the secular culture of the land of his birth. Not so his Sephardic counterparts, Morais and the Mendeses. A large part of their educational training was not in the world of the rabbis but in the realm of general knowledge. The Italian-born Morais attended the University of Pisa, while the younger, British-born Mendes studied first at University College, London, and then earned a medical degree at the University of the City of New York. Still, from early youth they were destined to become rabbis. Family traditions or, in Morais's case, close association with a leading rabbi of the home country provided the basis for their interest in and training for the Orthodox ministry of Western Europe and finally of America.[7]

On the other hand, the road to the Orthodox rabbinate of American-born Bernard Drachman and Henry W. Schneeberger was by no means preordained. Drachman was born in New York City in 1861 to Galician and Bavarian parents and was raised in Jersey City, New Jersey, in a community which then housed but twenty or thirty Jewish families. By his own account, his earliest experiences in life were "very much like that of any American child in an ordinary American environment." He attended the local public schools and received his primary Jewish education first from a private tutor and later in a small talmud torah. A gifted student in both secular and religious studies, Drachman gained admission to Columbia University from where he graduated in 1882. He was recruited after grade school to be one of the first students at the Emanu-El Theological Seminary. This Reform-run "prep school" was designed "to give youths preliminary training required for the [Reform] rabbinate." "English-speaking rabbis," Drachman later recalled, "were then very rare in America and members of the organization were desirous of supplying this deficiency." Drachman was destined not to fulfill his patrons' expectations, for upon graduation from Columbia and Emanu-El, he shocked the religious school's officials by declaring that while he intended to travel to Germany to study for ordination, it would not be, as planned, at Geiger's Reform *Lehranstalt*, but rather at the more traditional, Frankel-founded Breslau Seminary. Drachman remained at Frankel's institution, which he defined as "in fundamental harmony on the basic concepts of traditional Judaism and its adjustment to modern conditions," and received ordination in 1885. He then returned to New York and began his career as a spiritual leader who "insisted on maintaining the laws and usages of traditional Judaism," possessed both of a rabbinical degree conferred upon him by Dr. Manuel Joel of the Breslau Seminary and of that city's Neue Synagogue and a Ph.D. from the University of Heidelberg.[8]

Henry W. Schneeberger, Drachman's colleague in the American-born rabbinate, was born in 1848, also in New York City. The son of a prosperous merchant from Central Europe, he attended New York's public schools and Columbia Prep before enrolling in the university in 1862. His early religious training also paralleled Drachman's; he received his primary Jewish education from private tutors, among whom was the famous anti-Christian polemicist Professor Selig Newman. Upon graduation from Columbia in 1866, he too set off for Europe, but in his case to study with Rabbi Azriel Hildesheimer, a man who, according to his student, stood for "moderate orthodox views and its conservative principles." Schneeberger dedicated himself to his mentor's philosophy of uniting "an unimpaired culture of the Jewish national religious sciences with a firm and solid fundamental general education . . . to make . . . good Jews and at the same time furnish them with social accomplishments that can make them useful to society." Schneeberger returned to New York in 1871 not only with Hildesheimer's ordination but also with a Ph.D. from the University of Jena.[9]

These differences in training were strongly reflected in the way each rabbi looked at the broader Jewish and general worlds around him. The Sephardic rabbis were raised and educated not only among non-Jews but with Jews of every denomination and ethnic expression. Morais and Mendes were thus inured to interdenominational cooperation when they joined in the establishment of the Seminary. And although their work there was intended to stop Reform theological progress, they still perceived the Cincinnati-led group as an equal partner in community-wide campaigns against common outside threats like the omnipresent missionary problem.[10] Schneeberger and Drachman had even less difficulty working with the forerunners of the American Conservative movement. After all, Schneeberger and his Conservative counterpart Aaron Wise had both been ordained by Hildesheimer, and

Drachman, like Kohut, had been trained at Breslau. And although Wise and Kohut had broken with what Drachman and Schneeberger still defined as Western European Orthodoxy, they were still considered valuable colleagues in the battle for "the harmonious combination of Orthodox Judaism and Americanism which [for Drachman] was the true concept of the ancient faith of Israel."[11] Not surprisingly Drachman and Schneeberger too viewed Reform leaders as allies against outside threats.

Rabbi Jacob Joseph did not share these perceptions. Even if he could accept the legitimacy of the ordination of his more liberal Orthodox associates, he certainly had no time for or interest in those "colleagues" who had broken from the Orthodox fold.[12] From his European background, he knew of but one expression of Judaism, and it was to help save the faith from America that he had come to this country. Sabbath observance, the supervision of kosher meats, and the provision of immigrant children with a Jewish education were all in sorry disarray. He viewed it as his high task to lead a religious renaissance dedicated to the re-creation on voluntary American soil of the traditions left behind in Europe.[13]

Rabbi Jacob Joseph's more Americanized Orthodox counterparts shared his concern for the upgrading of traditional Jewish communal functions. Drachman later became head of an Orthodox Jewish Sabbath Alliance, which endeavored to convince Jewish shopkeepers to close their establishments on Saturday and petitioned the state legislatures to repeal blue laws which undermined the economics of traditional behavior.[14] But the motivation which drove and directed Drachman and his fellows' efforts stemmed from an altogether different understanding of the unique role to be played by Orthodox rabbis in America. They were trained to believe that resistance to modernization, in this case Americanization, was futile, and that any attempt to approximate in this country that which existed in the Old World was destined to fail. It was thus the job of the Orthodox rabbi in America to help his people mediate between their willing acceptance of the demands of acculturation and the increasingly problematic requirements of their ancestral identity. To them alone was given the task of creating a viable, truly American traditionalist alternative to the attractions of reformers. Rabbi Jacob Joseph, to their minds, was not equipped to address these issues.[15]

On a practical level this meant that while Rabbi Jacob Joseph harangued his listeners over their noncommitment to the Sabbath, Drachman worked to change American law to facilitate increased Jewish comfortableness with traditions. And while the East European spent most of his time supervising the meat markets, the Americanized expended their energies primarily in bolstering and modernizing Jewish education.[16] When Rabbi Joseph and his generation of downtowners looked at the *heder*, they would lament the low level of learning achieved by students and bemoaned the pitifully poor salaries paid to *melamdim*.[17] His Americanized counterparts too were appalled by the ineffectiveness of Jewish education, but for them, the solution began with the elimination of the European form of pedagogy and the providing of decent salaries to American-trained Jewish educators, who would teach a traditional Judaism relevant to the needs of new generations.

These categories of difference so apparent here among individuals and groups of rabbis each piously declaring themselves to be Orthodox has continued to characterize that denomination's rabbinate over the last one hundred years.[18] With certain notable exceptions or important subtle variations, training, institutional affiliations, and personal attitudes toward both emerging events and outside organizations have polarized the American Orthodox rabbinate into two camps: resisters and accommodators. The former have attempted to reject acculturation and disdained cooperation with other American Jewish elements, fearing that alliances would work to dilute traditional faith and practice. The latter have accepted the seeming inevitability of Americanization and have joined arms with less-traditional elements in the community so to perpetuate the essence of the ancestral faith. While the central issues facing each generation were different and the relative strength of each point has fluctuated, the basic split within the denomination has remained constant and from all contemporary indications will long endure.

II. The Issue of Immigrant Adjustment

If in 1887 Rabbi Moses Weinberger acknowledged and respected uptown traditional society, and Rabbi Jacob Joseph was at least ambivalent toward Drachman, Mendes, and their cohorts, East European

Orthodox rabbinic opinion by 1902 was decidedly opposed to and strident in its nonrecognition of the Americanized Orthodox rabbinate. On July 29 of that year a group of sixty Orthodox rabbis hailing from Russia, Poland, and Austria-Hungary met in the auditorium of the Machzike Talmud Torah on New York's East Broadway to formalize the creation of the Agudat ha-Rabbanim (Union of Orthodox Rabbis of the United States and Canada).[19] These clerical representatives of immigrant Jewish communities from Montreal, Toronto, Bangor, Omaha, and Denver were summoned to New York by Rabbis Asher Lipman Zarchy, Yehudah Leib Levine, Moses Zebulun Margolies (Ramaz), and Bernard Levinthal of Des Moines, Detroit, Boston, and Philadelphia, respectively. The midwesterners had already, in a circular letter to their colleagues in July 1901, expressed their distress over "the constant desecration of the Torah" and spoke of a divine "obligation to unite and form a union of Orthodox rabbis."[20] The easterners helped concretize this declaration several months later when, in May 1902, they chaired a meeting of predominantly New England–based rabbis at Ramaz's Boston home.[21] There they drew up an agenda of concerns and set a tentative date for a national Orthodox rabbinic conclave for July in New York.[22]

The sobriety of this call was matched only by the somberness of the delegates as the deliberations began. The meeting was convened on the day of Rabbi Jacob Joseph's funeral. The senior rabbi had been a broken man from years of struggle to bring order to immigrant Jewish religious life and died a relatively young man of fifty-nine the very day representatives arrived for the conclave. And yet it seemed somehow appropriate that the business of the rabbis continued through the days of mourning, for theirs was the task of solving through a national organization the same problems which had confounded and, to a great extent, defeated their late, revered teacher.[23]

The assembled rabbis sought means of recalling back to Judaism immigrants and their children who were daily drifting from the faith and practices of the past. Jewish education, they determined, had to be upgraded, individuals and institutions had to be encouraged to observe the Sabbath more punctiliously, kashruth supervision had to be more scrupulously monitored, and the all-too-often-abused marriage and divorce laws had to be upheld. The delegates also declared which individuals were qualified to lead this religious revival by restricting membership to "those rabbis ordained by the well-known scholars of Europe" who were "spiritual leaders of Orthodox congregations in the United States (and Canada)." In addition, all educationally pre-pared candidates had to abide by the association's regulations, which provided, among other stipulations, that no rabbi occupy a pulpit in a city served by a fellow member without the approval of the organiza-tion's executive board. The prevention of encroachment of a different kind was in the delegates' minds when they further resolved that "if an unqualified person settles in a community and poses as a rabbi, the *Agudah* will attempt to quickly influence him to leave. If . . . unsuc-cessful then the annual convention will determine his future."[24]

Under these provisions, three types of self-declared Orthodox rab-bis were to be denied leadership roles in Agudat ha-Rabbanim's ef-forts to reach immigrant generations as well as the mutual aid and charity benefits of organizational ties.

1. *The unqualified rabbi.* The Reverend Samuel Distillator, who advertised his varied talents of *shochet, mohel,* and *mesader kidushin* in local New York newspapers around the turn of the century, typifies the unwanted entrepreneurial rabbi who seemingly served constituen-cies without benefit of clerical certification.[25]

2. *The politically uncooperative rabbi.* It is noteworthy, but not surprising, that at least two of Rabbi Jacob Joseph's contemporaries, Rabbis Hayim Yaacov Widerwitz of Moscow and Joshua Segal, were not charter members of the Agudat ha-Rabbanim. The former was educated "at Hasidic yeshivas" and served in Moscow for fifteen years until 1893, when he settled in New York. His colleague, the so-called Sherpser Rav, arrived in the United States in 1875 and lived out his life in the metropolis. These men were better known by their respective American titles of "Chief Rabbi of the United States" and "Chief Rab-bi of the Congregations of Israel," "counter"-chief rabbis who op-posed Rabbi Jacob Joseph's hegemony, particularly in the area of ko-sher meat supervision, in the 1890's. Men like Widerwitz and Segal were less than beloved to those who had mourned Rabbi Jacob Jo-seph's passing. And for their part, they had little interest in surrender-ing their autonomous authority, including their control of numerous abattoirs and butcher shops, to any ecclesiastical committee.[26]

3. *The American Orthodox rabbi.* By 1902 Rabbis Drachman, Schneeberger, and Mendes had been joined in the Americanized Or-

thodox rabbinate by Western European–trained colleagues Joseph Asher, David Neumark, and Henry S. Morais, and by men like Joseph Hertz, Herman Abramowitz, Julius Greenstone, and Mordecai Kaplan of the first pre-1902 generation of Seminary graduates.[27] None of these clerical figures was invited to join the Agudat ha-Rabbanim. But they were not written out of organizational affiliation because of the place and method of their ordination; the Agudat ha-Rabbanim's own house historian declared in 1902 that "the first students that graduated from there [the Seminary] were full-heartedly for the faith of Israel and its Torah."[28] Their nonacceptance was predicated more directly upon their divergent views on how to best solve the problems articulated by the Agudat ha-Rabbanim and upon their perceived attempt to undermine immigrant confidence in ghetto rabbinic authority.　The Agudat ha-Rabbanim's policy of nonrecognition of and noncooperation with the American Orthodox rabbinate was expressed most emphatically two years after its founding when it announced its opposition to the Union of Orthodox Jewish Congregations of America, a synagogal association founded by Mendes and his Americanized associates just six years earlier.[29]

The Orthodox Union was called into existence in 1898 to protect "Orthodox Judaism whenever occasions arise in civic and social matters . . . and to protest against declarations of Reform rabbis not in accord with the teachings of our Torah."[30] Practically this meant that Drachman, Mendes, and some younger colleagues fought against blue laws, protected the rights of Sabbath observers, advocated the modernization of Jewish educational techniques, and argued that they, far more than the uptown Reform forces, had the best Jewish interests of the immigrants at heart. The Agudat ha-Rabbanim was unimpressed by their activities. To them, the Orthodox Union was a poorly disguised agent of Americanization which preached a synthesis of Jewish and American methods and values which threatened the continuity of the faith. To Agudat ha-Rabbanim minds, Orthodox Union leaders, bereft of their own constituency uptown, where Reform held sway, were sweeping into the ghetto and—not unlike the universally despised Christian missionaries—were seeking to wean East European Jews away from their traditional religious commitments.[31]

The Agudat ha-Rabbanim was probably most disturbed by the union's understanding of and approach to meeting the crisis of turn-of-the-century Jewish education. For the downtown rabbis, the American *heder* and yeshiva system had only to be faulted for its failure to produce scholars who would continue the intensive study of rabbinic law and who would ultimately produce talmudic novellae on American soil. The Jewish community had to be severely chastised for its unwillingness to support these traditional institutions of study. It refused to grant all due respect to the scholars from Europe who labored unnoticed in the intellectual wasteland of America. Probably most Agudat ha-Rabbanim members knew little of their Christian contemporary Hutchins Hapgood's writings on ghetto civilization. But had they read him, they undoubtedly would have agreed with his assessment of the life of "the submerged scholars" of the ghetto, men who "no matter what . . . attainments and qualities" were unknown and unhonored "amid the crowding and material interests of the new world."[32] The Agudat ha-Rabbanim attempted to solve this dilemma by approximating in America the internal conditions which sustained the great East European yeshivas they had left behind. Yiddish, they thus asserted, should be the preferred language of religious instruction, since it is "the language of the children's parents." English would be used only "when necessary," such as in communities where no Yiddish was spoken. The attainment of a solid, albeit separatistic yeshiva education was deemed the goal for all Jewish pupils. Indeed, the Agudat ha-Rabbanim's Yeshiva Committee was called upon to "supervise the . . . subjects taught in the yeshiva . . . lest the students regard the yeshiva simply as a stop over before they pursue advanced secular studies."[33]

Advocates of modern Jewish education shared none of these perceptions or prescriptions. Drachman expressed their position best when he defined the goals of Jewish education as the training of Jewish boys and girls through English-language instruction "to perform all the duties, to think all the thoughts and to feel the emotions which are the historical heritage of those of the household of Israel." This love for the Jewish heritage, he further emphasized, was unobtainable either in the *heder*, through private tutors, or through the all-day Jewish parochial school system. He spoke strongly for what would later be called "released time," an "ideal program" which would reach the disaffected and unaffiliated children of immigrants "during the day when children are awake and interested." But his greatest dream was of an

efficient Jewish after-public-school program, "a great system of Jewish public schools housed in their own buildings and equipped with all
pedagogic requirements to supplement the general public school system." There, of course, the traditions of the past would be transmitted
through the language of the new land.[34]

Agudat ha-Rabbanim leaders also witnessed with great concern the
efforts of Orthodox Union members to modify the trappings and
change the aesthetics of Orthodox synagogue life. It was the American
Orthodox rabbis' perception that a major cause of the disaffection
from Judaism of immigrants and even more of the second generation
was their uncomfortableness with the noisy and undignified landsmanshaft synagogue service. These congregations, linking Jews from
the same hometown or region, offered the opportunity to pray and
socialize in an Old World setting. For Agudat ha-Rabbanim members,
the landsmanshaft synagogue represented the institutional expression
of religious identity steeped in their European traditions.

But Orthodox Union members argued that "landsmanshaft Judaism" was in deep trouble. The immigrant synagogue undeniably
helped succor the newly arrived in encountering America by providing
him with the familiar ritual and social flavor of the other side. However, as the immigrant inevitably progressed in this country, and became
infused with new American mores, this Judaism rooted in what union
people felt was only nostalgia for the past was declared devoid of any
chance of surviving the external societal pressure upon him to live and
act as an American.

The Jewish Endeavor Society (JES), founded in 1901 by the early
students and first rabbis produced by the pre-Schechter Seminary,
sought to address this socioreligious dilemma. As students and later as
ordained rabbis, Herman Abramowitz, Julius Greenstone, and Mordecai M. Kaplan were among those inspired by their teacher Drachman to offer acculturating immigrants on the Lower East Side, and
later on in Harlem and Philadelphia, Jewish educational and cultural
programs and "dignified services" designed to "recall indifferent Jewry back to their ancestral faith." The "young people's synagogues"
established under the auspices of the JES held services on Sabbaths and
holidays, more often than not in the late afternoon, probably to attract
those who had been working until evening on these Jewish holy days.
The society's leaders characterized their services as Orthodox, an as-

sertion clearly buttressed by their use of the traditional prayerbook and their insistence upon the separation of the sexes. But in other ways, the services differed dramatically from those in the landsman-shaft synagogue. Recognizing the growing unfamiliarity of Jews with Hebrew, they instituted supplementary English-language prayers and considered the substitution of English translations for standard prayers. A weekly English sermon on topics related to the American Jewish experience was standard. Congregational singing in English and Hebrew was encouraged. And, of course, all overt signs of commercialism were eliminated from congregational life.[35]

Not surprisingly, these youthful efforts gained the quick and active support of rabbis associated with the Orthodox Union. Henry S. Morais, H. P. Mendes, Joseph M. Asher, David Newmark, and of course Drachman all lectured to the JES membership and taught society-run classes. Indeed the Jewish Endeavor Society could be fairly described during its nearly ten years of existence as the "youth division" of the Orthodox Union.[36]

This new approach to synagogue life was neither rapidly nor universally accepted by downtown society and its rabbinate. The itinerant preachers (*maggidim*) who spoke to crowds of worshippers on Sabbath and holiday afternoons did not appreciate the society's competition for synagogue space. More respected and established Agudat ha-Rabbanim constituents had more profound philosophical differences with the movement and its leader. Foremost was the fear that the infusion of American-style trappings and social activities was simply the first step toward the abandonment of traditional Judaism's theological teachings. Secondly, but almost as important, they were concerned that the leaders of the Orthodox Union, in their zeal to promote their Americanization-Judaism synthesis, consorted with Reform Jews who engaged in similar methods with the purpose of weaning immigrant Jews from their religious past. In April 1904 the Orthodox Union, which supposedly stood for "protest against declarations of Reform rabbis," sat with leaders of the Reform Emanuel Brotherhood, Temple Israel, and the West Side Synagogue to consider a report drafted by the interdenominational Board of Jewish Ministers to coordinate the endeavors of the several young people's synagogues which had sprung up since 1900. In the Agudat ha-Rabbanim's view, the Orthodox Union was at best lending unfortunate recognition to deviationist Jewish movements and at worst threatening the continuity of the faith through cooperation with the liberals.[37]

The Agudat ha-Rabbanim's nonrecognition of the Orthodox Union also led to the seemingly unnecessary duplication of efforts on issues of common concern. Rampant nonobservance of the Sabbath, for example, was a problem which exercised traditionalist leaders of all stripes. The Agudat ha-Rabbanim placed Sabbath preservation beside educational improvement as its highest communal priority and maintained a standing Sabbath Committee "to strengthen its observance among our people." The Orthodox Union also spoke out both institutionally and individually for the cause. Drachman specifically served for more than a quarter century as president of the Jewish Sabbath Observers Association, founded in 1894. But there is no evidence of the Agudat ha-Rabbanim and the union working together to promote the Sabbath cause during the organizations' first generation of activity.[38]

This evident lack of teamwork, however, did not lead to large-scale waste through the duplication of communal energies. The Agudat ha-Rabbanim and the Orthodox Union each attacked the problem somewhat differently, reflecting their own unique understandings of the functions of the Orthodox rabbinate in leading the immigrant community. Downtown leaders perceived as a prime concern the identification for the truly observant of those establishments, particularly butcher shops and bakeries, which violated the Sabbath. They encouraged their followers not to patronize such concerns and exhorted both these public violators and the Jewish community at large to return to traditional behavior. The Agudat ha-Rabbanim initiated forays for the cause outside its own circumscribed constituency when it appealed to Jewish trade unionists to make "Sabbath-day off" a demand in owner-worker negotiations. And it hoped to influence "Jewish charitable organizations to set up divisions to seek employment for Sabbath observers." But it stayed away from external community-directed efforts, the hallmark of the Orthodox Union actions.[39]

The American rabbis disdained preacherlike exhortations and addressed themselves to American conditions which encouraged religious violations. They communicated with Jewish businessmen and employers, but their primary brief was with the American legislative system, which grudgingly retained discriminatory blue laws. These regulations prevented Jews from trafficking on Sunday, forcing them to desecrate their Sabbath to work an economically viable week. The Orthodox Union also spoke out clearly against the practice of holding State Regents, school, and civil service examinations only on Saturday. And they protected Jewish children destined to be punished for skipping school on Jewish holidays. The members of the Jewish Sabbath Observers Association worked hardest to promote traditional practice through Albany legislation. The leaders of the Agudat ha-Rabbanim held sway more comfortably on East Broadway.[40]

The Orthodox Union rabbis' self-perception as public protectors of the immigrant's religious rights in America also led them to the forefront of campaigns against school sectarianism and outright missionary activities. To be sure, Henry P. Mendes's interest in these concerns clearly predated the founding of his organization. He was instrumental in the creation in 1880 of the Envelope Society, which helped sponsor the Hebrew Free School Association, established to fight missionary successes downtown. As leader of the Orthodox Union, he presided over organizational deputations to public school officials to eliminate Christian celebrations from the schools. The Orthodox Union would ultimately sponsor a successful boycott of the New York schools in 1906. Mendes, Drachman, and Asher were among the names always associated with the establishment of Jewish mission schools in the ghetto to combat the Christian mission homes. Through its lay leadership the Orthodox Union went so far as to join hands with a Catholic priest in fighting Protestant so-called nonsectarian influences in the poor Jewish and Catholic areas.[41]

The Agudat ha-Rabbanim did not criticize these activities, but it neither joined the union's antisectarianism fight nor initiated any parallel campaign of its own. Its more narrow, internally-looking communal agenda spoke to other issues—problems which, significantly, the Americanized rabbis did not emphasize.

Ultimately, the Agudat ha-Rabbanim was less concerned that American law respect the immigrant Jew and more interested that the new American continue to respect Jewish law. The organization's view of the problems of immigrant Jewry was probably best summed up by Rabbi Jacob David Willowski of Chicago. Earlier in his life Willowski had declared from Europe that "America is a *treif* land where even the stones are impure." Nonetheless he eventually found his way to these shores, and in 1904 he wrote: "All [these problems] are to be blamed on the land [of freedom] where groups with varying viewpoints and opinions came to be settled and no one recognizes any authority."[42]

So disposed, Agudat ha-Rabbanim members worked to reinvigorate the transplanted rabbis' authority in voluntaristic America as a means of leading immigrant Jews back toward greater observance of traditional Jewish law, often clearly in resistance to the pressures of Americanization. Orthodox Union rabbis formulated their labors based on the assumption that the clerical figure who saw Judaism as a faith in opposition to America would fail to sustain both himself and his community. Rather it was the job of the American rabbi to help present the essence of Jewish identity to the immigrant, regardless of his degree of traditional religious practice, as compatible with the inevitable American identity. And as we will presently see, Orthodox Union rabbis also recognized that they could not do the job alone.

In the winter of 1909, the opportunity for Orthodox rabbis to cooperate with Jews of varying stripes in reinvigorating the immigrant's sense of belonging to his community came to hand in the form of the New York Kehillah. This citywide umbrella organization was initially called into existence as a response by Jews—both immigrants and established Americans—to anti-Semitic allegations of Jewish criminality on the Lower East Side. It soon began to address itself to the broader questions of Jewish religious and cultural survival. High on its list of communal priorities was the creation of the Jewish "public school system" Drachman and others had earlier called for, attractive to new immigrants and capable of calling back to Jewish identification those who were rapidly assimilating. Temple Emanu-El's Rabbi Judah L. Magnes served as the chairman of the movement, which numbered such German-Jewish Reform lay worthies as Jacob H. Schiff, Felix Warburg, Daniel Guggenheim, and Louis Marshall as its major financial backers. As the Kehillah idea moved closer to realization, Orthodox rabbis were faced with the following dilemma: could they work with, indeed trust, Reform Jews in the development of their own Orthodox institutions in America? Clearly, cooperation with the rich philanthropists would bring significant sums to the impoverished field of Jewish education. But would cooperation eventually lead to co-optation, as Reform Jews forced both American and assimilatory ideologies upon the consciousness of Jewish youth?[43]

The American Orthodox rabbis associated with the Orthodox Union did not fear association with the Kehillah. Though loyal to their union's mandate to "protest against declarations of Reform rabbis not in accord with the teachings of our Torah," they had no predisposition toward opposing all efforts led by Reform Jews solely because of their denominational label. True to this formula, the Orthodox Union lent support to the Kehillah in 1909, albeit with some reservations, arguing that the institution should be given a chance "if the Kehillah can help not merely Judaism but Orthodox Judaism." They agreed with the Kehillah's plan to make the talmud torah system a bastion of both Americanization and Judaism, so long as instruction would be in keeping with Orthodox traditions when Judaism was taught. And if they harbored fears that their liberal brethren did not really understand the faith's requirements, they kept their apprehensions to themselves. Besides,they trusted their own ability to monitor the educational activities from within. Drachman and Mendes were charter members of the Jewish Community's ruling executive committee, and Mordecai Kaplan served on the Kehillah's first education committee.[44]

The East European–born Orthodox rabbinate—primarily but not exclusively those affiliated with the Agudat ha-Rabbanim—was initially highly suspicious of the Kehillah's designs. They feared that this American institution, led by unreliable Reform leaders and laymen, would ultimately seek "to undermine the Orthodox institutions of the Jewish Quarter." Soon after the Jewish Community became a reality, however, Agudat ha-Rabbanim leaders recognized that Kehillah power and money might be utilized, ironically, to strengthen their hold as religious authorities in the ghetto. As thoughts of a tenuous *modus vivendi* began to be expressed in East European Orthodox circles, some rabbis even started to consider the possibility of co-optation by their fellows of the citywide construct.[45]

This change of attitude stemmed directly from the Kehillah executive committee's call in December 1909 for the establishment within its multifarious city-wide structure of a Vaad ha-Rabbanim, "a committee of recognized and authoritative rabbis for the control of the whole matter of kashruth and schechita and other religious matters." Perceptive Agudat ha-Rabbanim members immediately understood that in its desire to bring all groups of Jews and all Jewish issues under its banner, the Kehillah was willing to formally recognize men like them as the officialdom in charge of "all matters such as kashrus, milah, mikveh (etc.), concerning which no differences of opinion as to the *Din* exist." An infrastructure was being created, albeit by the "wrong people," which could ultimately lead to the resuscitation of the traditional Jewish community, with powerful rabbis at the head, in religiously barren voluntaristic America. If direction of Jewish education could only be wrested away from the Kehillah's acculturationist cum assimilationist Reform Jewish founders and their American Orthodox rabbinic supporters, they could emerge from this initial limited partnership in effective control of the New York Jewish community. Through these most roundabout of means, the dreams of Rabbi Weinberger and the hopes of Rabbi Jacob Joseph would be fulfilled. So disposed, twenty-three of the Agudat ha-Rabbanim's forty-six New York–based members joined the thirty-two-member Kehillah Vaad ha-Rabbanim, founded in 1912. Their game-plan was to use the threat of immediate withdrawal from the Kehillah to extend their influence in the field of education, a strategy which Kehillah officials staunchly resisted.[46]

With all its inherent weaknesses and potentialities for conflict, this tenuous marriage of interests could not have even been considered without the efforts of two highly influential pre–World War I Orthodox leaders who simply did not fit the mold of the transplanted East European rabbi, Rabbi Philip Hillel Klein of Harlem's First Hungarian Congregation Ohab Zedek and Ramaz (Rabbi Moses Zebulun Margolies) of Yorkville's Congregation Kehilath Jeshurun. The basic sympathies of these exceptional men were with the harmonization of Judaism with American values, and they perceived American Orthodox rabbis, if not Conservative rabbis and Reform leaders, as worthy colleagues. But as astute communal politicians, they still aspired to maintain influence in all religious power bases, even going so far as to stand at the head of avowed anti-Americanization institutions. Accordingly, both of these men were leaders of the Agudat ha-Rabbanim. Ramaz was its long-time president, and Klein, for several years, was an honorary president. Yet while both stood at the helm of an organization which opposed the Kehillah's Americanization assumptions and which seemingly did not recognize other rabbis as equal colleagues, they simultaneously served as members of the Kehillah's governing executive committee. In the latter capacity, Ramaz and Klein served with Drachman and Mendes on the committee of religious organization, which developed the Vaad ha-Rabbanim proposal. And in 1911, Ramaz participated in the executive committee's Educational License Bureau, a committee which included Rabbi Mordecai M. Kaplan, then principal of the Jewish Theological Seminary's Teachers Institute, a Dr. Langer, principal of the German Reform–run Educational Alliance School, and Dr. Samson Benderly, director of the Kehillah's own Bureau of Education.[47]

These seemingly conflicting affiliations surprised no one who had followed either man's American career. The Hungarian-born Klein arrived in the United States in 1890, eleven years after his ordination by Rabbi Azriel Hildesheimer. Possessed also of a Ph.D. from the University of Jena, Klein, as rabbi of a growing, prestigious immigrant congregation, found he had much in common with the Western European–trained Rabbis Drachman, Asher, Henry Morais, and Mendes. His shared interests and concerns led him to join in the founding of the Orthodox Union in 1898. And yet six years later, he emerged as an early member of Agudat ha-Rabbanim, which did not recognize his friends and opposed their organization. In fairness, one might suggest that Klein, by virtue of his "modern" Orthodox training with Hildesheimer and his secular university degree, may not have initially agreed with the Agudat ha-Rabbanim's philosophy. This conceivably marginal member of Agudat ha-Rabbanim was indeed not among the American-based European rabbis called to the initial gathering of the Agudat ha-Rabbanim. But election to that rabbinic body did not change him. In fact, as he rose in the organization, he continued to work with the American Orthodox rabbinate. And finally, in 1909, when his own congregation moved up from downtown's Norfolk Street to Harlem and attracted both new immigrants and more acculturated and second-generation Jews to his pulpit, he agreed to engage Drachman as his rabbinic associate. Klein preached in Yiddish and Hungarian, primarily to the older generation; his colleague spoke in English. No greater recognition of the reliability of the American Orthodox rabbinate could be given by a leader of Agudat ha-Rabbanim than to share his pulpit with the Orthodox Union's "second in command."[48]

Ramaz's activities and associational patterns also belied his position as a head of the Agudat ha-Rabbanim. Rabbi Margolies was born and raised in Kroza, Russia. He attended yeshivot in his hometown, Bialystock, and Kovno before serving as rabbi in Slobodka (1877–99). He migrated to America in 1899 and served as unofficial chief rabbi of Boston. It was, strikingly, in his New England home that the agenda for the founding of the Agudat ha-Rabbanim was drawn up. Though seemingly in accord with his organization's definition of rabbi, upon assuming the post of rabbi of an affluent, uptown New York pulpit in 1905, he acceded to working with Rabbi Mordecai M. Kaplan, a graduate of the pre-Schechter Seminary and a major spokesman for the Jewish Endeavor Society. As in the case of Klein and Drachman, Margolies and Kaplan shared ministerial duties. Margolies appealed to the older generation; Kaplan began building his career of youth-centered activities.[49]

Ramaz also broke with the Agudat ha-Rabbanim's policies when he served on the board of education of the Uptown Talmud Torah, beginning in 1908. By 1911 he had become head of that group, which included Rabbi Israel Friedlaender of the Seminary and German Reform lay leaders Schiff and Marshall. This organization advocated, even before 1910, many of the American educational innovations which Drachman wanted and which ultimately became part of the Kehillah's programming. Thus it was quite natural that Ramaz, like Klein, informed by almost a decade of cooperation with Jews of varying stripes in searching for American Jewish solutions to the problems of immigrant identification, would find his way into the leadership of the Kehillah. How and why he and Klein remained powerful in the rejectionist Agudat ha-Rabbanim is a separate question.[50]

The hoped-for working alliance between the Vaad ha-Rabbanim and the Kehillah did not, however, long survive. Magnes's group zealously protected their authority over Jewish education. They stated categorically in 1912 that while the Kehillah would "at all times welcome every recommendation that may be made to it . . . by the Vaad ha-Rabbanim," it would not bind "itself to same." The Vaad, for its part, led by Rabbi Shalom Elkanah Jaffe of Norfolk Street's Beis Medrash Ha-Gadol and East Harlem's Rabbi Samuel Glick, held its ground as ritual authority and worked to extend its influence to education. Its activities prompted Israel Friedlaender to quip "that it was in bad taste to connect the matter of kashrus with that of education."

As time went on, even the powers granted the Vaad did not go unchallenged. In December 1912 Mendes stated that "while the rabbis of the Board were perfectly competent to deal with the matters of schechita and kashrus, there were other subjects, such as 'get,' Sabbath legislation, and milah which required the activities of rabbis and laymen who were in better touch with conditions in this country." By 1914, its dream of communal co-optation now dead, the Vaad's leaders decided it had no stake in the Kehillah. Contending that "the session or time allowed for daily instruction by the [Kehillah's Education] Bureau, for the schools affiliated with it, was insufficient for effective religious training," Vaad members seceded from the Jewish Community and began working independently.[51]

Leading the Vaad out of the Kehillah were the very men who had brought it in initially, Rabbis Klein and Margolies. In August 1914 both resigned from the executive committee. Klein cited "poor health" and complained that the committees he served upon did not "call upon [his] specialized sphere of knowledge." Ramaz resigned with the allegation that in "all matters pertaining to religion [that] should be referred to the Board of Rabbis to be acted upon . . . the Board of Rabbis was ignored entirely."[52]

The departure of Klein and Margolies from the Kehillah did not mark a decline in their dedication to the spirit of the Kehillah's endeavors or to participation in Americanization efforts. It certainly did not end their close collegial association with American Orthodox rabbis. Klein continued to work harmoniously with Drachman in the Ohab Zedek pulpit through the beginning of the 1920's. Ramaz continued to serve on the Uptown Talmud Torah's board of education even as that school became one of the Kehillah's flagship institutions. This institution was the home of the Seminary-run, Kehillah-financed Teachers Institute, which, strikingly, Mordecai Kaplan directed. Most significantly, in 1913, after some three years of serving alone in his synagogue's pulpit, Ramaz agreed to the appointment of Rabbi Herbert S. Goldstein, an American-born and trained rabbi, possessed of a unique dual ordination. He had been ordained as an Orthodox rabbi by Rabbi Shalom Jaffe, an Agudat ha-Rabbanim worthy, and in 1913 he had received a rabbinical diploma from the Seminary, where he had been a student of Kaplan's.[53]

Significantly, Goldstein's Schechter-era Conservative ordination did not disqualify the Columbia University–educated cleric, one of the last of the Drachman-Schneeberger generation of Orthodox rabbis, in Ramaz's eyes. The senior rabbi was also seemingly untroubled by Goldstein's outspoken public criticism of the social capabilities of the East European Orthodox rabbinate. In a front-page editorial in the *Hebrew Standard*, published in June 1915, Goldstein declared that the preservation of "the Judaism of the future" lay solely in the hands of "the young, university-trained Orthodox rabbi." Only they, he argued, could assist the "scientifically-trained, skeptical young Jew, reconcile what he learned in the public school and college with the ancient doctrines of his faith." Only those "reared on American soil, who have breathed the ideal of American democracy, who have been born and bred like other Americans," could minister to the acculturated intent on breaking down the ghetto walls to "live as their neighbors, their fellow citizens, the Americans."[54]

Ramaz overlooked Goldstein's difference in training and tacitly accepted his social orientation, because to a great extent he agreed with his colleague's understanding of Judaism's requirements in America. Ramaz and Goldstein apparently worked harmoniously in the Kehillah Jeshurun pulpit for five years. Ramaz ministered to the first generation, Goldstein attended their children. Finally, in 1917, ambition and the drive for even greater youth-directed programming led Goldstein to leave Yorkville to found the Institutional Synagogue in neighboring Harlem.[55]

Though Rabbis Klein and Margolies were the most renowned East European–born and trained clerics who willingly and consistently cooperated with Jews of differing theological confessions both within the Kehillah and without, they were not the only New York–based immigrant Orthodox rabbis to lead lives dedicated to the harmonization of Jewish tradition with Americanization. The thoughts and activities of Rabbis Shmarya Leib Hurwitz and Zvi Hirsch "Harris" Masliansky also departed forcefully from the patterns of rabbinic attitude and behavior promoted by the Agudat ha-Rabbanim. Masliansky was generally recognized as the most outstanding Yiddish-language preacher on the Lower East Side at the turn of the century. But he did not share the common proclivity of the downtown *maggidim* to oppose religious innovation. Born in 1856 in Slutzk, Minsk, Russia, into a rabbinic family, he was educated in yeshivot in Mir and

Volozin. Ordained in 1880 by Rabbi Isaac Elchanan Spector of Kovno and Rabbi Samuel Mohilever of Bialystock, he spent the early years of his rabbinate as a teacher and preacher in Eastern Europe. There he worked enthusiastically to increase popular support for the then nascent Zionist cause. Banished from Russia in 1894 for his controversial public utterances on Jewish nationalism, he migrated to the United States and immediately began to speak out for Zionism and for the Jew's need to acculturate to America short of abandoning tradition.[56]

Masliansky's attitude toward Americanization soon became known to German-American Jewish leaders, who in 1898 appointed him the first official lecturer in Yiddish at the Educational Alliance. Masliansky's appointment represented a signal departure from the Americanizing institution's earlier policies of disdaining the cultural-linguistic baggage of its immigrant clients. Now, through him, the alliance sought to begin bridging the widening chasm between Yiddish-speaking parents and their quickly acculturating children. Similar awakened sensitivities led Louis Marshall, four years later, to call upon Masliansky's assistance in launching his *Yiddishe Welt* as an organ dedicated to encouraging rapid acculturation through the medium of the Yiddish tongue.[57] It is thus not surprising to find Masliansky at the founding of the Orthodox Union in 1898, in the forefront of supporters of the Jewish Endeavor Society in the early 1900's, and as a consistent support of the Kehillah from its inception to its ultimate decline. Masliansky publicly expressed his approach toward cooperation with the Drachmans and Mendeses of the Jewish community, not to mention the Marshalls and Schiffs, when he declared in homiletic fashion that before Orthodox Jews vocally opposed the miscasting of Jewish tradition represented by the Reform movement, let them first learn from their liberal colleagues how to organize communal life, "how to honor leaders, and how to give charity." "There will come a time," he prophesied, "when Judah [Orthodoxy] and Ephraim [Reform] will be united, but first let Judah be united in its own territory."[58]

Shmarya Leib Hurwitz also had credentials as a preacher from Eastern Europe, but he built his reputation in this country primarily as a Jewish educator who, possessed of an impeccable Orthodox pedigree, accepted the modern pedagogic methods promoted by the Kehillah. Hurwitz was born in the town of Kritchev in the province of Mogilev, Russia, in 1878. A scion of a Chabad Hasidic family, he attended

yeshivot in Mstislav and Shamyachi before serving as a rabbi in Yeka-
terinoslav from 1899 to 1906. Arriving in New York, he quickly
earned a reputation in downtown society as an able preacher. Satur-
day- and holiday-afternoon services in major ghetto-based synagogues were spiced by his addresses to the appreciative crowds. In
1908 he moved to Harlem's Congregation Bnei Israel Anshe Sameth,
lured uptown by real estate operator Joseph Smolensky, who reportedly enticed Hurwitz with a lucrative contract which spared him
"from the poverty which most rabbis find themselves in." In 1909
Hurwitz moved to create the Rabbi Israel Salanter Talmud Torah to
meet the educational needs of the thousands of children residing on
the outer ridge of Jewish Harlem who were then untouched by modern
Jewish education. By 1910 the talmud torah was home to 350 children
in twelve different after-school classes.[59]

When the Kehillah became a reality, Hurwitz gave it his full-hearted
support. He backed the founding of the Bureau of Education, supported its "model school" program, and permitted the creation of a boys'
preparatory junior high school on its premises.[60]

Significantly, Hurwitz's advocacy of modern pedagogic methods
and his association with non-Orthodox Jews did not endear him to all
the members of his congregation. But then again, they probably had
problems with his views of Orthodox synagogue life in general. In
April 1912 Hurwitz declared, in an article entitled "The Necessity to
Found Synagogues Here in America," that so long as synagogues were
dirty, the services too long, disorderly and basically unintelligible, and
the sermons dealt with esoteric midrashic and talmudic subjects,
youngsters would not find Judaism attractive. Indeed Hurwitz severed
his connections with his immigrant congregation and preferred to
work with his patron Smolensky to help strengthen American Judaism
primarily through the talmud torah system.[61]

Finally, the career of Philadelphia's Rabbi Bernard Levinthal suggests that the pre–World War I clerical ability to serve the Agudat ha-
Rabbanim while personally promoting the harmonious synthesis of
Judaism with Americanization through cooperation with Jews of
varying theological opinions was not entirely a metropolitan New
York area phenomenon. His multifarious communal activities, rang-
ing from the founding of a modern, communal talmud torah to charter membership in both the German-dominated anti-Zionist Ameri-

can Jewish Committee and the later Zionist American Jewish Congress, to early leadership of the Federation of American Zionists and the Orthodox Union, led one sympathetic biographer to describe him as "the most Americanized of the strictly Orthodox rabbis in the country." All these distinctions were achieved while he served as a long-time honorary president of the Agudat ha-Rabbanim.[62]

The so-called chief rabbi of Philadelphia (he oversaw the activities of some six congregations) predicated his activities upon his understanding that "a rabbi is a rabbi of all Israel, not merely of Orthodox, Conservative or Reform." He reportedly declared that in communal work, one has to "stand above all positions and denominations."[63]

As with his fellows, particularly Margolies and Klein, Levinthal was not simply a seeker after communal influence and honor regardless of ideological inconsistency, though none of these men was immune to the pursuit of power and self-aggrandizement. They were, rather, strident Americanizers who used their connections to promote their perception of Judaism's requirements. As such, they were destined to serve as role models for a new generation of American-born Orthodox rabbis—trained at the Rabbi Isaac Elchanan Theological Seminary (RIETS) and elsewhere—who emerged after World War I.[64]

III. The Challenges of Interwar American Judaism (1920–1940)

The Agudat ha-Rabbanim, for all its ideological difficulties with Orthodox Union rabbis in the pre–World War I period, had to admit that its Americanized opponents almost always displayed deference to their East European colleagues as the recognized officialdom in ritual matters.[65] This authority was more than merely a source of honor or responsibility or even power in the American Jewish community. It was, specifically in the areas of kosher supervision, a most important source of steady income for many an immigrant rabbi seeking financial stability, if not economic advancement, in this country. Rabbis Asher Lipman Zarchy, Hirsch Grodzinski, and Moses Matlin did not migrate to Des Moines, Iowa, Omaha, Nebraska, and Sioux City, Iowa, respectively, with the primary goal of building great Jewish communities in these areas. Rather, they were drawn by the large stockyards of these cities and the pecuniary rewards to be earned as overseers for companies which distributed kosher meats throughout the United States. Others did not have to trek that far to find gainful rabbinic employment. There were religious constituencies desirous of a "chief rabbi" to bring order to religious practice within cities that were but a few hours from the major immigrant centers.[66] That control of Jewish industries rested solely within the East European rabbinate did not mean, however, that colleagues did not frequently compete with each other for a given city's meat stipend. The most celebrated instance of pre–World War I rabbinic rivalry was the challenge to Rabbi Jacob Joseph by Rabbi Widerwitz and Rabbi Segal. Their attack upon his control of New York's meat and poultry abattoirs and butcheries and their emergent counter–chief rabbinate effectively undermined whatever authority Rabbi Joseph had in communal affairs. Indeed, the Agudat ha-Rabbanim was set up to some degree to remedy this problem. But it had only limited success. The 1903 Chicago battle between Rabbis Judah David Willowski and Zvi Album was probably that era's most striking case of rabbinic noncooperation. Album was a charter member of the Agudat ha-Rabbanim, and Willowski, one of late-nineteenth-century world Jewry's most renowned rabbinic writers, was honored as *zekan ha-rabbanim* ("elder rabbi") by the Agudat ha-Rabbanim in 1903, the year of his immigration. Both were committed to upholding their organization's policy of nonencroachment by one rabbi upon a colleague's territory. Yet Willowski's attempt, as the newly elected chief rabbi of Chicago, to impose his suzerainty upon the butcheries under Album's domain led to a citywide battle punctuated not only by vicious polemics between angry supporters of each faction but by fistfights in local synagogues.[67]

Kashruth competition was even more acute among Orthodox rabbis not bound by Agudat ha-Rabbanim strictures. In 1906 Rabbi Luntz fought Rabbi Selzer in Paterson, New Jersey, creating two chief rabbinates there. Rabbi Gabriel Z. Margolis, chief rabbi of Boston beginning in 1907, battled Rabbi Federman, the city's incumbent kosher meat overseer. And while Agudat ha-Rabbanim leaders sought to use kashruth supervision as a weapon in Kehillah negotiations over Jewish education, other East European rabbis publicly challenged their authority to represent Orthodox Jewry in the area of meat regulation.[68]

Internecine rivalries over kashruth control were already quite commonplace when, in the 1920's, a new generation of American-born and/or trained rabbis entered the fray. These modern clerics neither shared the East Europeans' negativism toward Americanization nor consistently deferred to their elders, as had the previous generation, in matters of Jewish ritual regulation. For Agudat ha-Rabbanim members the emergence of a new group of English-speaking Orthodox rabbis was undoubtedly a source not only of consternation but also of embarrassment. Ironically, these rising leaders were products of an institution which the Agudat ha-Rabbanim had been instrumental in founding and maintaining—the Rabbi Isaac Elchanan Theological Seminary.

This school, later and better known as the division of Yeshiva University dedicated to the training of American Orthodox rabbis, was organized in 1897. It grew out of the desire on the part of several graduates of Yeshiva Etz Chaim, the first elementary-level all-day yeshiva in the United States, for further and more intensive talmudic study combined with a modicum of general studies. Lithuanian-born kosher wine supervisor Rabbi Yehudah David Bernstein, a founder of Etz Chaim, and Rabbi Moses Matlin, the father of an Etz Chaim student, joined with layman David Abramowitz in inaugurating the institution. In its early years, RIETS was decidedly not, as its sympathetic historian put it, "a rabbinical training seminary in the modern and professional sense of the term."[69] A goodly number of its early students were already ordained rabbis or ritual slaughterers from Russia who saw in RIETS a European-style yeshiva overwhelmingly dedicated to the advancement of rabbinic scholarship.[70] It was thus understandable that the delegates would rally to the cause when Rabbi Bernstein rose at the Agudat ha-Rabbanim's second convention, in 1903, to propose formal recognition and support for RIETS. It was also not surprising that Agudat ha-Rabbanim members would champion the acute fundraising needs of RIETS. After all, several early Agudat ha-Rabbanim members—Rabbis Matlin, Bernstein, Alperstein, and Kaplan—were among the first *roshei yeshiva* (talmud instructors) at the school.[71]

Three years later the ongoing relationship between school and rabbinical association was cemented when a Semicha Board was created at RIETS under the control of the Agudat ha-Rabbanim, specifically through members Margolies, Klein, Levinthal, and Samuel Z. Wein. This authority would ordain men who had the same training and qualifications for the rabbinate as candidates back in Europe. To this point little official thought had been given to the very different prerequisites for service in an American pulpit.[72]

Soon, however, the question of what types of competencies a man needed to possess in order to serve effectively as a rabbi in America became a major point of dispute at RIETS. The student body's composition had been changing as the first decade of the twentieth century passed. By 1908, according to one contemporary estimate, the majority of students were native-born sons of immigrants.[73] For these students, attendance at RIETS was their or their families' answer to the public school–*heder*/talmud torah educational marriage. They wanted the intensive talmudic education on the European model offered by a traditional yeshiva. But they simultaneously desired improved secular studies to permit them to ultimately compete with fellow Jews and other Americans in the marketplace, universities, and professions of this land. Only a few of these new-style students sought careers as rabbis in America, but they too sought to be competitive.[74] They entered RIETS hoping to become knowledgeable in the ways of American science and civilization and equipped as English public speakers comfortable with homiletic messages attractive to fellow new Americans.

The pressure to Americanize RIETS peaked in 1908, when the students struck the institution. They demanded a broader, more systematic secular curriculum, instruction in the English language and "in the art of public speaking" as well as in the "softer" Jewish disciplines of Hebrew literature and Jewish history. The yeshiva's predominantly lay directors apparently recognized the potency of the ideology which backed this demonstration and responded almost immediately by electing the student-sympathetic Ramaz as their new president.[75] That change began a protracted process which, through Ramaz, Levinthal, Klein, and significant Orthodox lay support, redefined the RIETS mandate. From that point on, RIETS evolved to ultimately stand as an institution of Torah and *hakhma*, "secular knowledge," capable of training Orthodox spokesmen "according to the spirit of the times." The battles of 1908 ultimately led to the reincorporation of a merged RIETS and Etz Chaim in 1915 as the Rabbinical College of America under Rabbi Dr. Bernard Revel.[76]

Dr. Revel stood unequivocally in favor of "Torah and *hakhma*." His own life story was proof of the possibilities in the harmonization of

Torah scholarship with the secular. Born in Kovno in 1885, young Revel earned the reputation of an *illui* (budding talmudic "genius") at the Telshe Yeshiva, where he was ordained. But Revel's purview went beyond talmudic erudition. While still in Russia he evinced much interest in the Western-oriented disciplines of the Wissenschaft des Judenthums. He also, interestingly, demonstrated more than a passing interest in the ideology of Bundism (Jewish socialism), a highly unOrthodox modern expression of Judaism.[77]

This uncommon young Orthodox rabbi migrated to the United States in 1906 and quickly found RIETS hospitable to his need to continue rabbinic learning. New York University simultaneously met his desire for intensified secular studies, and he graduated with an M.A. degree in 1909. From there, Revel's quest for higher study in the world of Jewish Wissenschaft brought him to Dropsie College, America's first nontheological Jewish academic institution. This institution, which was destined to develop close spiritual and personal ties with the Jewish Theological Seminary, graduated Revel as its first Ph.D. in 1912.[78] Thus, when called to the Rabbinical College (RIETS) in 1915 to assume the presidency, at the age of thirty, Revel had achieved, through his own initiative and perseverance, what the school hoped to provide succeeding generations of American Orthodox rabbis. He was an "immigrant" rabbi comfortable both in his parents' universe and in the ways of America, capable of training students and colleagues to aid Jews in their harmonization of conflicting cultural and traditional values.

To help Revel in his labors were the two "grand old men" of American Orthodoxy, Rabbis Mendes and Drachman. The former was appointed professor of homiletics; the latter, as professor of pedagogy, "acted in various instructional capacities," teaching both Hebrew studies and the German language. Several years later, Mendes's spot on the faculty was assumed by Herbert S. Goldstein, one of the most renowned Orthodox preachers of his era. For Mendes and Drachman the reorganization of RIETS undeniably represented a new start for the "seminary idea" of 1887, which to their minds had been waylaid by the liberalizing innovations of Schechter. True advocates of traditional Judaism in America would now again be produced, theologically prepared and socially competitive in the marketplace of American ideas and denominational expressions.[79]

For members of the Agudat ha-Rabbanim, the reorientation of RIETS forced a most troubling major policy decision. Could they continue to support and service an institution which now did not mirror the desire to recreate an East European yeshiva environment in America and instead strove to reflect the immigrant's attempted accommodation of Judaism with America? For men like Ramaz, Klein, and Levinthal, who had manned the RIETS Semicha Board from 1906 and/or the Agudat ha-Rabbanim's Rabbinical College Committee set up in 1917 to monitor the school's activities, support for the changes was a natural extension of their philosophy of positive acculturation. But what of the aforementioned Rabbi Jaffee, also a member of the 1917 committee, who had previously avoided frequent institutional association with Drachman and Mendes and Americanization efforts in general? And what of the less-famous committee members like Eliezer Preil of Trenton, Eliezer Silver of Harrisburg, and Israel Rosenberg of Jersey City, not to mention the rabbis who held classes at RIETS? None of these men had previously championed Margolies/Klein/Levinthal policies. How could they reconcile the apparently sharp deviation from the long-standing organizational policy of non-recognition of Americanization programs?[80]

Several factors may have contributed to the Agudat ha-Rabbanim's acceptance of the change in RIETS. First was the recognition that in member Revel the American Orthodox seminary was being led by a man of impeccable rabbinic training who, whatever his acculturating proclivities, understood the feelings of his colleagues. Second, they perceived that the idealized old-style yeshiva, for all its scholarly grandeur, could not compete effectively for American-born students, or ultimately for Jewish souls, against the seminary's traditionalism. They were forced to move somewhat from their position of almost complete nonaccommodation. They decided to stay with the Rabbinical College of America as its "rabbis," working in typical Agudat ha-Rabbanim style from within to achieve their organization's ultimate goals. They would be the traditional teachers of the next generation of rabbis, bulwarks against all except the most necessary changes. They would ordain students whose loyalty they hoped to retain.[81]

It was not long before Agudat ha-Rabbanim members recognized that many of the ordainees did not intend to remain obedient disciples. The RIETS-Rabbinical College produced during its first generation some fifty trained-in-America rabbis.[82] While the vast majority found positions in the metropolitan area either as pulpit rabbis or as heads of large communal talmud torahs, some ventured to other venues and to smaller Jewish communities previously served only by one or two East European rabbis, creating an immediate potentiality for rabbinic competition.[83]

Such was the case in 1931 when a young RIETS graduate, hired by a Portland, Maine, congregation for the Passover holidays, began to "buy his community's *chometz*" and received a stipend for his services. The resident Agudat ha-Rabbanim rabbi, who depended upon holiday honoraria for his economic survival, was outraged. He complained to the Agudat ha-Rabbanim that "this young chick whose eyes have not yet opened has pushed me aside after my ten years in the community. Please declare his rulings void and his ordination nullified."[84]

An even more vexing incident took place that same year in Massachusetts when another RIETS-trained rabbi "overruled" the chairman of the Agudat ha-Rabbanim–backed Council of Orthodox Rabbis in a matter of kosher meat slaughtering. The younger rabbi characterized the Agudat ha-Rabbanim decision as "foolish." And when asked if he knew the chairman of the rabbinic council he "acted as if the Chairman wasn't worth knowing and he boasted that he had no desire to be a member of an organization such as the Agudat ha-Rabbanim."[85]

The Agudat ha-Rabbanim responded to these charges and to the more generalized complaint that the American rabbis were undermining old-line authority in Jewish localities.[86] Under the leadership of its new president, Rabbi Eliezer Silver (elected in 1923), deputations and protests were addressed to Revel urging him not to send yeshiva graduates to communities led by Agudat ha-Rabbanim members without the specific permission of the resident senior rabbi. Secondly, Silver launched a program to bring the already ordained American rabbis into the Agudat ha-Rabbanim's fold and under its control.[87] He offered them organizational collegiality and mutual aid, provided that they could pass the more stringent *yadin yadin* ordination required of members.[88]

Silver drew heavily upon his own wide experience as a rabbi in the field in tendering this plan. Born in the Lithuanian town of Abel in 1881, he had gained his earliest training from his father, Rabbi Bunim

Tzemah Silver, before receiving advanced rabbinical training in Dvinsk, Vilna, and Brisk. He was awarded ordination from Rabbis Hayim Ozer Grodzinski and Shalom Ha-Kohen of Vilna. Unlike so many of his Orthodox rabbinical colleagues, Silver, upon his arrival in the United States in 1906, did not settle in New York. Rather, with the assistance of Rabbi Levinthal, he established himself in Harrisburg, Pennsylvania, where he remained until 1925. He then moved on to Springfield, Massachusetts, for six years before assuming a pulpit in Cincinnati, Ohio, a position he would hold until his death more than fifty years later.[89]

From his vantage points "outside of New York," Silver witnessed and participated in numerous controversies over kashruth and overall communal control in the smaller Jewish communities. He understood the fears of the rabbanim threatened by insurgent rabbis and dedicated himself to clerical unity under the Agudat ha-Rabbanim's banner.

Rabbi Revel, for his part, was desirous of maintaining good relations with the Agudat ha-Rabbanim. Their continued approbation of his graduates lent all-important legitimacy to the institution. The promise of membership in the Agudat ha-Rabbanim for his students was also welcome. Accordingly, Revel took steps in the early 1930's to develop a rabbinical curriculum that would prepare his yeshiva men for the more advanced degree. But at the same time, he recognized that Silver's demands threatened the very existence of his school. To Revel RIETS had been reorganized to offer American-born youth the opportunity to become American Orthodox rabbis. They were to compete effectively with Seminary-trained Conservative ordainees for leadership of an Americanized Jewish community. But how attractive could his school be to potential students if they knew that their ultimate job placement was to be effectively controlled by a coterie of East European–oriented rabbis? Faced with such a conflict, Revel seemingly adopted a fence-straddling policy—officially sensitive toward the Agudat ha-Rabbanim's position when specific conflicts arose, and simultaneously encouraging East European rabbis to accept his younger generation. He also tried to sensitize his disciples to respect the provinces of their elders.[90]

Revel's American-trained rabbis were not captivated by the Agudat ha-Rabbanim's offers, nor did they share their mentor's seeming great concern over RIETS'S institutional legitimacy. First, few were then qualified for full membership in the Agudat ha-Rabbanim, and fewer saw the necessity for more advanced study to enter the lists. More importantly, the younger clerics viewed the senior rabbinic alliance as out of touch both structurally and ideationally with contemporary issues, unable to serve the rapidly emerging second-generation Jewish community of the interwar period. The Agudat ha-Rabbanim was, to their minds, an organization which preached rabinical unification to standardize Jewish ritual practice and yet was rife with discord both from within and from without. Its combative members were seen as unaware of the negative impact their often notorious behavior made upon masses of acculturated Jews. And the popular perception of the Orthodox rabbinate was, for RIETS graduates, no mean issue. While the older immigrant laity which backed the Agudat ha-Rabbanim rabbis knew and "understood" the roots of these internecine rivalries, their children did not. And it was precisely these younger Jews, whom Agudat ha-Rabbanim members were ideologically and sociologically unable to reach, that they were seeking to influence. Membership in the Agudat ha-Rabbanim would be of little help to the American-trained Orthodox rabbi, then in the early throes of competition with the rising Conservative rabbinate, in projecting himself as a legitimately modern traditional pastor.

These critical evaluations of the East European rabbinate took permanent organizational form in 1935 with the founding of the Rabbinical Council of America (RCA).[91] This new clerical organization was in truth an amalgamation of two separate but similar-thinking organizations, the Rabbinical Council of the Orthodox Union and the Rabbinical Association of RIETS. The former organization was formed in 1926 by, among others, the rabbis of three of Manhattan's most established modern Orthodox synagogues—Herbert S. Goldstein of the Institutional Synagogue, David De Sola Pool, Mendes's successor at Shearith Israel, and Leo Jung, who replaced now Conservative/Reconstructionist Rabbi Mordecai Kaplan at the Jewish Center. These men, who were reminiscent of, if not identical to, the earlier Drachmans and Mendeses in their rabbinical training and orientation, sought to help bring American concepts of standardization to the kashruth industry through the OU symbol.[92] The Orthodox Union brought together RIETS men who either could not qualify for the Agudat ha-Rabbanim or did not want to join it. Chaim Nachman, H. Ebin, Ben Zion Rosenbloom, and Joseph H. Lookstein sought both to help their alma mater and to assist themselves in pulpit placement and congregational problems.[93] The amalgamation of these groups into the RCA consti-tuted a signal enduring link between two generations of American Orthodox rabbis.

The RCA set as its dual mandate the bureaucratization and stand-ardization of kashruth and the promotion of its own brand of Ameri-can traditional Judaism above and beyond the power of the Conserva-tive movement. Toward the first goal, the RCA fought for more than a generation, and with only a modicum of success, to end the practice of individual rabbis negotiating the right to oversee a particular prod-uct's kashruth. As the RCA saw it, this chaotic system of sometimes secret agreements lowered public esteem for the rabbinate when it did not encourage imposters or unscrupulous supervisors in the field. The RCA campaigned for the concentration of all kashruth under the OU banner, a public statement that control of this industry was a commu-nal responsibility and not an individual rabbi's sinecure. The RCA commissioned and controlled competent supervisors and publicized the OU symbol as authoritative. It also sought to encourage the great-er observance of kashruth both by the Jewish public and by national Jewish organizations, then notorious in Orthodox minds for their un-kosher-catered meetings and banquets.[94]

The actuation of these plans required that RCA members surrender their autonomy to the national body, a personal and financial conces-sion to communal priorities that many were loath to make. Indeed, it was not until 1954 that the RCA could officially prohibit its members from granting personal *hechsherim* (certifications). And even then compliance was not uniform either within or without the organiza-tion. Certainly Agudat ha-Rabbanim rabbis and innumerable other unaffiliated clerics unbound by this bureaucracy resented the under-mining of their authority. But then again, the RCA's methods in the second major area of its interest, the battle against Conservative Juda-ism, elicited even less Agudat ha-Rabbanim support.[95]

The Conservative movement had emerged during the interwar peri-od as American Jewry's numerically predominant religious denomina-tion. Offering its communicants a sociologically sophisticated mix-ture of liturgical traditionalism and ideological liberalism, it attracted vast numbers of second-generation Jews uncomfortable with their parents' European-looking Orthodoxy and put off by the "church-like" religious radicalism of Reform. American Jews were good family men who wanted to pray seated next to their wives and family. And they found in Conservatism a theology and practice attuned to the slowly developing suburban life-style, prepared to make religious accommodations to America's work clock and transportation revolution and yet still remain philosophically and practically within older Jewish traditions. Masses of Jews saw in the Conservative rabbi an adroit mediator between the ancestral faith of the past and the exigencies of the American future. These leaders could communicate their approach in impeccable English understandable to Jews and Gentiles alike. Orthodox rabbis, in their view, did not truly understand the demands of the acculturated, and Reform rabbis had yet to be sensitized to their fears of assimilation and of intermarriage.[96]

Agudat ha-Rabbanim rabbis, whose policies of resistance to Americanization possessed little currency with most second-generation Jews, had little to offer the acculturated in response to Conservatism's appeal, except well-articulated contempt for its perceived corruption of rabbinic tradition. The innumerable proclamations against and excoriations of the Conservative rabbinate, for all their intensity, had little practical effect.[97] The Yiddish-speaking followers of the Agudat ha-Rabbanim, those who knew and were influenced by the organization's ordinances, were Jews with relatively little interest in Conservatism's American social appeal. And those attracted to the liberal-traditionalists were drawn from among those disinterested in and unaware of old-line proclamations and attitudes.

RCA rabbis, on the other hand, staunchly believed that they could compete effectively against the Conservative rabbinate for spiritual leadership of the next generation. Through a tripartite policy of simulation, inclusion, and cooperation, they sought to prove that the American Orthodox rabbinate and its laity could be as attuned to American mores as their more liberal brethren without doing violence to the tenets of the ancestral faith.

RCA board member Joseph H. Lookstein of Manhattan's Congregation Kehilath Jeshurun was probably the organization's staunchest advocate of simulation. The Orthodox synagogue could be as architecturally modern, its services as decorous and appealing, its liturgy as linguistically intelligible, and its English-language sermon as compel-

ling as any Conservative temple. Born in 1902 in the province of Mogilev, Russia, Lookstein was brought at age seven to the United States
and settled with his family first on the Lower East Side and then in the
Brownsville section of Brooklyn. He received his basic Jewish and
secular education at the all-day Rabbi Jacob Joseph School on Henry
Street and then moved a few blocks over on the Lower East Side to the
Talmudical Academy, the RIETS "prep school." Significantly, while
studying for ordination, Lookstein pursued an advanced secular degree at City College of New York. It was during his university years
that this talented and culturally versatile young man was called to
assist Ramaz as student rabbi in the Yorkville pulpit previously occupied by Mordecai Kaplan and Herbert S. Goldstein.[98]

Ordained by RIETS in 1926, Lookstein served as assistant to Ramaz during the last ten years of the senior rabbi's life. While in this
post, he earned graduate degrees from Columbia University, was appointed by Revel professor of homiletics and practical rabbinics at
Yeshiva University, and emerged as a leading spokesman for the RCA.
Blessed with a gift for English sermonizing and possessed of an impressive academic and professional resume, Lookstein bore witness
that a RIETS graduate could be as worldly and Americanized as any of
his seminary counterparts.[99]

One sympathetic family biographer has suggested that Lookstein's
simulation idea grew out of his rejection while an adolescent of "the
noise, the tumult and the general disarray of the Orthodox *shuls.*"
Impressed by the aesthetics and dignity that were characteristic of
Reform and Conservative synagogues, he "strove to combine warmth
with dignity, the enthusiasm of Orthodoxy with the aesthetics of Reform, the tradition of four thousand years of Jewish practice with the
modern active tempo." That meant weekly English-language sermons,
prayers in English as well in Hebrew, special-theme Sabbaths, and
guest speakers. In 1937 Lookstein even invited Judah Magnes, then
chancellor of the Hebrew University in Jerusalem, to speak from the
Kehilath Jeshurun pulpit on Kol Nidre night. All these policies and
programs dated back to Drachman and the beginnings of American
Orthodoxy at the turn of the century and to Goldstein in the 1910's.
But by Lookstein's time these activities were more characteristic of the
Conservative synagogues.[100]

Lookstein was also a prime exponent of simulation in Jewish education. Clearly disdaining the Agudat ha-Rabbanim's concept of a yeshiva and taking Drachman's early idea that Orthodox Jewish education should emulate the public schools, Lookstein, in 1937, founded the Ramaz School, the prototype of many of today's modern day schools. Lookstein believed he could simulate the best aspects of the integrationist, acculturationist philosophy of the public schools in a homogeneous Jewish school environment. The student at Ramaz would receive the intensive Hebraic and Judaic training unobtainable in released-time or supplementary programming, while learning with equal intensity the values and mores of American society. Lookstein argued that the Jewish school calendar should correspond directly to the public school schedule; there would be no classes on Sundays, and Christmas vacation, renamed winter vacation, was instituted to permit maximal social integration with non-Jews and less Jewishly committed co-religionists.[101]

Unfortunately for the RCA, not all Orthodox rabbis possessed Lookstein's leadership capabilities or served congregations as content as the Yorkville synagogue with his aesthetic innovations and nondoctrinal changes.[102] Far more frequently, the interwar-period American Orthodox rabbi found himself in conflict with congregants who wanted to attend an "Orthodox" synagogue, defined here as a synagogue served by an American-trained Orthodox rabbi, but at the same time wanted to adopt the egalitarian mixed seating characteristic of Conservative temples. And when they were not debating pew patterns, conflicts raged over the equally crucial question of standardizing the time of Friday evening services. RIETS men serving such congregations had to deal with frequent lay requests that the synagogue precincts be used on weekday evenings for mixed-dancing congregation-sponsored socials. They also had to decide whether men known to be public nonobservers of the Sabbath could be allowed the honor of leading services, as well as whether a man married to a non-Jew could be accepted into full synagogue membership. They even had to take positions on such seemingly less compelling problems as whether and when pulpit flowers might be used in the synagogue.[103]

For many rabbis the answer to all these queries was yes, sometimes unabashedly, sometimes reluctantly. To compete against the more liberal traditionalists, many rabbis felt they would have to accommodate congregational pleasures and take simulation beyond the limits of theological acceptability, although without formal or programmatic assent. At the same time, these rabbis wished to see themselves as Orthodox rabbis and as members of the RCA, and to be so considered by their colleagues.[104]

This approach to synagogue life and congregational ritual was particularly prevalent among those rabbis serving in midwestern pulpits, graduates of either RIETS or the relatively new Chicago-based Hebrew Theological College (HTC). The latter seminary was founded in 1922 by a group of Midwest-based rabbis to train local youths for rabbinic pulpits. Committed from its inception to producing "modern leaders of Orthodox Jewry," its curriculum emphasized not only "intensive study of the Talmud and the Codes . . . and mastery of the *Tanach* [Bible] but also a thorough knowledge of Jewish history and literature and a comprehensive grasp of the problem of contemporary Jewish life." As such, this rabbinic training school had much in common with the early pre-Schechter Seminary while sharing many of the ideological perspectives of the Revel-organized RIETS. It stood for little that would satisfy the Agudat ha-Rabbanim's understanding of the goals and methods of a yeshiva. In any event, its modern ordained rabbis, far removed from the metropolitan hub, fought the "battle for Orthodoxy" against powerful Reform and Conservative forces. They almost universally acquiesced at least on the issue of mixed seating. Still as graduates of an American Orthodox training center, they sought RCA membership, posing a critical policy dilemma for the national organization.[105]

The RCA adopted a policy of inclusion both for HTC graduates and for those RIETS alumni who led what would come to be known as "traditional" congregations. Undoubtedly faced with a choice between accepting the situation of their colleagues as it was and driving them into the arms of the Conservative Rabbinical Assembly (RA) and the United Synagogue of America, the RCA by 1942 opted for inclusion. Its articulated policy was to admit all rabbis ordained at RIETS, HTC, or any other recognized Orthodox institute or authority. National office-holding in the organization, however, was to be reserved for rabbis serving in separate-seating congregations.[106]

The RCA strove to garner additional respect for Orthodoxy and its rabbinate through cooperation with more liberal Jews on interdenominational issues. In 1936, in a move highly reminiscent of Drachman and Mendes's willing participation in the New York Kehillah, the RCA became a constituent member of the Synagogue Council of America, an amalgam of Conservative, Reform, and Orthodox groups which dealt, inter alia, with church-state concerns and problems of anti-Semitism, issues upon which seemingly all denominations could agree. Ten years earlier the Orthodox Union and its Rabbis Goldstein and Pool had been among the founders of the council. And in 1939, RCA leaders sat down with Central Conference of American Rabbis (CCAR) and RA spokesmen to explore their mutual concerns over "the secularization in the Jewish centers and federations." To be sure, the usual fears were expressed that cooperation on nonreligious or interreligious matters would lead to theological co-optation. But to many RCA people, the possibility of projecting themselves as leaders not only of their community but of the entire Jewish community was all too compelling.[107]

These RCA policies, to be sure, did not sit well with the Agudat ha-Rabbanim. Harkening back as always to the European model which dominated its perspective and fueled its energies, the Agudat ha-Rabbanim contended that the rabbi's job was primarily to lead and not to be the servant of his community. Jewish law, it countered, set certain standards which may be neither suspended nor abridged on the basis of the popular will. And those clerics who would undermine the immutable halacha had no place in the Orthodox rabbinate. The Agudat ha-Rabbanim could see no social, political, or religious legitimacy to American colleagues serving in mixed-seating synagogues. And the RCA apologia that once ensconced in his pulpit a rabbi would hopefully change things for the "better," held for no currency for its members. Indeed, they even had difficulty with the seemingly innocuous simulation idea that Orthodox synagogues could hold Friday-evening lectures on "secular" topics to attract the uncommitted, because it emulated Conservative practice.[108]

Acting on these beliefs, the Agudat ha-Rabbanim in 1939 called upon the seventeen men who maintained memberships in both the Agudat and the RCA to leave the American association in protest over its articulated policies. The resignation of these distinguished rabbis from the RCA, it was hoped, would effectively undermine that clerical body, leading to the reestablishment of a separate RIETS alumni society clearly under the hegemony of the Agudat ha-Rabbanim.[109]

One year later, the Agudat ha-Rabbanim sought to assert its rabbinical suzerainty in a far more dramatic way, through a takeover of RIETS. The death in 1940 of Bernard Revel, at the age of fifty-five, left Yeshiva University in disarray. Gone was the synthesizer who had fused, for students and American Orthodox rabbis alike, the positive goals of acculturation with the maintenance of the Old World faith. American Orthodoxy was bereft of the spokesman who could crystallize and articulate its distance from Conservative Judaism and its differences with the Agudat ha-Rabbanim brand of Orthodoxy. With Yeshiva at bay, some rabbinical students gravitated toward the Seminary. Meanwhile, the Agudat ha-Rabbanim tried to step into the vacuum. Rabbi Silver suggested to the RIETS board that an Agudat ha-Rabbanim committee be appointed to administer the school. With his men in charge, Silver could monitor the types of men leaving RIETS and the pulpits they were to assume.[110]

The university's board politely but firmly sidestepped Silver's initiative. Instead they appointed a primarily in-house executive board to manage the school while a search for a new president could be conducted. In 1943, Rabbi Samuel Belkin emerged as a worthy successor both to Revel's post and as expositor of his philosophy. A thirty-one-year-old professor of classics at Yeshiva College and Talmud instructor at RIETS, Belkin was in personal background, educational training, and philosophical orientation remarkably similar to his predecessor. Like Revel, Yeshiva's new president had been recognized while a child as a potentially, prodigious talmudic scholar. He was ordained at age seventeen at the yeshiva of Rabbi Israel Meir Ha-Kohen Kagan in Radun, Russia. But like Revel, Belkin also manifested a voracious appetite for secular humanistic learning. His quest for the latter form of scholarly training led him to the United States and to American universities, where in the years between his arrival in this country and his appointment to Yeshiva's faculty, Belkin not only mastered the English language but earned a Ph.D. in classics at Brown University and was elected to Phi Beta Kappa. In him, Yeshiva had once again found a leader whose life spoke to its commitment to living harmoniously in both the world of Jewish faith and the universe of secular knowledge and society. It would be Belkin's agenda through his more than thirty years at Yeshiva's helm to expand the purview of the university and to deepen the parameters of Revel's message. He would sit atop of a theological seminary that aspired to produce a type of rabbi who was truly conversant with, if not comfortable in, the American environment. RIETS graduates would continue to be occasionally objectionable to the Agudat ha-Rabbanim.[111]

It was RCA leaders who played a large role both in blocking the Agudat ha-Rabbanim takeover and in the selection of Belkin, thus ensuring that Yeshiva stayed Revel's course. Having asserted their independence from the respected East European rabbis, they lobbied hard to maintain their alma mater as an institutional bastion of support for their ideas and activities.[112] While that struggle raged, the RCA proceeded to place even greater distance between itself and the senior rabbis by creating its own Halacha Commission. Through this agency, which responded to questions on religious law and practice submitted to it by individual members, the American rabbis formally asserted that as a group they were competent not only to teach Judaism in this country but also to adjudicate problems of ritual observance. No longer would American–born rabbis have to defer to the learning of the members of the Agudat ha-Rabbanim. Through the Halacha Commission, a statement was implicitly and explicitly made that a man trained in the ways of the modern Jewish world as well as the world of Torah was better equipped to apply precedent and procedures to the needs of the Americanized lay majority. It was to this committee that questions regarding mixed dancing, the permissibility of autopsies to advance medical science, and the use of microphones during Sabbath and holiday services were submitted, and authoritative answers were rendered.[113]

The RCA, however, probably could not have made, or sustained, this broad assertion of its authority in American Jewish life without the philosophical backing and practical support of another uncommon East European–born rabbi, Joseph B. Soloveitchik.[114] The "Rov," as he came to be known to his disciples within and without Yeshiva University, emerged in the 1940's as the towering ideologue of American Orthodoxy.

Soloveitchik was born in 1903 into a world-renowned rabbinic family. His grandfather, Rabbi Haym Soloveitchik, the so-called Brisker Rov, is credited with revolutionizing the methodology of talmudic study in the East European yeshivot. The "Brisker method," in the words of one of its present-day exponents, relied upon an "insistence on incisive analysis, exact definition, precise classification and critical independence." Soloveitchik learned this system under the close tutelage of his father, Rabbi Moses Soloveitchik, with whom he studied almost exclusively through his teen years. While still a young man, Joseph Soloveitchik came to believe that a systematic knowledge of general philosophy would enhance his understanding of the Torah and its applicability to the modern condition. He enrolled in the University of Berlin in 1925 and studied there for six years under the Neo-Kantian philosopher Heinrich Maier, earning a Ph.D. in 1931 with a dissertation on the philosophy of Hermann Cohen.[115]

While the younger Soloveitchik sought his own road to more advanced religious understanding, Rabbi Moses Soloveitchik was recruited by Revel to head the RIETS faculty in 1929. His appointment did much to solidify the traditional talmudic and codes core of the rabbinic training at RIETS, while Revel introduced mechanisms for the ancillary skill development so much required of an American cleric. With Rabbi Moses Soloveitchik on the faculty, few could effectively question the scholarly reliability of men who studied at RIETS.[116]

In 1932 Rabbi Joseph Soloveitchik migrated to these shores, was accepted as unofficial chief rabbi of Boston, and affiliated with the Agudat ha-Rabbanim. During his early American years, Soloveitchik, bred in a tradition that emphasized the intellectual rather than the pastoral functions of the rabbinate, devoted himself primarily to the dissemination of Torah scholarship through public and private lectures and through the creation of the first Hebrew day school in New England, Boston's Maimonides School. This school's approach and curriculum more closely resembled those of the recently founded Ramaz than the older Etz Hayim.

It was not until 1941 and the death of his father that Rabbi Joseph Soloveitchik brought his talmudic excellence and affinity for the study of philosophy to Yeshiva University.[117] The Agudat ha-Rabbanim asked Rabbi Soloveitchik to head up the RIETS Talmud faculty. His acceptance assured the rabbinic body that a high level of rabbinic scholarship would continue to characterize Yeshiva while it went through the throes of replacing President Revel, but, as time went on, Soloveitchik's political nonalignment with the Agudat ha-Rabbanim in its dealings with the younger Orthodox rabbis led the organization to be less than satisfied with him.[118]

For RIETS students and their more senior alumni colleagues in the RCA, Rabbi Soloveitchik's emergence came to mean something entirely different.[119] Here was a man possessed of the highest East European rabbinical credentials and yet philosophically and psychologically capable of relating "the ideal *halakhic* system to the basic realities of human life" and able to formulate "a creative philosophy, conservative and progressive, keeping intact our Jewish tradition even as he was developing it further," who would become their spiritual guide and legal mentor.[120]

In practical terms this ultimately meant that Rabbi Soloveitchik not only understood and accepted the forces and pressures which had created the RCA tripartite approach to religious life—simulation, inclusion, and cooperation—but was prepared to assist in setting authoritative parameters for each of these policies. In the sociological realm of simulation, Soloveitchik granted those who sought his advice the widest latitude. He applauded those who could show "the American Jew that it is possible to have a synagogue conform to the *Shulkan Aruk* . . . and at the same time . . . excel as far as good behavior, cultivated manners and beautiful sermons are concerned." And in certain specific situations, he acceded to a RIETS graduate accepting a pulpit in a mixed-seating congregation, if that congregation demonstrated a willingness to be convinced to conform to Orthodox strictures. In one case, after being informed that a mixed-seating congregation was willing to install a temporary *mechitza* during the trial Sabbath of an RCA member, Soloveitchik, in his own words, "inclined to take the more liberal view of the situation . . . [but] only to a situation in which there is at least a vague probability that the visit of the rabbi might pave the way for bringing that synagogue into the fold." At the same time, as adviser to the RCA's Halacha Commission in the 1940's and as its chairman in the early 1950's, Soloveitchik vigorously opposed so-called Orthodox congregations which adopted the Conservative practice of having the cantor face the congregation rather than the ark in prayer and/or showed no interest in moving in the direction of separate seating. He also rendered a final, negative opinion on the issue of the permissibility of a microphone at Sabbath and holiday services. That decision further distinguished the Orthodox from the more liberal congregations.[121]

Finally, he staunchly supported the RCA policy of cooperation with

the less traditional in broad communal agencies. In a poignant statement on the need for Jewish unity against hostile outside forces, Soloveitchik declared:

> When representation of Jews and Jewish interest *klapei chutz* [towards the
> outside world] are involved, all groups and movements must be united. There
> can be no divisiveness in this area for any division in the Jewish camp can
> endanger its entirety. . . . In the crematoria, the ashes of Hasidim and Anshe
> Maseh [pious Jews] were mixed with the ashes of radicals and freethinkers and
> we must fight against the enemy who does not recognize the difference between
> one who worships and one who does not.[122.]

At the same time he advised RCA members to tread warily when
dealing with Conservative and Reform rabbis on issues affecting the
internal life of the Jewish community.

Although Rabbi Soloveitchik's leadership did much to legitimize
the RCA's approach toward meeting the problems of mid-twentieth-
century American Jewish denominational life, his influential voice did
little to effectively reconcile Agudat ha-Rabbanim and RCA disagree-
ments. If anything, the Soloveitchik years (ca. 1940 to the present)
witnessed the widening of the gap between groups of Orthodox rabbis
operating in America. RCA stalwarts, possessed of the Rov's imprimatur and thus confident of their authenticity, have organizationally
resisted, although with some notable individual exceptions, the gravi-
tational pull of the East European–trained rabbis. At the same time,
the Agudat ha-Rabbanim has become more and more attuned to a
very different Torah voice which has solidified and further formalized
its resistance to the harmonization techniques characteristic of the
American Orthodox rabbinate. This new era of immigrant Orthodoxy, which we will presently discuss, began on a large scale during
and after World War II, and to a great extent its adherents have
eclipsed the indigenous prewar Agudat ha-Rabbanim leaders as the
staunchest resisters of Americanization. In so doing, they have challenged the assumptions of both the Agudat ha-Rabbanim and the
American Orthodox rabbinate.

IV. A New Era of Immigrant Orthodoxy (ca. 1940–1980)

Through all its early years of disagreement and conflict with American
Orthodox rabbis, the Agudat ha-Rabbanim proudly projected itself as

the institutional bastion of resistance against Americanization's in-roads into traditional faith. But not all East European rabbis who shared the Agudat ha-Rabbanim's basic point of view aligned them-selves with that organization. In its earliest days, some Galician- and Hungarian-born or trained rabbis disdained affiliation with the pre-dominantly Lithuanian rabbinic alliance on ethnic grounds.[123] For others nonalignment with the clerical association meant continued freedom to pursue their own pecuniary interests in the kashruth field.[124] Finally and most significantly, there were rabbis who believed that the Agudat ha-Rabbanim's antiacculturation and antimoderniza-tion policies did not go far enough. They looked askance at the Agudat ha-Rabbanim's continued support for RIETS, especially as creeping Americanization slowly transformed that East European–style yeshi-va into Yeshiva University. And they had theological difficulties with the organization's consistent backing of modern Jewish nationalism, albeit through the somewhat separatistic Mizrachi (Religious Zionist) movement.

Rabbi Gabriel Wolf Margolis was one individual who opposed the Agudat ha-Rabbanim both practically and philosophically. And in the early 1920's, he unified varying strains of East European rabbinic disaffection with Agudat ha-Rabbanim into a competing organiza-tion, Knesset ha-Rabbanim ha-Orthodoxim (Assembly of Hebrew Orthodox Rabbis). The Vilna-born Margolis, scion of a Lithuanian rabbinical family, had served communities in the Russian Pale cities of Dubrovno, Horodno, and Yashinovka for close to forty years before migrating to the United States and settling in Boston in 1908 at the age of sixty. This senior scholar, the reputed author of several European-published rabbinic tracts, quickly elected chief rabbi of several New England–area congregations, saw little personal value in affiliating with the still relatively new rabbinic organization.[125] If anything, he recognized the Agudat ha-Rabbanim as an organizational establish-ment which stood in the way of his economic and rabbinic-political advancement through the kashruth industry. Indeed, upon his remov-al to New York in 1912 to head up the Adath Israel Congregation and burial society, and upon his recognition that the kashruth industry in the metropolis was then under Agudat ha-Rabbanim control through its rabbinic officialdom of Klein, Ramaz, and Jaffe, he undertook a decade-long campaign to undermine the reliability of Agudat ha-Rabbanim within New York Orthodox circles. Not only did he speak out against the Agudah's move toward cooperation with the Kehillah, he charged his opponent Ramaz with incompetence in his monitoring of slaughtering procedures. And he also pointedly accused Jaffe of falsely certifying unkosher products. Finally, Margolis violently opposed the Agudat ha-Rabbanim's support for a 1919 strike by the Butcher Workmen Union and the Union of Live Poultry Workers. This dispute gave him the opportunity to declare that the Agudat ha-Rabbanim was itself a "union" designed to prevent competent competitive rabbis from establishing themselves in the United States. But despite all his efforts, Margolis was unable to effectively wrest kashruth control from the incumbent supervisors.[126]

In the early 1920's it became clear that Margolis's difficulties with the Agudat ha-Rabbanim went well beyond questions of money and rabbinic power and propriety. Margolis was, firstly, troubled by his opponents' support for Zionism. As he saw it, Jews had no right to actively participate in their own political redemption. God alone would decide when the exile should end, and therefore no true-believing Orthodox Jew could associate with that modern national movement. Using the traditional liturgical rendering of Maimonides' Creed as his source, he announced that "God will send at the end of days his redeemer to save those who wait for him. For God and for no one else. And as he took us out of Egypt, so he will show us miracles soon and in our own day."[127]

Margolis also had difficulty with the Agudat ha-Rabbanim's continued association with the Americanized RIETS. Rabbi Isaac Elchanan Spector, he declared, "would turn over in his grave if he knew that a seminary had been built bearing his name where [general] philosophy, the humanities and all other meaningless matters were taught." RIETS, he believed, had lost its way as it sought, under Dr. Revel, to emulate Columbia University and the hated Jewish Theological Seminary of America.[128]

These philosophical concerns, coupled with his long-standing practical opposition, led Margolis in 1920 to organize some 135 like-minded critics of the Agudat ha-Rabbanim into the Knesset ha-Rabbanim ha-Orthodoxim. This assembly placed high on its agenda of priorities the reformation of what it called "the politics of kashruth." And not unlike the organization it opposed, the Knesset called for the strengthening of traditional Jewish education in the United States, the greater observance here of the Sabbath, and help for afflicted Jews across the seas. Not surprisingly, it also adroitly refrained from recognizing Zionism as an international Jewish reality in this post-Balfour period. But for all the noise and furor of their criticism and protests, Margolis and his followers failed to unseat the Agudat ha-Rabbanim as the most representative voice of the East European rabbinate in America.[129]

Rabbi Yehudah Heschel Levenberg's contemporaneous, quiet institutional challenge of the Agudat ha-Rabbanim, on the other hand, was ultimately of tremendous, enduring significance. In the 1910's and the early 1920's, the Slabodka-trained chief rabbi of New Haven organized the Beis Ha-Medrash Le-Rabbanim (Orthodox Rabbinical Seminary), the first European-style yeshiva in the United States offering no secular studies.[130] This inaugural institutional statement that Torah Judaism need not, on any level, accommodate Americanization attracted to its faculty such future luminaries as Rabbis Moses Feinstein, Yaacov Ruderman, and interestingly enough, the young, newly arrived Samuel Belkin.[131] Although the school would survive but a few years—it declined precipitously when Levenberg moved himself and his school to Cleveland—it set an ideological standard which at least Rabbis Feinstein and Ruderman would uphold in their respective yeshivot, Mesivta Tifereth Jerusalem of New York and Baltimore's Ner Israel, both founded in the 1930's.

These schools were two of the five enduring institutions formed or transformed during the interwar days which challenged the RIETS/ Agudat ha-Rabbanim monopoly on rabbinic training and leadership, and their shared, if somewhat strained, assumptions about the limits of Americanization. Williamsburg's Mesivta Torah Vodaas, led by Rabbi Shraga Feivel Mendlowitz, Rabbi David Liebowitz's Brooklyn-based Yeshiva Chofetz Chaim, and Brownsville's Yeshiva Rabbi Chaim Berlin, headed by Rabbi Yitzchok Hutner, joined their Manhattan- and Baltimore-based colleagues in standing four-square against the combination of advanced secular and religious studies within one institutional setting. But significantly, none actively opposed their students attending schools like the City College of New York at night. These yeshivot were not producing American Orthodox rabbis, as was RIETS. Rather, they were educating Orthodox rabbis in

America who would acquire their advanced degree of integration with the host society in other, secular institutions. Such were the limits of the approaches to religious educational life even in the circles that were the most resistant to Americanization during the pre–World War II days. There was no rabbinical group or individual who would or could attempt to shut out America totally from the lives of religious students.[132]

The coming of World War II broadened tremendously the limits of Orthodox rabbinic resistance to Americanization. Hitler's invasion of Poland in 1939 and of Russia two years later forced to these shores a new breed of Orthodox Jews to a great extent previously unseen in America. These were men and women who during the period of mass migration had heeded the words of Rabbi Israel Meir Ha-Kohen Kagan (the Chofetz Chaim): "Whoever wishes to live properly before God must not settle in these countries."[133] They were now entering this country—when immigration laws permitted—only because the Europe they knew was in the process of being destroyed. Individually this meant that people who had not broken to any great extent with the traditional past to seek their fortune and new world in America were reinvigorating the Orthodox community. The desire to become like all other Americans was far less pronounced among them than it had been among those who preceded them. Obversely, their zeal to recreate European institutions on American soil was far more emphatic than that of the immigrant Orthodox of the turn of the century. Institutionally, this new migration came to mean the settlement and sustaining in America of two new religious organizational forms, the refugee yeshiva and the leader-oriented sect.

Cleveland's Telshe Yeshiva and the Beis Medrash Govoha in Lakewood, New Jersey, best represent the Torah institutions founded or reestablished in this country by rabbis, students, and their followers who successfully, and in some cases miraculously, escaped the European Holocaust. In the former case, Rabbis Elya Meir Bloch and Chaim Mordecai Katz led their community halfway around the world from western Russia through Siberia to Japan and then to Seattle, Washington, before reassembling their lives and yeshiva in 1941 in an Ohio suburb. There, on American soil, they proceeded to recreate almost intact both the methodology of talmudic study and the insulated spirit of their old-country home. Two years later, Rabbi Aharon Kotler, formerly head of the Polish Kletsk Yeshiva, after a similarly arduous journey, resettled in America. Possessed of an even greater drive to recreate the Jewish religious world then being destroyed by the Nazis, he founded his yeshiva in a rural New Jersey community. There, theoretically removed from the assimilatory influences of the metropolis, an institution was built which would not only block out America but would even deemphasize the "utilitarian" goal of training young men for the active rabbinate. His school stood for the East European ideal of "Torah for its own sake." Men would study there not so much for ordination but for the love of learning. American talmudic scholars would there be produced worthy of what would have been Lithuanian Jewry's highest scholarly accolades.[134]

The arrival in America of leader-oriented Orthodox immigrant groups was also a product of the dislocations which accompanied and followed the Second World War. In 1939 Rabbi Joseph Breuer moved from Frankfurt am Main, by way of Belgium, to New York's Washington Heights, bringing with him the Orthodox traditions of Samson Raphael Hirsch and quickly attracting to his new residence a considerable following of German immigrant Jews. In 1940, Rabbi Joseph Isaac Schneersohn, the leader of the Lubavitcher Hasidim, made Brooklyn's Crown Heights his home, beginning a process which led thousands of wartime and postwar Russian Hasidic refugees to that locality. The year 1946 witnessed the settlement of Hungarian Satmar Rebbe Joel Teitelbaum and his followers in Brooklyn's Williamsburg. And these years and the next decade witnessed Hasidic groups from Romania, Hungary, and Galicia following their leaders to these shores. The Hasidic groups differed from each other somewhat in matters ritual, social, and ideological, and overall the approach of the East European Hasidim to religious life certainly varied significantly from the teachings of the Hirschian Western European contingent. But what they all held in common was the Orthodox community structure, resistant of rapid Americanization, rooted in their allegiance to their respective chief rabbis.[135]

Unlike poor Rabbi Jacob Joseph, who after his arrival in the United States searched for a constituency which would resist the inroads of the new land, Rabbis Breuer, Schneersohn, Teitelbaum, and the others led their followers to America with their individual authority and power remaining intact. Committed to recreating the lost communities of Europe on American soil and resisting, each to its own degree, the pressures of immigrant acculturation, these leader-oriented groups quickly established their own networks of schools, self-help charitable institutions, and social organizations. Chief rabbinates were now truly being established in this country, but with one major difference. None of these men, with the possible exception of the Jewish-proselytizing Lubavitcher Rebbe, attempted to extend their formal suzerainty beyond the community of their true believers.

These new, growing, and confident Orthodox elements impacted dramatically on the status, thinking, and practice of such indigenous Orthodox groups as the Agudat ha-Rabbanim. No longer were these long-time Orthodox rabbis in America the most strident force against Americanization. Though the circumstances that brought the newcomers to America were entirely different from those which directed the earlier generation, they were nonetheless showing that traditional faith could progress in this country without any accommodation to the host environment. This meant, for example, that an Americanized RIETS/Yeshiva University, even in its most traditional of incarnations, was not, to their minds, a necessary evil to attract a lost generation back to the ancestral faith. Why, Lakewood or Telshe devotees asked rhetorically, trim one's ideological and social sails to represent the entire, seemingly uncaring American Jewish community, when there now existed a strong, ever developing, committed religious population which accepted the law of the Torah and wanted only those rabbis trained as in the past to lead and guide them?[136]

This newly arrived Orthodox leadership also questioned the Agudat ha-Rabbanim's long-standing commitment to Zionism, as expressed through its support of the Mizrachi movement. Many, if not all, of the newcomers were backers of the Agudath Israel. That religio-political party, founded in Central and Eastern Europe in 1912, linked in its opposition to Zionism a diverse group of Hirschians, Hasidim, and Lithuanian yeshiva spokesmen. At its inception the Agudath Israel criticized modern Jewish nationalism on strong theoretical and practical theological grounds. In its view, Jewish tradition had ordained that the Jews were in exile for their sins and were destined to remain in Diaspora until Providence willed their miraculous return. Accordingly, the contemporaneous Zionist manifestation was a false messianic movement, led mostly by men and women who had broken with the Jewish religious past, which threatened the continuity of the people's existence. Significantly, the Agudath Israel was particularly strident in its upbraiding of Mizrachi religious Zionists, seeing them as the worst transgressors of all. They spoke and behaved daily like Orthodox Jews and yet they supported the apostate movement.[137]

The cataclysmic and climactic events of the 1930's and 1940's, which witnessed Zionism's emergence not only as a major political reality but more significantly as a practical refuge of necessity, caused the Agudath Israel to modify its position. It had become increasingly difficult to oppose this projected sovereign refuge haven for one's people in a Hitlerian world, even when one opposed the Zionist movement. Accordingly, the Agudath Israel deemphasized its theological difficulties with Jewish nationalism and refocused its attention on the fact that Israel was being built by secular Jews unconcerned with and unbridled by the law of the Torah. Now occupying an ideological position still significantly different from the Mizrachi's—the latter had always considered itself the "watchdog" for Judaism *within* the Zionist movement—the Agudath Israel in the 1930's and 1940's charted its own separatist role in "building Eretz Yisrael in accordance with Torah and the guidance of the sages." Practically this meant that it would remain outside of the Zionist political system, while creating its own religious institutions and fighting for greater traditional religiosity in the Yishuv. By World War II's end only a small minority from the original Agudath Israel coalition, the Naturei Karta of Jerusalem and their Satmarer cousins, remained opposed to the rise of Israel.[138]

The Agudath Israel in its original form—Rabbi Gabriel Margolis notwithstanding—made no appreciable impact upon the Orthodox rabbinate in America through the mid-1930's. Agudat ha-Rabbanim and RCA members seemingly shared leadership in the relatively small but vibrant American Mizrachi movement. Indeed an American branch of the Agudath Israel did not appear until 1938. And even then, under the guiding hand of the Agudat ha-Rabbanim's president, Eliezer Silver, a major goal of the American branch was to find mechanisms for all Orthodox Jews concerned with the Yishuv to cooperate in promoting their religious institutional life.[139]

The Torah-world leaders who arrived during and after World War II rejected this cooperating, seemingly half-hearted approach. Transplanting the European Agudath Israel's position to America, they endeavored to chart a course for their movement in line with their group's worldwide position. Rabbis Kotler, Bloch, Katz, and Grozovsky all became, as early as 1941, part of the Council of Torah Sages, an Agudath Israel presidium in America which effectively replaced the indigenous American-born leadership. Implicit here was the newcomers' critique of the old-time American rabbis' nonadherence to uncomprising principles.[140]

The Council of Torah Sages also championed, and with characteristic intensity, long-standing Agudat ha-Rabbanim causes. The older organization had from its inception argued that Yiddish was the most appropriate language for Jewish religious instruction. But it allowed, however, that English might be used as a secondary tongue, particularly in geographical areas where Yiddish had been forgotten. In 1947 Rabbi Kotler declared that Yiddish must be the sole language for teaching the tradition. "Mass assimilation among the gentiles," he pronounced, "will result if we utilize the language of the land. Our Jewish children will then emulate non-Jewish practice."[141]

The council's 1956 categorical condemnation of Orthodox rabbis cooperating with their Conservative and Reform counterparts in the Synagogue Council of America and on local boards of rabbis gave another of the Agudat ha-Rabbanim's old-line principles its fullest articulation. In a ban signed by eleven *roshei yeshiva*—including Rabbis Kotler, Feinstein, and Ruderman, two Mesifta Torah Vodaas instructors, Yaacov Kamenetsky and Gedalia Schorr, and two refugee RIETS scholars, Lifshitz and Zaks—colleagues were "forbidden by the law of our sacred Torah to be members" of such organizations. Significantly, Rabbi Eliezer Silver, still president of the Agudat ha-Rabbanim, did not sign the proclamation. For him, such a written testament—despite his basic philosophical agreement with its thrust—would effectively cut off Yeshiva University men whom he still hoped to influence both from his organization and from the wider, growing yeshiva world.[142]

Men like Eliezer Silver were undoubtedly filled with bittersweet sentiments by the rise of this new era of immigrant Orthodoxy. While they could only applaud the rapid and comprehensive growth of a truer-than-ever Orthodox community in this country which was seemingly well-resisting America's pressures and recreating reasonable facsimiles of Old World life-styles, they had to be saddened that the realization of that which they had originally set out to do was being achieved by others. Indeed, by the mid-1950's, long-time Agudat ha-Rabbanim members could not help notice that even their organization was no longer in their hands. In 1958, the majority of the organization's members were wartime immigrant rabbis, and the Agudat ha-Rabbanim's presidium was now controlled by Council of Torah Sages men like Kotler, Feinstein, Kamenetsky, and Lifshitz among others. The strictest of the Orthodox of one generation had been eclipsed by the new yeshiva world with its army of new immigrants. In 1960, the Agudat ha-Rabbanim officially opposed members belonging to mixed rabbinical groups. It solemnly declared that any rabbi who belonged to such organizations as the Synagogue Council and/or the New York Board of Rabbis (NYBR) would forfeit his membership. And with an eye toward the Orthodox Union/RCA it declared that "all Orthodox rabbis must also resign from the Board of Rabbis."[143]

This new generation of immigrant Orthodox rabbis also made its impact on the thoughts and behavior of RCA members. Although the Council of Torah Sages denigrated their education and deplored their outlook, some RCA men have been either unwilling or unable to ignore the new immigrant rabbis' teachings and influence. This sensitivity to what renowned, transplanted European figures were thinking and saying was seen most graphically in the RCA's reaction to the aforementioned 1956 ban. With Rabbis Kotler, Feinstein, and others officially on record as opposed to their membership in the Synagogue Council, and/or the NYBR, a group of RCA spokesmen led by then President Rabbi David Hollander argued that the RCA had no choice but to submit to higher Torah law. Although Hollander's view never acquired the majority necessary to change RCA policy, the influence of the council had made inroads. Its uncompromising position had detached from the American Orthodox rabbinical ranks a clerical segment willing, after a generation of struggle for independence, to surrender its autonomy to a body of immigrant rabbis.[144]

The yeshiva world has influenced the American Orthodox rabbinate in other ways, less easily documented, but equally significant. As one contemporary sociologist discovered, the RIETS student of today is far different from his counterpart of prewar days. He too has felt the impact of the yeshiva world's uncompromising ideology. Indeed, many have come to redefine our term "simulation" to mean the attempt to approximate the talmudic learning environment of a Chaim Berlin or a Lakewood while participating to an ever decreasing degree in a university setting. And while all RIETS men revere Rabbi Joseph Soloveitchik, and a goodly proportion still evince an interest in the secular, for some the rabbinic role-model is a Rabbi David Lifshitz (a signatory of the 1956 ban) or any number of younger *roshei yeshiva* who have themselves sought to emulate the East European rabbinical style. Significantly, RIETS has responded to these demands and proclivities through the establishment, beginning in the 1950's, of its own Kollel (postgraduate, "Torah for its own sake") programs, as well as, in 1970, the *yadin yadin* program, first conceived of by Revel two generations ago. Finally, although Rabbi Haskel Lookstein, following in his own father's footsteps, may have been assigned by RIETS to teach students homiletics, many present-day rabbinic candidates believe that their ability to rise in congregational life is predicated less on their capacity to deliver articulate English-language sermons and more on their reputation as a talmudic scholar attractive to an increasingly learned Orthodox laity.[145]

V. Reflections on the Current Generation of Accommodators (ca. 1940–1980)

For all the inroads immigrant Orthodox rabbis have made during the post–World War II years upon the thinking and practices of their American-trained colleagues, the traditions begun by Drachman and Goldstein,[146] institutionalized by Revel and Belkin, formalized by Lookstein, and delimited and crystallized philosophically by Rabbi Soloveitchik have by no means disappeared. The current generation of RCA rabbis still constitutes for the most part a hard core of support for the established principles of simulation, inclusion, and cooperation. For some, continued backing for the idea that Orthodox rabbis must represent the entire community, and should cooperate with and include less-traditional colleagues to the extent that they can, is an exigency of life as a minority denomination in the suburbanized contemporary Jewish community. This point of view was clearly apparent in the reaction of rabbis serving communities far removed from the New York metropolis to Hollander's anti-SCA position. "A local rabbi who would follow Hollander's intolerant footsteps," one Colorado-based source declared, "would be hooted out of town or consigned to obscurity."[147] But for most of the clerics who tacitly ignored the 1956 ban, the decision to avoid self-segregation was less a product of necessity and more an act of faith. Indeed RIETS produced, from the late 1930's to the 1950's, a coterie of graduates who not only supported umbrella defense and interdenominational organizations but personally rose to leadership positions in these cooperative institutions.

Significantly, men like Rabbis Emanuel Rackman (RIETS, '32), Israel Miller (RIETS, '41), and Herschel Schacter (RIETS, '42) were all initiated into the practical world of Jewish intragroup cooperation as chaplains in the United States Armed Forces during the Second World War. As volunteers willing to serve both their country and all its Jewish elements, they entered the military already predisposed toward representing a broad ethnic polity. Their close observation, if not eyewitnessing, of Hitler's atrocities sensitized them further to Rabbi Soloveitchik's message that Jew-hatred drew no ideological lines.[148]

Returning to America in the late 1940's, all three of these men built multifaceted careers as leaders of second-generation American congregations, spokesmen for the RCA and for Religious Zionism in America, and as Orthodox representatives in a myriad of intragroup organizations. Each has served in the Executive and other high-ranking capacities in the Jewish Agency, the American Zionist Federation, and the World Zionist Organization. Miller and particularly Schacter were among the first to join the contemporary community-wide battle for Soviet Jews.[149] Rackman was president of the New York Board of Rabbis from 1955 to 1957. And not surprisingly each has served as chairman of the Jewish Welfare Board's Commission on Jewish Chaplaincy. Most significantly, in 1968 Schacter was elected chairman of the Conference of Presidents of Major American Jewish Organizations, the first Orthodox rabbinical leader to speak for that umbrella organization. The principle of cooperation was thus fully articulated as a RIETS/RCA man represented to the American and world governments the interests of some thirty Jewish organizations running almost the gamut of Jewish commitments and postions. In 1974–76 Miller served in this powerful and prestigious post. And in 1982, Rabbi Julius Berman, a 1959 graduate of RIETS and president of the Orthodox Union, became the third Orthodox-based chairman.[150]

Architectural, sermonic, and ancillary congregational simulation is also still advocated by most RCA members. And in the most recent decade, Orthodox simulation has added an additional dimension, for at least some RCA members, through their advocacy of increased women's participation in all aspects of synagogue life. The rise of the feminist movement has impacted substantially upon American Jewish denominational life. Dramatic change has both taken place and has been resisted in the more liberal movements. Women are now trained and ordained as rabbbis at the Reform Hebrew Union College–Jewish Institute of Religion and at the Reconstructionist Rabbinical College. And their sisters have now battled successfully for admission to the Jewish Theological Seminary's rabbinical program. On the local level, Conservative women have struggled for greater liturgical access and participation, and both Conservative and Reform women have petitioned for increased control over the political dimensions of synagogue life.[151]

Americanized Orthodoxy, too, has not been immune to these currents of change. Although a goodly proportion of the RCA membership has resisted to date either debate over or concession to women's goals, another smaller contingent has been searching, textually and sociologically, for the limits to which they can accommodate within the Orthodox reading of Jewish law that which is becoming part of the more liberal Jewish theological/sociological world. Accordingly, many Orthodox congregations now permit their women to serve on lay boards of trustees, and some even permit female membership on synagogue ritual committees. Most strikingly, a few rabbis have placed their imprimatur upon separate women's tefilot (prayer services) within their communities. Interestingly, by 1982 this latter initiative had become pervasive enough for the Agudat ha-Rabbanim to declare in a tone somewhat reminiscent of eighty years ago:

> God forbid this should come to pass. A daughter of Israel may not participate in such worthless ceremonies that are totally contrary to Halacha. We are shocked to hear that "rabbis" have promoted such an undertaking which results in the desecration of God and his Torah. We forewarn all those who assist such "Minyonim," that we will take the strictest measures to prevent such "prayers," which are a product of pure ignorance and illiteracy. We admonish these "Orthodox rabbis": Do not make a comedy out of Torah.[152]

In 1976, Rabbi Norman Lamm was elected Yeshiva University's

third president. A self-described disciple of Rabbis Belkin and Solo-veitchik, this American-born and Yeshiva College-trained, RIETS-or-dained leader was in his early career a junior colleague of Joseph Lookstein at Yorkville's Kehilath Jeshurun and later served as successor to Leo Jung at the West Side, New York, Jewish Center.[153] During his relatively brief administration to date, Lamm has committed himself forcefully to many of the now century-old principles which have directed the Americanized Orthodox rabbinate. But, as we have seen, the Orthodox world in America today is quite different from the one his predecessors first knew. The refugee-yeshiva/leader-oriented communities, now in their own second generation, are strong, resolute, and growing. The simulators and cooperators seem to be represented more in his own generation than in the one being trained and emerging from his own theological seminary.

Lamm, for his part, has urged lay and rabbinical leaders "to broaden our horizons beyond our immediate needs and the concerns of our narrow constituency to embrace all of the Jewish community throughout the world." And he has spoken out in a historical vein against "right wing . . . authoritarianism which . . . has largely abandoned the fierce intellectual independence which had always been the hallmark of the European yeshiva scholar in all segments of religious life." On a more philosophical level he has declared similarly:

> We are committed to secular studies, including all the risks that this implies, not only because of vocational or social reasons, but because we consider that it is the will of God that there would be a world in which Torah be effective; that all wisdom issues ultimately from the Creator and therefore it is the Almighty who legitimizes all knowledge.

Finally, he has charged his fellow Americanized Orthodox rabbis to take their unique message, different from what is offered both by the more liberal denominations and by the world of transplanted Europe, to the larger American Jewish community as teachers, rabbis, and communal leaders. Time will tell how strongly his voice will be heard both within and without the American Orthodox seminary that he champions.[154]

Jeffrey S. Gurock is Associate Professor of American Jewish History at Yeshiva University and the author of *When Harlem Was Jewish, 1870–1930.*

Notes

The author would like to thank Rabbis Berish Mandelbaum and Herschel Schacter for their bibliographic assistance in the preparation of this article.

The following abbreviations are used:

AH   *American Hebrew*
AJH   *American Jewish History*
AJHQ   *American Jewish Historical Quarterly*
AJYB   *American Jewish Yearbook*
EJ   *Encyclopaedia Judaica* (Jerusalem and New York, 1971–72)
HS   *Hebrew Standard*
JCR   *Jewish Communal Register* (New York, 1917–18)
MA   Judah L. Magnes Archives. Jewish Historical General Archives, Jerusalem, Israel; copy of file at American Jewish Archives, Cincinnati, Ohio.
Min CED Minutes of the meeting of the Committee on Education of the Jewish Community of New York
Min ECK Minutes of the Executive Committee of the Kehillah
MJ   *Morgen Zhurnal*
PAAJR   *Proceedings of the American Academy for Jewish Research*
PAJHS   *Publication of the American Jewish Historical Society*
UJE   *Universal Jewish Encyclopedia,* edited by Isaac Landman (New York, 1939–43)
YT   *Yiddishes Tageblatt*

1. Moshe Davis. *The Emergence of Conservative Judaism* (Philadelphia, 1963), p. 237; Bernard Drachman, *The Unfailing Light* (New York, 1948), pp. 177–182; Cyrus Adler, "Semi-Centennial Address," in *The Jewish Theological Seminary of America: Semi-Centennial Volume,* ed. Cyrus Adler (New York, 1939), pp. 5–7; Henry Pereira Mendes, "The Beginnings of the Seminary," ibid., pp. 35–42.

2. The dividing lines between "Orthodox" and "Conservative" rabbis involved in this initiative were much less the differences in their rabbinical training than in their philosophy and practices in American pulpits after ordination. The similarity in their rabbinical training, whether they are indicated in the text as "Orthodox" or "Conservative," is evidenced by the following comparisons. Among those of Ashkenazic origins, both Drachman and Kohut were graduates of the Breslau Seminary, the former in 1885, the latter eighteen years earlier. Schneeberger was ordained by Azriel Hildesheimer in Berlin in 1871, Aaron Wise was ordained by the same man a few years earlier when Hildesheimer was still in Eisenstadt, Hungary. Wise and his older colleague Kohut significantly were students at the Pressburg Yeshiva in Hungary, the school of Rabbi Moses Sofer (the *Hatam Sofer*), before gaining ordination among more modern, liberal exponents of traditional Judaism. Bettelheim was ordained in the 1860's by Rabbi Shlomo Yehudah Leib Rappaport, the famous traditional rabbinical pioneer of the Haskalah and supporter of *Wissenshaft des Judenthums*. Marcus Jastrow, ordained by Rabbis Moses Feilchenfeld of Rogasen and Wolf Landau of Dresden, clearly received at least as traditional a training as the other American-serving rabbis, both Orthodox and Conservative. Probably the most traditionally trained rabbi in the group was Rabbi Moses Maisner. He was ordained by Rabbi A. S. B. Sofer of the Pressburg Yeshiva. Drachman described his colleague as a "strong adherent of Orthodox teachings who served Adath Israel Synagogue of New York. See *AJYB* 1903–4, p. 77, and Drachman, p. 179. Importantly, all the rabbis here mentioned, including Maisner, were recipients of Ph.D.s from recognized Central European universities. See below for a discussion of the levels of Orthodox training received by those who defined themselves as Orthodox in the

America of the 1880's. For now, the heterodoxy of practice among those defining themselves as Conservative is evidenced by the fact that Kohut of New York's Ahavath Chesed, Wise at the city's Rodef Shalom, and Jastrow at Philadelphia's Rodef Shalom all came to pulpits which had already broken with totally distinct Orthodox practices. Bettelheim was rabbi in the Baltimore Hebrew Congregation, which used the Jastrow-Szold prayerbook and permitted mixed seating during the services. Significantly, his Orthodox colleague Schneeberger served that city's Congregation Chizuk Emunah, whose members had broken away from the Baltimore Hebrew Congregation over the issue of mixed seating.

Among the Sephardic rabbis, the Mendeses, father and son, were members of a British-based rabbinical house. Both received secular training at English-style schools and universities and were trained for the rabbinate primarily at home through family tutors. Their father and grandfather was London Rabbi David Aaron De Sola. Meldola De Sola of Montreal, another of the fourteen Seminary founders, was also a grandson of David De Sola. Sabato Morais, commonly acknowledged as the greatest guiding spirit behind the Seminary, was privately trained for the rabbinate in Italy and ordained by Rabbi Abraham Baruch Piperno of Leghorn. Henry S. Jacobs, born in Kingston, Jamaica, rabbi of Ashkenazic Congregation B'nai Jeshurun of New York in 1886, also claimed Sephardic heritage and received similar training. He was ordained by Rabbi N. Nathan of Kingston and served at Shearith Israel (New York) for two years before moving on to B'nai Jeshurun. There he was more comfortable with the abridged Torah reading and other variations which made that congregation, in the words of its historian, "classified as Conservative-Reform, together with Jastrow of Philadelphia and Szold of Baltimore."

Rabbis Weil and Davidson are the remaining rabbis mentioned in the sources as involved with the founding of the Seminary. I have been unable to find any background information on these two figures except for the random remark in an *AJYB* listing of rabbis and cantors in 1903–4 that a Rabbi D. Davidson served Congregation Agudath Jesharim in New York City. For more details on these rabbis, see Davis, pp. 329–366; Israel Goldstein, *A Century of Judaism in New York* (New York, 1930), pp. 160–163; Isaac Markens, *The Hebrews in America* (New York, 1888), pp. 275–308; Isaac Fein, *The Making of an American Jewish Community: The History of Baltimore Jewry* (Philadelphia, 1971), pp. 118–119. David De Sola Pool and Tamar De Sola Pool, *Old Faith in a New World* (New York, 1955), pp. 192–194, 425; Guido Kisch, ed., *Das Breslauer Seminar: Judisch-Theologisches Seminar (Fraenkelscher Stiftung) in Breslau 1854–1938* (Tubingen, 1963), pp. 381–403.

3. This denominational historiographic point of view is clearly most reflected in Davis's *The Emergence of Conservative Judaism*. See also on this trend, Herbert Parzen, *Architects of Conservative Judaism* (New York, 1964), pp. 18–25.

4. Mendes, pp. 35–41. See also on the purposes of the early Seminary, Davis, p. 237; Adler, pp. 5–7; and Drachman, pp. 177–182. There is a significant difference of opinion among both historians and contemporary observers as to the relative strength of the so-called Orthodox as opposed to the Conservative factions in the organizing of the Seminary. Clearly reflecting later denominational tensions and prejudices, Drachman's autobiography suggests that Kohut "was the only rabbinical representative of Conservative Judaism." See Drachman, p. 179. Cyrus Adler, in his contribution to the Jewish Theological Seminary festschrift, talks of a highly heterogeneous grouping "reflecting varying views." See Adler, p. 5. Davis's work suggests a view of these events similar to Adler's. In like manner, Drachman is clear in his understanding of the early Seminary as having an "uncompromising adherence to the tenets of Orthodox Judaism [although] the term 'Orthodox' is not used." See Drachman, pp. 181–182. Davis emphasizes the heterogeneity of opinion which pervaded the Seminary. For our purposes it is clear, however, that the self-defined Orthodox leaders in the institution saw their work as strictly Orthodox, albeit

looking, as Drachman put it, "for the harmonious combination of Orthodox Judaism in America which to me was the true concept of Judaism." See Drachman, p. 206.

5. Abraham J. Karp, "New York Chooses a Chief Rabbi," *PAJHS*, March 1954, pp. 129–194. Jonathan D. Sarna, trans. and ed., *People Walk on Their Heads: Moses Weinberger's Jews and Judaism in New York* (New York, 1982), pp. 22, 111–114.

6. The suggestion that the rabbis here engaged in organization building viewed themselves as Orthodox rabbis creating Orthodox institutions in America is evidenced either by their contemporary statements or by their later activities. Morais, for example, argued during the deliberations over the founding of the Seminary that it should be called "The Orthodox Seminary." See Davis, p. 235. Drachman, as noted previously, argued that "although a certain proportion of the organizing delegation and participating rabbis belonged to the Conservative wing of Judaism, the principles of the Seminary . . . were those of uncompromising adherence to the tenets of Orthodox Judaism." See Drachman, p. 181. The Mendeses and Schneeberger were founder-leaders of both the Seminary and the later Union of Orthodox Jewish Congregations of America, which was formed in 1898 to promote "Orthodox Judaism whenever occasions arise in civic and social matters." See Israel M. Goldman, "Henry W. Schneeberger: His Role in American Judaism," *AJHQ*, December 1967, p. 179, and *AH*, January 4, 1901, pp. 231–233. Additionally, not only did the men see themselves as Orthodox, but they were perceived as such by some significant contemporary observers. Rabbi Joseph H. Hertz, a student of Morais, eulogized his teacher as "the trusted leader of Orthodox Judaism in America." See J. H. Hertz, "Sabato Morais: A Pupil's Tribute," in Adler, p. 47. Drachman himself referred to Morais, H. P. Mendes, and Schneeberger as "splendid representatives of the Orthodox ministry." See Drachman, pp. 177–182. But probably the most significant "testimony" to Morais's Orthodoxy is the appreciation of him expressed by the Agudat ha-Rabbanim, which, as we will immediately see, represented transplanted East European forms of Orthodoxy in America. Its *Sefer ha-Yovel shel Agudat ha-Rabbanim ha-Ortodoksim de-Artsot ha-Brit ve Canada* (New York, 1928) recounted the history of the Jewish Theological Seminary and stated that "the founder of the Seminary, Dr. Sabato Morais, was indeed an upholder of the old traditions . . . and the early students who emerged from there were full-hearted for the faith of Israel and its Torah." The *Sefer ha-Yovel* then contrasts Morais's upholding of old traditions with the later "conservatives, so-called 'upholders of old traditions' who did not deserve to be called such." See *Sefer ha-Yovel*, p. 18. To be abundantly fair, it should be noted that the publication of Davis's book sparked an important historiographic debate as to how the designations "Conservative" and "Orthodox" may be used in dealing with nineteenth-century figures. One of the most spirited exchanges was between Abraham J. Karp and Charles Liebman on the question of Morais's designation as Orthodox. Liebman claimed that "Morais . . . must be reclaimed to Orthodoxy," based upon his textual-based understanding that when Morais used the term "enlightened conservatism" he was referring to modern forms of Orthodoxy. If "conservatism" did not mean Orthodoxy, it is unlikely he would have used the term "Orthodox" in his defense of the Seminary to Reform Rabbi Richard Gottheil as an "Orthodox institution which will win many converts to intelligent conservatism." Liebman also notes historiographically that in other writings Davis characterized Morais as "the unflagging champion of traditional Judaism." For Liebman "the first head of the Seminary was apparently fond of the term 'conservative' as a synonym for Orthodoxy." Karp, on the other hand, while admitting that Morais called himself Orthodox and "espoused the cause of Orthodoxy," said he displayed many un-Orthodox philosophical and practical features uncharacteristic of "the Orthodoxy of a rabbi living in the 19th century." Morais, for example, worked with non-Orthodox elements in both nontheological, communal endeavors and in the founding of Maimonides College. Morais also chose as his colleagues on the advisory board of the Seminary men like Jastrow, Szold, Kohut,

etc.—for Karp "hardly an Orthodox rabbinic body." Most significantly, Karp quotes Morais as advocating liturgical change and philosophical departures deviating from Orthodox belief. Our suggestion is that Morais may be characterized as an Orthodox rabbi based on his self-definition and activities, his acceptance as such by his American Orthodox colleagues, and most notably his acceptance by the Agudat ha-Rabbanim. Clearly Karp is right in arguing that Rabbi Hayim Soloveitchik of Brest-Litovsk, Isaac Elchanan Spector of Kovno, or even Samson Raphael Hirsch of Frankfurt am Main might not have called Morais an Orthodox rabbi. But that conceivable nonrecognition does not make him a Historical School rabbi by default. Rather he and his generation of Orthodox rabbis—Drachman, Schneeberger, et al.—as we will see below, are spiritual, when not actual, antecedents of the "Orthodoxy espoused and practiced by the Rabbinical Council of America in the present decade of the 20th century," a basis of judgment of Orthodoxy which Karp feels cannot be used in evaluating Morais. See on this debate, Charles Liebman, "Orthodoxy in Nineteenth Century America," *Tradition*, Spring–Summer 1964, pp. 132–140, and Abraham J. Karp, "The Origins of Conservative Judaism," *Conservative Judaism*, Summer 1965, pp. 33–48. There is, of course, no historical debate or question concerning the Orthodox affiliation of Rabbi Jacob Joseph.

7. Karp, pp. 143–144; Max S. Nussenbaum, "Champion of Orthodox Judaism: A Biography of Sabato Morais" (D.H.L. diss., Bernard Revel Graduate School, Yeshiva University, 1964), pp. 1–10; *JE*, vol. 8, pp. 486–487. The elder Mendes, though not a university graduate, was well versed enough in secular culture to run Northwick College, a school for Anglicized Jewish youths.

8. Drachman, pp. 3, 100, 151, 165, 167, and passim.

9. Goldman, pp. 153–159 and passim.

10. The elder Mendes was born and raised in Kingston, Jamaica, where he established the Beth Limud School of Kingston. He resigned that post when he moved on to England for his "family-based" rabbinical training. After service in a pulpit in Birmingham he was elected to a pulpit in London, where he built Northwick College, a Jewish boarding school. H. P. Mendes attended his father's school, which drew to its student body the children of Anglicized upper-middle-class families of varying religious commitments. It offered them a combined secular and religious curriculum. On the Mendeses' early training and associational patterns, see *JE*, vol. 8., p. 468, and Eugene Markovitz, "Henry P. Mendes: Builder of Traditional Judaism in America," (D.H.L. diss., Bernard Revel Graduate School, Yeshiva University, 1961), pp. 4–5. Morais, similarly, had a broad associational pattern with Jews of all stripes as well as non-Jews. He counted among his closest Jewish friends Emanuel Felici Veneziani, who was destined to be named Chevalier of the Crown of Italy, Israel Costa, later Chief Rabbi of Leghorn, and Raffaelo Ascoli, lawyer and writer. His membership in the Order of Free Masons of Italy testified to his associational history with non-Jews, particularly Italian patriots, in his youth and young manhood. See Nussenbaum, pp. 7–10. For an example of Morais's communication, if not participation, on nontheological issues with Reform rabbis, see Nussenbaum, p. 150, for a discussion of Jastrow, Mendes, and Joseph Krauskopf mediating an 1890 Philadelphia cloakmakers' strike. The Mendeses showed their interdenominational orientation in their activities in the founding and early leadership of the New York Board of Jewish Ministers, later the Board of Rabbis. See Markovitz, pp. 133–153, for discussions of their combined antimissionary and promodern Jewish education work.

11. Drachman, pp. 100, 206. Drachman insisted in an appended note to his autobiography, that he did not agree with the view which saw Hildesheimer's Berlin Seminary as Orthodox and by analogy his education as less than Orthodox. For him, Breslau, which advocated "the bindingness of Jewish law," and Berlin, which advocated "the harmonious union of Orthodox faith

and modern culture," were both Orthodox institutions. He did, of course, note that some other Orthodox rejected even the Orthodoxy of Hildesheimer. For him, Breslau and Berlin were both "in fundamental harmony with the basic concept of Traditional Judaism and its adjustment to modern conditions."

12. Although the committee that chose the chief rabbi was concerned about the "various shades of Orthodoxy . . . in America," Rabbi Jacob Joseph himself never spoke out publicly in criticism of the legitimacy of the Orthodox ordination claimed by his English-Sephardic and American-born Ashkenazic colleagues. Indeed, there is some evidence that at least one of his contemporaries both recognized the existence of an American Orthodoxy uptown that was different from theirs and was pleased with its activities. Weinberger, in a letter to a friend in Hungary, spoke of "uptown congregation named Orach Chayim, whose members are enormously wealthy and completely German . . . who go there daily for the afternoon prayers and to engage in Torah study." See Sarna, p. 116. Polish-born Abraham Neumark, trained at rabbinical seminaries in Berlin and Breslau, was spiritual leader of that congregation. His educational profile is clearly not unlike Schneeberger's or Drachman's. See Ben Zion Eisenstadt, *Anshe Hasheim b'Arzeis Ha-Bris* (St. Louis, 1933), p. 21, for Neumark's biography.

Despite this "character witness," additional questions could have been raised, and would still be cogent today, as to the acceptability of the ordination of the Seminary Orthodox group to those of East European heritage. Critics of the Sephardim would have relatively little difficulty with the ritual and philosophical Orthodoxy of those who ordained Morais and Mendes. But they might question the levels of knowledge of traditional Talmud and rabbinic sources achieved by their colleagues. The Sephardim might be seen as Orthodox but not as highly revered or respected as Orthodox rabbis. Observers seeking to denigrate Schneeberger's legitimacy might also criticize his early training and facility with traditional texts. And questions could be raised about his teacher Hildesheimer. Though widely seen as an Orthodox rabbi by German Jewry, it is clear that he moved his seminary from Eisenstadt to Berlin because of opposition to him emanating from Hungarian rabbis, disciples of the Hatam Sofer, who deplored his modernism. See on Hildesheimer, *EJ*, vol. 8, col. 478, and Leo Jung, ed., *Jewish Leaders (1750–1940)* (New York, 1953), pp. 220–221. However, it also should be noted that Hildesheimer was "orthodox enough" for the committee which selected Rabbi Jacob Joseph to solicit his opinion about possible candidates for the chief rabbinate of New York. See Karp, p. 137.

Bernard Drachman's case presents far more problems. He might be "disqualified" from the Orthodox rabbinate on the basis of his early training as well as the background of his teachers. At the Breslau seminary, Drachman counted as his teachers a most heterogeneous faculty which included Heinrich Graetz, Manuel Joel, Israel Lewy, David Rosin, Jacob Freudenthal, and Baruch Zuckerman. All of these scholars were advocates of Reform and of the philosophy of *Wissenschaft des Judenthums*, and friends, colleagues, or disciples of Zachariah Frankel. Although Drachman claimed for himself a belief "in the bindingness of the authority of tradition upon the individual conscience," he was ordained by Joel, a recognized contemporary supporter of Frankel, who clearly questioned the untrammeled validity of the oral law. See on the history of the Breslau seminary, Isaac Heinemann, "The Idea of the Jewish Theological Seminary 75 Years Ago and Today," in Kisch, pp. 85–101. At all events, I believe that Drachman proved his Orthodoxy not so much at the Breslau seminary but immediately thereafter, when he left one of his earliest pulpits, at New York's Congregation Bikur Cholim, over the issue of the synagogue trustees' demand that he support their initiative toward mixed seating in the services. That act, more than philosophical pronouncements and educational background, might ultimately prove to be the most effective historical guideline between American Orthodoxy and American Conservatism in the nineteenth century.

Even if Rabbi Jacob Joseph could have accepted this appreciation of Drachman as Orthodox, he might still have had difficulties with the ongoing affiliation of Drachman and his associates with the Jewish Theological Seminary. They all called their work Orthodox, but an examination of the institution's earliest curriculum would raise additional questions. Not only were they part of a most heterogeneous faculty but they were training rabbis in a way more reminiscent of Breslau—if not Geiger's Berlin—than of Volozin. The Bible was "the principal text book of the Seminary . . . selected portions of the Talmud form[ed] a part of each year's instruction," Jewish history would be taught primarily for "its bearing upon the history of the world," and all graduates were to be required to have a secular education. Additionally, words like "critical accuracy" and "Historical Judaism" were used to describe the approach toward study, phrases that could be construed as supporting either American Orthodoxy or Conservatism but certainly not the Orthodoxy of East European Rabbi Jacob Joseph. See Davis, pp. 240–241, for the Jewish Theological Seminary statement on curriculum.

13. Karp, p. 188.

14. Benjamin Kline Hunnicutt, "The Jewish Sabbath Movement in the Early Twentieth Century," *AJH*, December 1979, pp. 196–215.

15. Clearly Mendes, Morais, et al. had no cause to denigrate the legitimacy of Rabbi Jacob Joseph's Orthodox ordination. But they did outspokenly question his effectiveness as an American Orthodox rabbi. H. P. Mendes wondered out loud, "will he be able to take up the fight against the encroaching steps of Reform in America? Do not give way to false hopes. Those who come after you will be Americans, full-blooded Americans like your brethren in faith uptown." And Morais chimed in, "[Rabbi Joseph] is not a cultured man. He does not possess the knowledge nor the literary attainments which a rabbi should possess." See *American Israelite*, March 30, 1888, and *New York Herald*, July 31, 1888, quoted in Karp, p. 153.

16. It is interesting to note that in attempting to recreate rabbinic authority in America, specifically on the kosher meat issue, Rabbi Joseph ultimately had to turn to his uptown American Orthodox colleagues H. P. Mendes and Drachman for help in bringing the wholesale butchers into line. Drachman and Mendes aided their downtown associate, although for them meat monitoring was not the highest communal concern. See Karp, p. 169.

17. Sarna, pp. 51–56.

18. The Orthodox rabbinate in America, of course, predates the 1880's. Rabbi Abraham Rice of Baltimore is generally acknowledged as the first ordained rabbi to serve in this country. A student of Rabbis Abraham Bing and Wolf Hamburger of the yeshiva in Wuerzburg, he arrived in the United States in 1840 and served in Baltimore, Maryland. He was joined in the American Orthodox pulpit in 1853 when Rabbi Bernard Illowy arrived from Hungary. A student of Rabbi Moses Schreiber of Pressburg and later the recipient of a Ph.D. from the University of Budapest, Illowy served in pulpits in New York, Philadelphia, and New Orleans before becoming Rice's Baltimore-based colleague in the 1860's. Representatives of the East European Orthodox rabbinate in the United States pre-1887 include Rabbis Abraham Joseph Ash of New York, Abraham Jacob Lesser of Chicago, New York's Joseph Moses Aaronsohn and, of course, Moses Weinberger. Ash served Beis Hamedrash Ha-Gadol intermittently from 1860 until his death in 1887. His passing helped precipitate the search which led to Rabbi Jacob Joseph's selection. Rabbi Lesser, trained at yeshivas in Mir and Minsk, came to the United States in 1880 and served in Chicago until 1900, when he moved to Cincinnati. Rabbi Aaronsohn was, in the words of one contemporary Hebrew journalist, Zvi Hirsch Bernstein, "the first Orthodox rabbi in America with the exception of Rabbi Abraham Joseph Ash." See on these early rabbinical figures, Fein, pp. 54–55, 95, and passim; Israel Tabak, "Rabbi Abraham Rice of Baltimore," *Tradition*, Summer 1965, pp. 100–120; David Ellenson," A Jewish Legal Decision by Rabbi Bernard Illowy of

New Orleans and Its Discussion in Nineteenth Century Europe," *AJH*, December 1979, pp. 174–195; Sarna, pp. 4–5; Judah D. Eisenstein, "The History of the First Russian-American Jewish Congregation," *PAJHS*, 1901, pp. 63–74; *Sefer ha-Yovel*, p. 137; Zvi Hirsch Bernstein, "On Jews and Judaism 35 Years Ago," *Yalkut Maarabi*, 1904, p. 129.

Of course, such notables as Rev. Gershom Mendes Seixas and Rev. Isaac Leeser served as ministers/hazzanim and spokesmen for traditional Judaism in this country from the late eighteenth through the mid-nineteenth century without the benefit of ordination.

19. For a graphic representation of the information extant on these founding members, see Benzion Eisenstadt, *Chachme Yisrael Beamerika* (New York 1903).

20. *Sefer ha-Yovel*, pp. 13–21.

21. The *Sefer ha-Yovel* reports that the organizational meeting at Ramaz's home in Boston took place "at the time of the Zionist meeting" in that city (undoubtedly the Federation of American Zionists meeting), raising the question of what impact Zionism's secular nature made on the founding of the Agudat ha-Rabbanim. The winter of 1901–1902 is, of course, a significant time-frame in general Zionist history. In December 1901, at the Fifth Zionist Congress, a resolution was passed favoring a program fostering global Zionist national education; the launching of secular Hebrew culture as part of the Zionist movement. Religious Zionists angered by the resolution's total omission of any religious orientation to the Zionists' Jewish cultural activities met four months later under the leadership of Rabbi Isaac Jacob Reines to organize as an independent body to protect the interests of religious Jews in the Zionist movement. The world Mizrachi movement would soon emerge out of these latter deliberations. Looking at America, the limited historiography on the early years of Zionism in this country indicates that East European Rabbis Margolies and Philip Hillel Klein, along with—and significantly so—Drachman and Mendes, were among the early backers of Hovevei Zion in New York. The Hebrew and Yiddish press of the day noted that these rabbis addressed Zionist cell meetings. Additionally, the *Encyclopedia of Religious Zionism* indicates that Rabbis Dov Baer Abramovitz, Abraham Eliezer Alperstein, Joseph Grossman, Bernard Levinthal, and Margolies—all charter members of the Agudat ha-Rabbanim—were consistent supporters of Mizrachi both here and abroad. Thus it is not surprising to find Levinthal, Ramaz, and others attending the New England conclave in May 1902. And although that convention did not deal with the Mizrachi question of East Europe, the problem of religious Judaism being overlooked might well have been on their minds when a resolution to condemn Dr. Emil G. Hirsch for asserting that "the Sabbath is dead" was considered out of order by some Zionist delegates who asserted that "the Zionist movement does not recognize religious questions." That may well have made some impact upon the Orthodox rabbis there at the convention. Of course, Sabbath observance would become a basic plank of the Agudat ha-Rabbanim's program.

In any event, it is important to note that both the organization and its member rabbis as individuals, though resisting of Americanization, were not anti-Zionist. In 1903, at the Agudah's second annual convention, "Zionism was unanimously accepted as part of the Conference program." A year later, a eulogy for Theodor Herzl was pronounced by Rabbi Margolies at the third convention. As late as 1936, the Agudat ha-Rabbanim could congratulate the American Mizrachi on its twenty-fifth anniversary. The era of anti-Zionism among Orthodox rabbis in America dates from a later period, clearly much later than the rise of organizational anti-Zionism of the Agudath Israel in Eastern Europe. See below for a discussion of postwar anti-Zionism among Orthodox rabbis. See on the foregoing discussion, *AH*, May 30, 1902, pp. 39–41; *AJYB*, 1903, p. 161, and 1904–5, p. 282; Hyman B. Grinstein, "Memoirs and Scrapbooks of Joseph Isaac Bluestone," *PAJHS*, 1939, pp. 53–64; Samuel Rosenblatt, *The History of the Mizrachi Movement* (New York, 1951), pp. 1–20; Pinchas Churgin and Leon Gellman, *Mizrachi: Jubilee*

Publication of the Mizrachi Organization of America (1911–1936) (New York, 1936).

22. There is some disagreement in the sources about the date of the meeting in Ramaz's home. The *Sefer ha-Yovel* states that the meeting was held in the month of Adar (February-March) at the time of the Zionist convention in Boston. That year, the Zionist convention in Boston met at the end of May. Our working assumption is that the Adar date is mistaken.

23. *Sefer ha-Yovel*, p. 24.

24. Ibid. For an English translation of the Agudat ha-Rabbanim's constitution, see Aaron Rakeffet-Rothkoff, *The Silver Years in American Orthodoxy: Rabbi Eliezer Silver and His Generation* (Jerusalem and New York, 1981), p. 316.

25. Jeffrey S. Gurock, *When Harlem Was Jewish* (New York, 1979), p. 23

26. Judah David Eisenstein, *Ozar Zikhronothai: Anthology and Memoir* (New York, 1929), pp. 77, 118. "Biographical Sketches," *AJYB*, 1903, p. 180. Eisenstein, the early historian of the East European Jewish religious community in the ghetto, recorded for posterity Rabbi Widerwitz's public appreciation of who made him chief rabbi of the United States: "The sign painter," he reportedly asserted. And to the question of "why of the entire United States?" he replied, "because it is impossible to bring together all American communities to dismiss me." Despite this humorous epigram, it should be noted that Widerwitz was nonetheless a scholar who had published, while still in Russia, the works of Rabbi Mendel of Lubavitch and who, according to Eisenstein, published numerous articles. Rabbi Segal was even more of a serious scholar than Widerwitz. Indeed Segal authored a most significant work of American halachah, *Eruv v'Hotzaah* (1901), a tract which argued the permissibility of carrying in New York's East Side on the Sabbath. His position was based on the reality that the Jewish Quarter was enclosed on three sides by water and the fourth side was considered legal "as a closed door" by virtue of the elevated railroads linked by raised columns north to south in Manhattan Island. Eisenstein tells us, significantly, that the "Hasidim who followed him carried their taleisim on the Sabbath." Eisenstein, p. 118. Of course, Widerwitz's and Segal's difficulties with Rabbi Jacob Joseph stemmed not from varying interpretations of "Sabbath texts" but rather the competition over the right of supervision in the crucially important "workaday" world of kosher meat supervision. See below for more on the split within the East European Orthodox rabbinate in America over the power of kosher regulation. It is also possible that Segal and Widerwitz, of Galician and Hasidic orientation, did not fit in the Agudat ha-Rabbanim's predominantly Lithuanian, non-Hasidic group of rabbis.

27. English-born Joseph Asher was educated secularly at Jews' College grammar school, Owens College, Manchester, and Trinity College, Cambridge University. As such his training was quite similar to that of the Mendes family. But he received his rabbinical training in Kovno, Russia, and was ordained by Rabbi David Tevel Katzenellenbogen of Kovno/Suwalk, qualifying him at least theoretically for Agudat ha-Rabbanim membership. Clearly his position as professor of homiletics at the Seminary, not to mention his role as rabbi and preacher at Conservative Congregation B'nai Jeshurun in New York before moving on to the Orthodox Orach Chaim in the same city, did not help his chances of being invited to joined. Asher identified closely with the Mendes-Drachman strain of Orthodoxy. So did his predecessor at Orach Chaim, David Neumark. As noted above in n. 12, the Polish-born Neumark was trained in the Breslau and Berlin rabbinical seminaries before coming to the United States and linking up with the American Orthodox group. Philadelphia-born Henry S. Morais was the recipient of an American secular education and was trained for the ministry by his father, Sabato Morais. He served congregations in Syracuse, New York, and Newport, Rhode Island, before beginning a very significant tenure at Congregation Mikve Israel in New York.

Henry Speaker (1895), David Wittenberg (1895), Bernard M. Kaplan (1897), Leon H. Elmaleh (1898), Morris Mandel (1898), Menahem M. Eichler (1899), Michael Fried (1899), Emil Friedman (1899), David Levine (1900), and Israel Goldfarb, Phineas Israeli, Hillel Kauvar, and Nathan Wolf, all of the 1902 pre-Schechter rabbinical graduating class round out the list of so-described "full-hearted (American Orthodox) rabbis." All also played an important role in the Jewish Endeavor Society, to be discussed below.

See for biographical descriptions: "Biographical Sketches," *AJYB*, 1903, p. 42; Adler, pp. 76–78; Eisenstein, *Anshei Shem*, p. 21.

28. *Sefer ha-Yovel*, p. 18.

29. Mendes, Abramovitz, Drachman, Greenstone, Kauvar, Morais, and Schneeberger were all officers and trustees of the Orthodox Union in 1903. See *AJYB*, 1903–4, p. 159. The decision to oppose the activities of the Orthodox Union was part of a blanket rejection by the Agudat ha-Rabbanim, at its third convention, of Rabbi Mendes's appeal to them to cooperate in (a) bringing "to the notice of the rabbis the fact that certain marriages legal in Jewish law are illegal according to the law of the State," (b) regulating the practice of milah, i.e., "mohelim not paying sufficient regard to surgical cleanliness," and (c) opposition to the "Cincinnati College" of the Reform movement. The Agudat ha-Rabbanim responded that they would abide by the state's laws and did not need to be reminded. They also averred that mohelim under their influence always used great caution in the operations. Most significantly, they rejected cooperation with Mendes in opposing Reform. They demurred that Seminary rabbis (now post-1902) "are not fit for the position of rabbi on account of lack of proper and sufficient preparation." Finally, the Orthodox Union was not recognized as a valued ally in the fight to perpetuate Judaism. The Agudat ha-Rabbanim noted that "our principal aim has always been directed to form and build up a union of real Orthodox congregations." See *AH*, July 8, 1904, p. 204, July 30, 1904, p. 282, and Markovitz, "Henry Pereira Mendes: Architect of the Union of Orthodox Jewish Congregations of America," *AJHQ*, March 1966, pp. 380–381.

Agudat ha-Rabbanim's nonacceptance of Seminary graduates post-1902 is understandable considering the change of administration and emphasis at the start of the Schechter years. Non-recognition of the Orthodox Union, an organization led by the Orthodox leaders of the old Seminary, cannot easily be based on the sudden invalidity of the Seminary. Rather, one might argue it was due to (a) unwillingness of the Agudat ha-Rabbanim to share leadership, (b) holding the American Orthodox to be guilty by association for working with Conservative leaders, and (c) the presently to be discussed Americanizing thrust of the union, which the Agudah rejected.

30. *AH*, January 4, 1901, p. 231.

31. Indirect impressionistic evidence supporting this view of the Orthodox Union rabbis as searching for a constituency to lead may be found in Drachman's autobiography. Commenting upon the lot of the American Orthodox rabbi around the turn of the century, he lamented: "It seemed for a time. . . . that there was no room, no demand in America for an American-born, English-speaking rabbi who insisted upon maintaining the laws and usages of Traditional Judaism. . . . Reform Judaism had conquered almost the entire field of Jewish life. . . . There were a few Orthodox congregations whose members were American-born . . . But there were no vacancies. Groups of East Europeans . . . adhered to Orthodox traditions of their native lands and wanted rabbis of that type." See Drachman, p. 167. In truth the leaders of the Orthodox Union were interested not so much in leading first-generation immigrants but in struggling for the second generation.

32. *Sefer ha-Yovel*, pp. 25–26; Rakeffet-Rothkoff, pp. 317–319. See Rabbi Zalman Jaccob Friederman, "Takanot Hachomim," *Ha-Peles*, 1902, pp. 469–471. For another look at how the Agudat ha-Rabbanim understood the picture of Jewish education at its inception, Hapgood focuses upon the career of Vilna-born Rabbi Moses Reicherson (1827–1903), a great Hebrew

grammarian. Arriving in New York in 1890, he authored articles for *Ner Maarabi, Ha-Pisgah*, and *Ha-Ivri* and edited *Ha-Techiya*. But his talents went almost unnoticed in New York, and he died a "melamed in the Uptown Talmud Torah." See Eisenstein, p. 106, Hutchins Hapgood, *The Spirit of the Ghetto* (New York, 1902), pp. 55–57.

33. *Sefer ha-Yovel*, p. 26, and Rakeffet-Rothkoff, p. 319. To be sure, not long after its founding, the Agudat ha-Rabbanim moved slightly off its staunchly separatistic stance. At its second convention, held in August 1903, leaders agreed both to work toward a systematic curriculum for "all talmud torahs and hedarim" in this country and to give financial aid to talmud torahs in smaller communities. Mention was also made of the need to establish Hebrew schools for girls. Equally important, it was decided to hire "graduates from the normal schools in the employ of the City Boards of Education" to teach secular subjects in the all-day yeshivot, a concession to United States law if not custom. A year later at the third convention, held in July 1904, authorities leading talmud torahs and yeshivas "were requested to institute lectures for the young on Saturday and Sunday afternoons." No mention was made of the language of discourse or the topics for discussion. In any event, for the Augdat ha-Rabbanim the ideal form of Jewish education remained the transplanted *heder*/yeshiva system from East Europe. See *AJYB*, 1903–4, p. 160; 1904–5, p. 282.

34. *AH*, May 30, 1902, pp. 37–38.

35. *HS*, October 18, 1901, p. 4; *AH*, January 18, 1901, p. 284; February 8, 1901, p. 379; April 5, 1901, p. 596; Drachman, pp. 225 ff.

36. *AH*, December 6, 1901, p. 118; February 7, 1902, p. 375; May 2, 1902, p. 725; December 25, 1903, p. 205. For more on the history of the Jewish Endeavor Society, see my "Jewish Endeavor Society," in Michael Dobkowski, ed., *American Jewish Voluntary Organizations* (Westport, Conn., forthcoming). Clearly the Jewish Endeavor Society was a critical first step toward what would emerge as the Young Israel Synagogue in the 1910's. See on that my "The Orthodox Synagogue in America," in Jack Wirthheimer, ed., *The History of the Synagogue in the United States* (New York, forthcoming).

37. Ironically the JES stood for one of the causes which most interested the Agudat ha-Rabbanim—putting the imposter rabbi and his "mushroom synagogue" out of business. See *AH*, October 17, 1902, p. 608, for the society's position on the privately owned and operated "congregations" which sprung up overnight yearly around High Holiday time ostensibly offering services to non-seat holding-downtowners in "rented rooms, saloons and dance halls." With reference to *maggidim*, we have the comments of one Endeavorer that his "services were successful but unfortunately a 'maggid' usually appeared on the scene followed by his hosts and naturally the services had to make room for the Yiddish preacher." See *AH*, January 16, 1903, p. 298.

The foregoing description of Agudat ha-Rabbanim opposition to the JES is based exclusively upon observations made by society proponents about the tenor of criticism which greeted their efforts on the Lower East Side. We are thus hearing only from Agudat ha-Rabbanim critics possessed of their own particular biases. A major bibliographical issue which must be addressed beyond this work is the specific opinions of individual Orthodox rabbis over (a) the permissibility of substituting vernacular prayers for the original Hebrew, (b) what are the obligatory prayers which had to be recited in the original, and (c) whether Yiddish-language sermons were inviolable and whether there exist certain "secular" topics that ought not to be discussed from the pulpit.

38. *Sefer ha-Yovel*, p. 26; Rakeffet-Rothkoff, pp. 319–320; *AJYB*, 1903, p. 160; Drachman, p. 229. When Drachman's association was first founded, Rabbi Jacob Joseph was one of the individuals who initially cooperated with him. Eisenstein, p. 77. And by the mid-1920's there are indications that the Agudat ha-Rabbanim had come to work not only with Orthodox Union

people but with more liberal Jews and non-Jews in promoting the five-day work week. See Benjamin Kline Hunnicutt, "The Jewish Sabbath Movement in the Early Twentieth Century," *AJH*, December 1979, pp. 196–225. But that era of semicooperation began a full generation after Drachman's organization came into being.

39. Again it should be noted here that Drachman's organization worked with Reform Jews from its very inception, which might have discredited that organization *a priori* in Agudat ha-Rabbanim eyes. See Hunnicutt, pp. 199–200.

40. See *HS*, October 24, 1902, p. 4; *AH*, February 7, 1902, p. 400; *HS*, June 12, 1903, p. 10, for examples of turn-of-the-century Orthodox Union lobbying efforts.

41. For Mendes's early anticonversionist efforts, see Markovitz, "Henry P. Mendes," pp. 53–54. On the Orthodox Union's early 1900's antisectarianism campaigns, see Leonard Bloom, "A Successful Jewish Boycott of the New York City Public Schools," *AJH*, December 1980, pp. 180–188; Jeffrey S. Gurock, "Jacob A. Riis: Christian Friend or Missionary Foe; Two Jewish Views," *AJH*, September 1981, pp. 29–47; idem, "Why Albert Lucas of the Orthodox Union Did Not Join the New York Kehillah," *PAAJR*, 1982–83. Parenthetically, my two aforementioned articles note the strong differences in opinion between Orthodox Union leaders and Reform Jewish spokesmen on how to deal with Christianity's impact on the immigrant Jew.

42. Jacob David Willowski, *Sefer Nimukei Ridbaz Perush al ha-Torah* (Chicago, 1904). For more on Willowski's United States career, see Aaron Rothkoff, "The American Sojourns of Ridbaz: Religious Problems within the Immigrant Community," *AJH*, June 1968, pp. 557–572. For his conflicts with other Orthodox rabbis, see below.

43. See Arthur Goren's authoritative history of the Kehillah, *New York Jews and the Quest for Community* (New York, 1970), particularly chapters 2 and 3, for the evolution of the "Jewish Community" idea and varying group reactions to its formulation.

44. *AH*, January 4, 1901, p. 235; *HS*, March 5, 1909, p. 12; Min ECK, April 7, 1909; *MA*, P3/1398; Min CED, April 10, 1910; *MA*, P3/1662.

45. Goren, p. 50.

46. Min ECK, December 12, 1909; *MA*, P3/1398; Min ECK, October 8, 1912; *MA*, P3/1400; Min ECK, October 10, 1910; *MA*, P3/1399; Min ECK, May 14, 1912; *MA*, P3/1400; *JCR*, pp. 292–293, 1187–1188.

47. *JCR*, pp. 1187–1188; Min ECK, April 17, 1909; *MA*, P3/1398; Min ECK, December 11, 1911; *MA*, P3/1400.

48. Rabbi Philip Hillel Klein was born in Hungary in 1848. He received his earliest training from his father, Rabbi Zeev Zvi Klein, a disciple of the Chatam Sofer. At the age of fifteen he began studying with Rabbi Hildesheimer while the latter still resided in Eisenstadt. Like his mentor Klein ultimately migrated to a more cosmopolitan setting, in his case, Vienna, where he studied secular subjects while teaching at a yeshiva led by Rabbi Zalman Shpitzer. In 1869, at the age of twenty-one, he was ordained by Rabbi Zvi Benjamin Auerbach of Halberstadt at Hildesheimer's Berlin Rabbinical Seminary. Klein ministered in Liebau, Russia, before migrating to the United States in 1890. See *Sefer ha-Yovel*, p. 140. Klein served with Drachman on the committee on resolutions at the second Orthodox Union convention in 1901. He was also honored at that occasion with the privilege of delivering the opening prayer to the delegates. See *AH*, January 4, 1901, p. 235. For Klein/Drachman's Harlem career, see Drachman, pp. 277–279; Gurock, *When Harlem Was Jewish*, p. 119; and First Hungarian Congregation Ohab Zedek, *Golden Jubilee Journal* (New York, 1923), passim. Drachman for his part, in his autobiography, lauded Klein as "a rabbi of the old ghetto-type, on a par with the great Talmudists of Poland and Russia, but he was a university graduate as well." See Drachman, p. 280.

49. See *EJ*, vol. 11, col. 959, and *AJYB*, 1903–4, p. 79, for basic biographical information on

Ramaz. For Ramaz's pulpit career and an in-house look at his relationship with Kaplan, pre-1910, see Joseph H. Lookstein, "Seventy-Five Yesteryears: A Historical Sketch of Kehilath Jeshurun," *Congregation Kehilath Jeshurun, Diamond Jubilee Year Book, 1946* (New York, 1946), pp. 17–236. Of course, more needs to be known about the early career of Kaplan in that Orthodox pulpit. The basic facts are that in 1902, upon his graduation from the Seminary, he was appointed, in the words of this congregational organ, "minister" of the synagogue. The journal continues that "the title of 'minister' was changed to that of rabbi when in 1908 ordination was conferred upon Rabbi Kaplan by Rabbi Isaac Reines of Lida, Russia," p. 24. In any event, for at least three years, Ramaz worked with a "non-Orthodox" rabbi who did not have dual ordination like that possessed by Rabbi Herbert S. Goldstein to be discussed below.

50. *AH*, January 31, 1908, p. 344; February 28, 1908, p. 444; *HS*, February 14, 1908, p. 1; Min ECK, 12/11/11; *MA*, P3/1400.

51. Min ECK, October 8, 1912; *MA*, P3/1400; Min ECK, December 10, 1912; *MA*, P3/1400. Moses Z. Margolies and Philip H. Klein to Executive Committee of the Jewish Community (Kehillah of New York), October 31, 1912, in Min ECK, October 21, 1912; *MA*, P3/1407; *JCR*, pp. 292–293.

52. Klein to Bernard G. Richards, *MA*, P3/1414; Min ECK, August, 11, 1914; *MA*, P3/1410.

53. For a history of the Uptown Talmud Torah's Americanization efforts and problems before and during the Kehillah era, see Gurock, *When Harlem Was Jewish*, pp. 99–108.

54. See *HS*, June 18, 1915, p. 1, for Goldstein's major statement on the role of the Orthodox rabbinate in America.

55. For more on Goldstein's career in Yorkville and beyond, see Isaac Berkson, *Theories of Americanization* (New York, 1920); A. Joseph Epstein, "The Early History of the Central Jewish Institute, 1915–1920" (M.A. thesis, Bernard Revel Graduate School, Yeshiva University, 1977); Aaron Reichel, "An American Experiment: The Institutional Synagogue in Its First Score of Years" (M.A. thesis, Bernard Revel Graduate School, Yeshiva University, 1974).

56. "Biographical Sketches of Jews Prominent in the Professions, etc., in the United States," *AJYB*, 1904–5, p. 152; Marnin Feinstein, *American Zionism, 1884–1904* (New York, 1925), pp. 132, 170–171, 209.

57. Moses Rischin, *The Promised City: New York's Jews, 1870–1914* (Cambridge, Mass., 1962), pp. 103, 239–240. Masliansky's memoirs indicate that prior to assuming his job at the Educational Alliance, he reportedly told Louis Marshall, "It is the goal of the Educational Alliance to warm the immigrant Jewish soul with his traditions which he has preserved over the thousands of years of his travails in Diaspora, because he will never become a good American if he loses his Judaism . . . we must Americanize the older generation and Judaize the younger souls." See Zvi Hirsch Masliansky, *Masliansky's Memoirs: Forty Years of Life and Struggle* (New York, 1924). See also for more on Masliansky, his *Sermons*, trans. by Edward Herbert, rev. and ed. by Abraham J. Feldman (New York, 1926), and *Droshes* (New York, 1908–9).

58. *AH*, January 4, 1901, p. 235. *JCR*, p. 72, indicates that as late as 1917–1918, three years after Klein and Margolies left the Kehillah's executive committee, Masliansky remained on that powerful cooperating board.

59. Eisenstadt, *Doros ha-Aharonim*, 2nd ed., vol. 2 (Brooklyn, 1937), p. 59; *MJ*, August 7, 1908, p. 5; August 19, 1908, pp. 7–8.

60. *MJ*, June 5, 1911, p. 5; June 3, 1910, p. 5; Hurwitz was more than just a school principal. He was a prolific writer in the field of Jewish education, authoring both textbooks for students and a philosophical tract on the goals of Jewish education in America. Among his books for youths and schoolchildren were *Dinai Yisroel Minhagav, Otzar ha-Yahadut, Hagim Zemanim*, **and twenty**-two other similar primers. His approach to Jewish education was best expressed in a

tract entitled *Ha-Dat ve ha-Hinuck* (1927) in which he argued that Jewish educational goals in America had to be different from those prevailing in Europe. He advocated a balanced curriculum of Jewish history, Bible, prophets, and Hebrew language and literature in addition to the traditional study of Talmud, ideas very much in keeping with those of the Kehillah innovators.

61. *MJ*, September 22, 1910, p. 7; June 5, 1911, p. 5; *YT*, April 15, 1912, p. 7. Given Hurwitz and Masliansky's attitudes, which clearly differed in many ways from those of the Agudat ha-Rabbanim, an organization which neither joined, it is not surprising that both helped found the Jewish Ministers Association of America (Agudas ha-Rabbanim ha-Matiffim) in 1916. Hurwitz was the organization's first secretary, and Masliansky was a charter member of the organization, which included in its membership such American-born or Americanized rabbis as Drachman and Moses Hyamson. See *JCR*, pp. 1189–1192. Noteworthy also is the fact that this organization was not the first attempt to bring Orthodox rabbis of varying backgrounds together. In 1896, Mendes attempted to establish an Orthodox Rabbinical Council of New York City. There were ten names in its charter of organization—Mendes, Drachman, and Meisner of early Seminary officialdom, plus seven other worthies: Rabbi Morris Wechsler, in 1895 spiritual leader of Congregation Brit Shalom of New York, and Rabbi Wolf Friedman, possibly the rabbi of Congregation B'nai Israel Anshe Sameth, and five otherwise unidentifiable rabbis named Bloch, Gur, Marcus, Yanowsky, and Tzinzler. See on this early group, Markovitz, pp. 374–375, and for brief biographical sketches, see *AJYB*, 1903–4, pp. 55, 104. Hurwitz and Masliansky did, however, stop short of joining the interdenominational Board of Jewish Ministers, an organization joined by Mendes, Drachman, and younger colleagues Hyamson and Goldstein. See *JCR*, pp. 298–300.

62. *AJYB*, 1903–4, p. 74; Naomi W. Cohen, *Not Free to Desist: The American Jewish Committee, 1906–1966* (Philadelphia, 1972), p. 563; Alex Goldman, "Bernard L. Levinthal: Nestor of the American Orthodox Rabbinate," in *Giants of Faith: Great American Rabbis* (New York, 1964), pp. 160–176; *Sefer Kavod Chachomim* (Philadelphia, 1935), passim. It is interesting to note that among the dignitaries offering greetings in honor of Levinthal's anniversary were such ideologically diverse communal leaders as the Jewish Theological Seminary's Cyrus Adler, identified there as head of the American Jewish Committee, Morris Rothstein of the Zionist Organization of America, Conservative Rabbi Julius Greenstone, American Orthodox Rabbi David De Sola Pool, and East European trained Yeshiva University worthies Joseph B. Soloveitchik, Moses Soloveitchik, and Bernard Revel. The Agudat ha-Rabbanim also sent greetings.

63. *Sefer Kavod Chachomim*, p. 75; Goldman, p. 167.

64. A clear thrust of the above presentation is the historiographical necessity of full-length studies of these exceptional East European rabbis who, as we will see, so influenced the next generation of Orthodox rabbis. For example, although Rabbi Levinthal supported Americanization efforts and as such should have been a role model for the next generation of Orthodox rabbis, an "oral tradition" about him, which needs amplification, maintains that he jealously protected his prerogatives in centralizing Philadelphia pulpits and keeping younger RIETS men out for more than a generation. Ramaz on the other hand, as we will see later, supported the goals of the newer colleagues.

65. There are, of course, instances where American Orthodox rabbis cooperated with East European colleagues in the hope of ensuring the latters' hegemony of kashruth supervision. As noted previously, Drachman and Mendes in 1888 helped Rabbi Jacob Joseph control the wholesale butchers of New York. And in that same year, both English-speaking rabbis conducted appeals in their synagogues to help save Rabbi Joseph's failing association. In the 1890's accusations were leveled against Drachman claiming that he was both awarding "tens of thousands of *heksherim* to *shohatim* and butchers who did not observe the Sabbath" and planning to usurp Rabbi Jacob Joseph's position as chief rabbi. Critics pointed to Drachman's Vaad ha-Rabbanim

Mahzike Hadath (Rabbinical Council—Strengtheners of the Faith) as the source of the problem. Drachman replied that his organization had a broad agenda for protecting observant Jews, not just kashruth, and that he had been brought into this area of controversy by problems of Jewish consumers.

If one accepts Drachman's apologia, it may be understood that kashruth supervision was not at the top of his communal concerns. At most he saw himself as a protector of Jewish consumers in the broader economic sense. Harold Gastwirth notes, for example, that in April 1899 Drachman was involved in the founding of the Orthodox Hebrew Society, dedicated to dealing with problems of Sabbath observance, Sunday blue laws, and Christian missionaries, but not kashruth. The Orthodox Union's list of concerns in its early generation did not prioritize kashruth supervision. To be sure in 1905 the Orthodox Union discussed the idea of certification of retail stores, and five years later talked about a set of universal requirements governing kashruth. But neither idea was acted upon. See on these Orthodox Union positions, *YT*, January 19, 1905, p. 8, and *AH*, March 25, 1910, p. 535. And, of course, as we have noted previously, Orthodox Union rabbis deferred to the Agudat ha-Rabbanim in Kehillah days and activities. For these and more details on the American rabbis' early relationship with Agudat ha-Rabbanim rabbis over kashruth, see Harold P. Gastwirth, *Fraud, Corruption and Holiness: The Controversy over the Supervision of the Jewish Dietary Practice in New York, 1881–1940* (Port Washington, N.Y., 1974), pp. 55–82.

66. Clearly much more needs to be known about what motivated East European–born rabbis to depart far away from the immigrant centers. In the case of Rabbi Matlin, *Sefer ha-Yovel*, p. 146, suggests that "illness and weakness forced him to move to western mountain states," but the choice of Sioux City, a town of at most several hundred Jews, was undoubtedly not a random selection. The growth of kashruth supervision as a profession was facilitated greatly in the post-1880 period by advances in the agricultural and railroad industries. The introduction of the refrigerator car "made it possible to slaughter the cattle and dress the meat in the west, thus substantially reducing the cost of shipping as compared with that of transporting a live animal." See Gastwirth, p. 27. At all events, it is important to note that the vast majority of East European rabbis did not move out of touch with the immigrant centers. Then as now, the lack of contact with colleagues and superiors, the unavailability of religious training facilities and spouses for their children, and the myriad of religious activities which require a Jewish community, seemingly kept these rabbis close to "home." A statistical analysis of the sixty charter members of the Agudat ha-Rabbanim residing in thirty-one American cities in 1902 reveals the following: A full quarter lived in New York City alone, and another third had settled in cities with Jewish populations in excess of fifty thousand. Only five rabbis ministered in cities with less than five thousand Jews: Providence, Rhode Island, Portland and Bangor, Maine, Des Moines, and Omaha. Thus Rabbis Grodzinsky and Zarchy were the only ones working in small towns remote from the Baltimore-Boston seaboard, east-of-the-Alleghenies segment of America which thirty-five of the sixty called home. (Rabbi Matlin moved out of New York after 1902.) The geographical homogeneity of this group is further highlighted by the fact that only five of the sixty lived west of St. Louis. Rabbi Zarchy, who during his career served in Lexington, Kentucky, was the only one of the sixty to preside south of the Mason-Dixon line.

Twenty-seven years later, the pattern of East European rabbinic settlement had not changed appreciably. There were 313 members of the Agudat ha-Rabbanim working out of eighty-six cities. But 152 of them—approximately one-half—lived in New York. An additional fifteen resided in Chicago, America's second-largest Jewish city. Nine more were based in Baltimore. Surprisingly only five were centered in Levinthal's Philadelphia, a city often seen as a bastion of Conservative Jewry. All in all, 207 of the 313 rabbis made the Baltimore-Boston seaboard their homes. Noteworthy also is the fact that the Agudat ha-Rabbanim had members in thirteen New Jersey cities within approximately three hours of New York and Philadelphia, and members in thirteen Massachusetts cities within approximately three hours of Boston or New York. An additional seventeen rabbis were based in western Pennsylvania and western New York State. An equal number ministered west of St. Louis, including four in Los Angeles, four in Minneapolis–St. Paul, and three in San Francisco–Oakland. Des Moines was by that time led by a Rabbi N. H. Zeichik, and Rabbi M. H. Braver worked out of Sioux City. Omaha continued to be served by Hirsch Grodzinsky, an individual whose perseverance alone is deserving of further study. The South could only boast of four rabbis, two in growing Atlanta and one each in Lexington and Norfolk, Virginia. Certainly the Agudat ha-Rabbanim's members did not comprise the totality of the East European rabbinate in America. But the sixty subjects in 1902 and 313 in 1929 constitute enough of a sample to make these reasonable judgments. All these statistics verify our suggestion that the East Europeans stayed close to the immigrant hubs until well into the twentieth century.

67. See Gastwirth, pp. 55–90, for the most complete discussion of Rabbi Jacob Joseph's difficulties with his competitors. The Willowski-Album dispute has been studied through the published writings of each. Album authored *Sefer Divrei Emet*, 2 vols. (Chicago, 1904–1912), where he defended his position. Willowski's introduction to his *Nimukei Ridbas al ha-Torah* (Chicago, 1903) offers his side of the story, along with a wide-ranging indictment of religious practice in America. That work, along with Weinberger's 1887 tract, ranks high within the rabbinic "protest" literature of the immigrant period. For the best secondary account of the dispute, see Aaron Rothkoff, "The American Sojourn of Ridbaz: Religious Practice within the Immigrant Community," *AJHQ*, June 1968, pp. 557–572. See also on the Ridbaz-Album battle, Gastwirth, pp. 90–92.

68. Gastwirth, pp. 92–118.

69. Gilbert Klaperman, *The Story of Yeshiva University: The First Jewish University in America* (London, 1969), p. 53. Klaperman notes significantly that although the school's New York State certificate of incorporation clearly states that among the objects of the school's concern was "preparing students of the Hebrew faith for the Hebrew Orthodox Ministry," the true agenda of the school was more in line with its public newspaper announcement in January 1897, which made no reference to training for the pulpit as a reason for establishing the school. See Klaperman, pp. 52–54.

70. It should be noted, however, that from its inception RIETS was never totally sealed off as an institution. Secular studies, albeit at this point a peripheral, necessary evil, were offered at the school seemingly to attract native-born students away from public school education. These students, we will immediately see, changed significantly the focii of the school. See Klaperman, pp. 52–54, 75.

71. It is important to note that not all of the RIETS faculty members were Agudat ha-Rabbanim members. Rabbi Joseph's nemesis, Hayim Yaacov Widerwitz, frequently lectured at the yeshiva. See Klaperman, pp. 69–70, 80.

72. Ibid., pp. 88–89.

73. The comparison of native-born to foreign-born students at RIETS here noted is taken from Klaperman's study, which is in turn based on an article by I. Cohen, "Yeshiva Rabbi Isaac Elchanan," in the journal *Aspaklaria* (Adar 1907). More scientific analyses of the nativity, not to mention the actual real numbers, of students at the institution are rendered impossible by the unavailability of RIETS records from its inception until its merger with Etz Chaim in 1915. Thus estimates of student enrollment in the early years are derived entirely from contemporaneous newspaper sources, memoirs, and interviews with early students and their families, dutifully

recorded by Klaperman.

74. This projection of the nature of student interest in studying at RIETS is based upon our knowledge of what was taught at the school and a sketchy awareness of what became of some of the members of the early class of 1901. Klaperman reports that of the twelve or so students known to have been in the school as of 1901, five later attended medical school, one became an English-language journalist, only two became Hebrew teachers, and one was destined to serve as a rabbi. See Klaperman, p. 78.

What is more interesting and unfortunately unknown is the question of where these students came from. Our understanding of immigrant history in this country tells us that most children of new Americans were sent to the public schools, and some were also afforded a supplementary Jewish education. What made the families of RIETS students different, allowing them to a great extent to ignore the usual tool of Americanization? More needs to be known about this significant self-selecting group.

75. The nature of the student demands and the formal decision of the directors to elect Ramaz are known from contemporary newspaper sources. See for a complete discussion of these accounts, Klaperman, pp. 93–106. The unavailability of internal documentation makes it, however, impossible to know why the directors (seven rabbinic, thirteen lay) moved so fast to stem the protest. One possible explanation is that fear of encroachments by the Jewish Theological Seminary upon the fledging Orthodox institution may have moved their hands. Klaperman reports that just a year before the strike three RIETS students had presented themselves to Dr. Solomon Schechter to discuss the possibility of their enrolling in the newly reoriented Conservative Seminary. It should be remembered, of course, that one of Schechter's mandates was to train East European Jews to minister to their Americanizing brethren. Fear of possibly losing good men to the more liberal denomination may have moved the hand of the RIETS directors. That same fear, as we will presently see, may have influenced the Agudat ha-Rabbanim to support the 1915 merger and reconstitution of RIETS.

76. See Klaperman, pp. 99–133, for a discussion of the tumultuous seven years between the student strike and the establishment of the Rabbinical College of America. Several times during that era, RIETS was threatened with closing. Student unrest continued, for substantive changes in curriculum were slow in catching on. Some students expressed their displeasure by actually moving on to the Seminary. As late as 1913, the ever-present and supportive-of-change Ramaz criticized RIETS's "unrealistic curriculum as a cause of student defection." See Klaperman, pp. 171–172. It was also a time which saw a rising group of concerned Orthodox laymen like David A. Cohen and Harry Fischel, who preached a practical synthesis of "Orthodox Judaism and Americanization." Fischel for one was quite forthright in asserting, upon the Rabbinical College's founding, that its goal was "to educate and produce Orthodox rabbis who will be able to deliver sermons in English, to appeal to the hearts of the younger generation."

It should also be noted that during these years, Rabbis Jaffee and Masliansky were among the prime movers of a Yeshiva Le Rabbanim, "a yeshiva to train rabbis." See Klaperman, pp. 117–118. Masliansky's participation is not surprising, given his already noted attitude toward Judaism and Americanization. What Jaffee, who showed no previous interest in types of synthesis, was doing there is hard to explain. Klaperman suggests that "Rabbi Jaffee was the stormy petrel on the rabbinic scene known as an impetuous non-conformist who rushed in without fear when his mind was made up." See Klaperman, p. 117. Jaffee, defined in this essay as one of the Agudat ha-Rabbanim's opponents of accommodation and cooperation, is another of the oft-mentioned rabbinic figures worthy of further study.

77. For a complete biography of the early years of the first president of Yeshiva University, see Aaron Rothkoff, *Bernard Revel: Builder of American Jewish Orthodoxy* (Philadelphia, 1972),

pp. 27–39 and passim.

78. Ibid., pp. 38–39. The close spiritual and personal ties between the Seminary and Dropsie were cemented through the activities of Cyrus Adler, president of both Dropsie, from 1908, and of the Seminary, from 1915. See also Ira Robinson, "Cyrus Adler, Bernard Revel and the Prehistory of Organized Jewish Scholarship in the United States," *AJH*, June 1980, pp. 497–505, for a discussion of the relationship between the Orthodox leader, Conservative leadership, and the rise of Jewish letters in this country.

79. See *Rabbinical College of America Register 5678 (1917–1918)* (New York, 1917), reprinted in Klaperman, p. 254, for a listing of the faculty positions held by Drachman and Mendes. See also Drachman, p. 368, for his description of his teaching duties at the yeshiva. Significantly, Drachman notes that he never taught Talmud at the Rabbinical College because it was the special domain of the East European rabbis, who were "inclined to consider Occidental and most especially American rabbis as inferiors." See also *Rabbi Isaac Elchanan Theological Seminary Register 5685 (1924–25)* (New York, 1925), which lists Goldstein as assistant professor of homiletics. An interesting subject for examination is the progression of the line of homiletics instruction at American Jewish theological seminaries from Drachman at the seminary through Mendes and Goldstein and ultimately to Rabbi Joseph H. Lookstein at Yeshiva University and its relationship to the greater history of denominational life. For more on this issue see below.

80. For a listing of the members of the Rabbinical College Committee, see *Rabbinical College Register* in Klaperman, p. 254. An intriguing question emerging here concerns Jaffee's relationship with Goldstein, his former student, who went from him to the seminary and then into the American Orthodox pulpit and ultimately to Revel's institution.

81. As was true of all previously noted important rabbinical political decisions in America, not all East European rabbis followed the organization's apparent line of thinking. See below for a discussion of early opposition to the Rabbinical College initiated by, among others, Rabbi Gabriel Wolf Margolis. This tentative reconstruction of Agudat ha-Rabbanim attitudes is based upon several of the organization's activities in response to episodic changes toward Americanization undertaken at RIETS. In 1905, the Agudat ha-Rabbanim called for its right to supervise both religious and secular studies and to monitor student behavior.

Indeed in 1902 it attempted to make the RIETS building, to be built ultimately on Montgomery Street, the center for its organization as well. See on this Klaperman, pp. 171, 207. See also his remark that "the Agudat ha-Rabbanim had long challenged the desirability of a secular education for rabbis." Of course the theme of fear of the Seminary is, as previously noted, a subject open for much more extensive study.

82. In 1917–18 *Rabbinical College of America Register* lists seventeen "alumni" of that institution. The 1924–25 RIETS *Register* counts thirty-three graduates since "the reorganized Seminary" came into existence. Clearly the latter group, who were ordained under the new curriculum, must be characterized as American-trained rabbis. As for the earlier group, Rothkoff suggests that the men ordained before the reorganization "had received the greatest part of their rabbinic training in European yeshivot." See Rothkoff, p. 51. These earlier rabbis might be seen simply as having finished their education in the United States, constituting in effect the next generation of Agudat ha-Rabbanim membership. Unfortunately, more detailed background information on these first graduates is unavailable, since the yeshiva's student records for those years are no longer extant.

83. Of the seventeen pre-1918 alumni listed, seven were noted as having positions in New York or Brooklyn synagogues or schools. Four others found pulpits in the Baltimore-Boston areas, and an additional three resided in western Pennsylvania or upper New York State. Omaha,

Seattle, and Canton were home to the remaining three rabbis. The latter listing also indicates that yeshiva graduates continued to settle in the New York area or in the outlying areas already served by Agudat ha-Rabbanim members. Of the thirty-three pre-1925 graduates, twenty-four found jobs in the New York–Brooklyn synagogues and schools. The Baltimore-Boston axis attracted two others, and western Pennsylvania and upstate New York became home to four others. The remaining three rabbis lived in Omaha, Ottawa, Canada, and Savannah, Georgia.

84. Rakeffet-Rothkoff, p. 107.

85. Rothkoff, p. 171.

86. Conflicts arose primarily when a young yeshiva graduate either simply assumed a full-time position or more problematically, as we will see below, accepted such deviations from Orthodox ritual in his synagogue as a low or nonexistent *mechitza* (partition separating the sexes in prayer). There were also instances, on the other hand, where East European rabbis would contact the yeshiva for an American rabbi to help conduct High Holiday services. The younger colleague would preach in English. See for an example, Rabbi Silver's 1939 letter of thanks to Rabbi Revel for sending him a rabbinical student assistant, quoted in Rakeffet-Rothkoff, p. 176.

87. See Rothkoff, pp. 169–180, for examples of pressure placed on Revel by Agudat ha-Rabbanim members. In 1930 Silver sent a questionnaire to many of the American-trained Orthodox rabbis to ascertain through some twenty-two specific questions their behavior patterns in the rabbinate, their relationships, if any, with rabbis of the more liberal denominations, their interests in the kashruth industry, etc. Rakeffet records sample reactions to these inquiries, which ranged from "the respectful to the polemical." Some were pleased that the established Agudat ha-Rabbanim was interested in their activities. Others perceived Silver's questions as an invasion of their privacy. See Rothkoff, pp. 99–105. These questions and answers, saved in the Silver Archives, remain still an invaluable trove for a social and attitudinal history of the early American Orthodox rabbinate.

88. Full membership in the Agudat ha-Rabbanim would be accorded to those trained to "adjudicate all areas of Jewish law" (*yadin yadin*). Associate memberships would be offered to those possessing only *yoreh yoreh*, the power "to decide matters of ritual." For these working definitions see Rakeffet-Rothkoff, p. 104.

89. Ibid., pp. 43–95, for a detailed biography of Silver's early years and the stages of his American rabbinic career.

90. This understanding of Revel's behavior is predicated upon documentation extracted from Rothkoff's biography. That volume notes that Revel frequently received letters from young rabbis in the field complaining about the inroads Conservative Judaism was making into their constituencies. Indeed, supporters of Yeshiva were very concerned that an Agudat ha-Rabbanim rabbi would drive congregants to the more liberal denomination. Rothkoff reports that Revel received a telegram in 1937 from laymen who wanted an American Orthodox rabbi to remain in a pulpit over the objections of an East European *rav*. The young rabbi, they said, was passing "the legacy of the Torah to our children . . . and our elder learned rabbi by his conduct setting a bad example to our young ones causing them to shift to Conservatives." See below for more on Conservatism's impact. At the same time, Revel had to continue to have the approbation of the East European rabbis to keep the religious reliability of his school at status quo. This led to the perceived fence-straddling position. For documentary evidence supporting this thesis, see Rothkoff, pp. 166–178.

91. For a discussion of the individuals and groups who came together to form the RCA in 1935, see Louis Bernstein, *Challenge and Mission: The Emergence of the English-Speaking Orthodox Rabbinate* (New York, 1982), pp. 9–12.

92. De Sola Pool and Jung were throwbacks to the Drachman/Mendes era or style of Ameri-

can Orthodox rabbis, based on their training at Western European seminaries and at secular schools and not East European yeshivot or at early RIETS in America. De Sola Pool, born in London in 1885, was trained at that city's Jews' College before studying in Berlin at Hildesheimer's seminary. He arrived in the United States in 1907 and assumed Shearith Israel's pulpit, a position he would hold until his retirement in 1956. For more on his life and career, see his own history of his congregation, *Old Faith in a New World: Portrait of Shearith Israel, 1654–1954* (New York, 1955). Leo Jung was born in Moravia in 1892. He moved to London in 1912, when his father, Meir Jung, was elected rabbi of the London Federation of Synagogues, only to return to Central European yeshivot before receiving ordination in the Berlin Rabbinical Seminary in 1920. He migrated to the United States that same year and after two years' service in Cleveland, assumed the Jewish Center pulpit in 1922. For more on Jung's career, philosophy, and approach to the American rabbinate, see his autobiography, *The Path of a Pioneer: The Autobiography of Leo Jung* (London and New York, 1980). See also Nima H. Adlerblum, "Leo Jung," in *The Leo Jung Jubilee Volume*, ed. by Menahem M. Kusher, Norman Lamm, and Leonard Rosenfeld (New York, 1962), pp. 1–40, and his collected sermons and essays, most specifically *Foundations of Judaism* (New York, 1923), *Crumbs and Character* (New York, 1942), *The Rhythm of Life* (New York, 1950), *Harvest* (New York, 1955), and *Heirloom* (New York, 1961). Goldstein, as noted before, had Jaffee's *semicha* and seminary ordination. It is not surprising that these men, each serving affluent, acculturated pulpits, gravitated toward each other and toward the Orthodox Union. The Jewish Center, of course, had been founded in 1918 by Kaplan, who had not yet formally broken institutionally with Orthodoxy. The prototype of the predominantly Conservative Jewish Center Synagogue was created under Orthodox auspices, and it is clear that Jung's congregation was keenly aware of the tensions between Orthodox and Conservative rabbis over leadership of the acculturated Jewish community.

93. The names of these rabbis and their agendas are derived from the *Program of the Third Annual Convention of the Rabbinical Association of the Rabbi Isaac Elchanan Theological Seminary, August 8–9, 1931.* Significantly, the convention dealt with four major issues: "The Problem of Placement," "The Relation of the Rabbinical Association to Existing Rabbinical Organizations," "Our Part in the Maintenance of the Yeshiva," and "The Cultural Program of the Yeshiva." A study of the some twenty-five or so men listed as committee members of the association, their backgrounds and their pulpit experiences, would cast much light on the growth of the early Orthodox rabbinate. We would like to know of the levels of conflict and cooperation which they encountered both with the Agudat ha-Rabbanim to their right and the Conservative colleagues to their immediate left.

94. For the many details on the evolution of RCA policies toward kashruth regulation, see Bernstein's chap. 4 on kashruth, pp. 91–121.

95. Ibid., p. 92 and passim.

96. Marshall Sklare, *Conservative Judaism: An American Religious Movement* (New York, 1966), is the standard and best starting point for understanding that movement's growth and development. See also, on the sociological-theological mix which made Conservative Judaism so attractive, Will Herberg, *Protestant-Catholic-Jew* (Garden City, 1955). And for an insightful look at the growth of Conservative Judaism within the New York metropolis, see Deborah Dash Moore's *At Home in America: Second Generation New York Jews* (New York, 1981).

97. *Ha-Pardes*, published out of Chicago by Rabbi Samuel Aaron Pardes beginning in 1927, made public many of the ordinances and exhortations promulgated by the Agudat ha-Rabbanim against synagogue modernization efforts. This organ reported that at the 1930 convention of the Agudat ha-Rabbanim, both Conservative and Reform rabbis were described as "enticers" seeking to lead Jews astray, and a prayer was proffered that Jews be saved from these forms of

"idolatry." More significantly, that same year the Agudat ha-Rabbanim opposed Orthodox synagogues conducting late Friday night lectures on "secular" subjects, since they emulated the more liberal denominations and might confuse the careless into believing all denominations were basically the same. In 1931, Silver denounced the Conservatives for teaching "a new Torah" and argued the necessity of his organization's continuing to pillory the activities of the deviationists. Of course, the Agudat ha-Rabbanim was publicly most exercised by the Conservative rabbinate's incursions into the realms of kashruth and marriage regulation. The liberal-traditionalists' attempt to solve the agunah problem in the 1930's was described as an "abominable act which threatens the future of the Jewish people." The Agudat ha-Rabbanim also declared all associations with Conservative rabbis in communal efforts off-limits to its members. See on these proclamations, *Ha-Pardes*, June 1930, p. 26; December, 1930, p. 6; June 1931, p. 28; May 1934, p. 2; June 1935, pp. 2–5. See also Agudas ha-Rabbanim de-Artzot ha-Brit ve-Canada, *Le-Dor Aharon* (New York, 1936), for a full-length polemic against Conservative activities in the areas of marriage and divorce.

98. Bernard L. Shientag, "Rabbi Joseph H. Lookstein: A Character Study by a Congregant," in *Congregation Kehilath Jeshurun Diamond Jubilee*, pp. 53–57 and passim. Lookstein's election as a student rabbinical assistant in 1923 followed the resignation of Rabbi Elias L. Solomon, a Seminary graduate and destined to be a leader of the Conservative Rabbinical Assembly. It marks, on a one-synagogue microcosmic level, the beginning of the competition between RIETS and seminary men. Until then, when looking for a university-trained, English-speaking rabbi, the upwardly mobile, acculturated congregation had to look for Seminary men Kaplan, Goldstein, and Solomon. Solomon, significantly, did not have the "benefit" of either prior Orthodox ordination before Seminary graduation, as in Goldstein's case, or subsequent ordination, as in Kaplan's case, before assuming an Orthodox pulpit. With Lookstein, one might argue, the congregation could have the correctly trained rabbi they wanted, prepared both sociologically and halachialy. This change is certainly worthy of further investigation and explication.

99. Lookstein's gift for the homily can be discerned through an examination of his compiled sermons. See his *The Sources of Courage* (New York, 1943), *Faith and Destiny of Man: Traditional Judaism in a New World* (New York, 1967), and *Yesterday's Faith for Tomorrow* (New York, 1979).

100. Haskel Lookstein, "Joseph: The Master of His Dreams" in *Rabbi Joseph H. Lookstein Memorial Volume*, ed. Leo Landman (New York, 1980), pp. 16–17.

101. Joseph H. Lookstein, "The Modern American Yeshivah," *Jewish Education*, April 1945, pp. 12–16. The Ramaz School was not the first modern day school in twentieth-century America. The Yeshiva of Flatbush preceded it by more than a decade. And, of course, more separatistic yeshivot like Etz Hayim and the Rabbi Jacob Joseph School, the latter attended by Lookstein himself, date back to 1886 and 1902 respectively. For more details on the history of American yeshivot, see Alvin Schiff, *The Jewish Day School in America* (New York, 1966).

102. It may be suggested that the contentment of Lookstein's congregation was also based on the geographical proximity of the members' residences to the work and business district of New York and their socioeconomic profile. Based in Yorkville, they were still living in the inner city, making commutation from work to home to synagogue without violating the Jewish Sabbath clock a logistical possibility. And as an upper-middle-class group, congregants may have been able to more easily adjust their work and life schedules to remain consistent with ancestral time traditions. Of course, more investigation needs to be done to explain their attitudes toward nonegalitarian synagogue seating patterns.

103. That each of the dilemmas noted here posed a real problem for the American Orthodox RCA members during the interwar period is evidenced by the fact that questions requesting

guidance on each issue were submitted by members to either the RCA Standards and Rituals Committee or to its Halacha Commission during the first fifteen years of that organization's existence. In submitting questions to their peers, members of the RCA made a significant statement of independence from senior East European–trained authorities. See Bernstein, pp. 39–51, for the RCA proclamations on these social-theological questions.

104. Bernstein, p. 15. It may be suggested that men trained as American Orthodox rabbis in the interwar period at RIETS and at the HTC can be classified into four categories when looking at that rabbinate's relationship with the Conservative rabbinate. There were those like Lookstein who competed with the Conservatives as Orthodox simulators without making theological accommodations. There are those noted here who liberalized ritual without formally going over to Conservatism and who remained in the RCA. Category three includes those who, either for financial considerations or out of sincere theological belief, left the Orthodox rabbinate and joined the RA. And there are those RIETS men in limbo who served mixed-seating congregations and felt comfortable neither in the RA nor in the RCA. Each of these varieties of RIETS alumni needs further amplifications.

105. During the first quarter-century of its existence, the HTC ordained some 132 rabbis and graduated some 200 Hebrew teachers. It also trained meat slaughterers who undoubtedly served midwestern communities. By the milestone year of 1947, the HTC complex included a Rabbinical Department, a Teachers Institute, a school for *shochetim*, and four prep-school classes, and served as co-sponsor of the Chicago Jewish Academy, a "Ramaz-style" day school. The alumni of this institution, men like Maurice Solomon of Kansas City, Manuel Laderman of Denver, Colorado, New York's Simon G. Kramer, and Baltimore's Uri Miller, who became head of the RCA, clearly made their mark upon American Jewry and have yet to be studied. We also need to know more about the background, training, and philosophy of Rabbis Saul Silber, Isaac Ha-Levi Rubinstein, Ephraim Epstein, and Abraham Cardon, who helped found the school. Noteworthy also is the fact that Rabbi Oscar Z. Fasman, an early ordainee, became in 1946 "the first American-born person to lead an institution granting Orthodox rabbinic ordination." See Saul Adelson, "Chicago's Hebrew Theological College," *Jewish Life*, December 1947, pp. 43–48, for a brief discussion of the history of that school. See also Eliezer Berkowitz, "A Contemporary Rabbinical School for Orthodox Jewry," *Tradition*, Fall 1979, pp. 56–64, for a discussion by an HTC faculty member about the goals of modern theological seminaries. See also, for a brief autobiography of Fasman, his "After Fifty Years, an Optimist," *AJH*, December 1979, pp. 159–178.

106. Bernstein, pp. 14–15.

107. Ibid., pp. 142, 135.

108. Rakeffet-Rothkoff, pp. 105–106.

109. Bernstein, pp. 128–129. The Agudat ha-Rabbanim suggested that the some "twenty percent" of the RCA members who were "more or less acceptable," i.e., at least separate-seat congregations, be admitted as full members. The others might become associates but without full privileges. Negotiations took place between RCA and Agudat ha-Rabbanim leaders in 1939 but to no avail.

110. See Rakeffet-Rothkoff, pp. 264–271; Klaperman, pp. 171–177; and Bernstein, pp. 10–11, for discussions of the history of Yeshiva from the demise of Revel to the election of Belkin.

111. A thorough biography of Belkin is clearly warranted but remains to be written. Basic biographical materials and short discussions of his philosophy are to be found in Leon Stitskin, "Dr. Samuel Belkin as Scholar and Educator," in *Studies in Judaica in Honor of Dr. Samuel Belkin as Scholar and Educator*, ed. by Leon Stitskin (New York, 1974), pp. 3–18, and Hayim Leaf, "Dr. Samuel Belkin—Scholar, Educator and Community Leader" (Hebrew), in *Samuel Belkin Memo-*

rial Volume (New York, 1981), pp. ix–xx. The former article also contains a partial list of Belkin's writings. For Belkin's years at Yeshiva, see Klaperman, pp. 177–184.

112. Rabbis Jung and Lookstein were key figures in the battle to prevent the imposition of Agudat ha-Rabbanim hegemony. Both were members of the Yeshiva board and were appointed to the executive board during the interregnum period. More importantly, they were the rabbis of Manhattan's two most affluent Orthodox congregations from where were derived many of the major financial contributors to the institution. Lookstein was also instrumental in galvanizing the RCA's official response to the Agudat ha-Rabbanim's challenge.

113. The Halacha Commission was a seven-man board led in the early 1940's by Rabbi Simcha Levy, a RIETS alumnus and rabbi in Perth Amboy, New Jersey. The other six men included both RIETS and HTC graduates. For more details on the issues faced and decisions rendered by the commission, see Bernstein, pp. 34–71.

114. It should be noted that by 1940, Rabbis Klein and Margolies, two of the most famous pre–World War I rabbis, who undoubtedly would have backed RCA activities, had passed away. Margolies's last connection with RCA rabbis was at their organizing meeting in 1935, where he gave his blessing. Margolies's policies were continued and developed further by Lookstein, his student, pulpit successor, and grandson-in-law. Significantly, Levinthal, who survived his fellows, did not show great enthusiasm for the younger rabbis, though he seemingly shared their point of view about America. Of course, Rabbi Soloveitchik clearly surpassed his earlier colleagues in support of the American rabbinate. Besides his practical backing, he gave the idea of harmonizing Judaism and Americanism a broader philosophical grounding.

115. Aaron Lichtenstein, "R. Joseph Soloveitchik," in *Great Jewish Thinkers of the Twentieth Century*, ed. and introduction by Simon Noveck (Clinton, Mass., 1963), pp. 282–285. There is no full-length biography or autobiography of Soloveitchik in his career or thought. Indeed, as Lichtenstein pointed out a generation ago, most of Soloveitchik's teachings have been orally presented and not published. Lichtenstein continues that "although Soloveitchik has published very little, he has written a great deal. . . . R. Soloveitchik himself once described it as a 'family malady.' Soloveitchik attributes this familial reluctance to the demands of perfectionism." See Lichtenstein, p. 287. More recently some of Soloveitchik's lectures and essays have been compiled. See, for example, Abraham R. Besdin, ed., *Reflections on the Rav: Lessons in Jewish Thought, Adapted from Lectures of Rabbi Joseph B. Soloveitchik* (Jerusalem, 1979), and Joseph Epstein, ed., *Shiurei ha-Rav: A Conspectus of the Public Lectures of Joseph B. Soloveitchik* (New York, 1974).

116. Rothkoff, pp. 118–122. Rabbi Moses Soloveitchik headed up a RIETS faculty of rabbis from Eastern Europe seemingly possessed of close ideological affinities to, if not membership in, the Agudat ha-Rabbanim. It would be interesting to know of the relationship both within the seminary and subsequently without between the East European teachers and the American students. To what extent did the teachers back or influence Agudat ha-Rabbanim policy, and to what degree did they support the American-born students? In other words, did Rabbi Joseph Soloveitchik's soon-to-be-discussed attitude toward his American disciples constitute a break in the RIETS faculty atmosphere?

117. Lichtenstein, p. 285.

118. Ibid., p. 286; Rothkoff, p. 214; Rakeffet-Rothkoff, pp. 267–271. Joseph Soloveitchik's contact with Yeshiva University did not abruptly begin in 1941. In 1936 he delivered a series of lectures on philosophy at Yeshiva College. See Rothkoff, p. 129. He taught general philosophy in the college during the early years of his tenure at the university. In 1940, he organized with Revel a Boston branch of RIETS; an institution which did not survive his moving to New York. It should, however, be noted that Soloveitchik did not give up his position of leadership and author-

ity in Boston when he began his formal connection at Yeshiva. He commuted for the next forty years between New York and Boston.

119. It should be noted that when Joseph Soloveitchik was appointed, there was some student opposition to the choice. See Rakeffet-Rothkofof, pp. 269–270. In the chaotic interregnum days, fears were raised that Soloveitchik would be the pawn of the Agudat ha-Rabbanim and help them dismantle the institution which Revel had built.

120. Lichtenstein, p. 282.

121. Joseph B. Soloveitchik, "Tribute to Rabbi Joseph H. Lookstein," in *Rabbi Joseph H. Lookstein Memorial Volume*, pp. vii–viii; letter, Joseph B. Soloveitchik to Israel Klavan, May 23, 1952, quoted in Bernstein, p. 49. It may be suggested that the use of the term "vague probability" can be applied to almost all situations where a RIETS man found himself in a "traditional" pulpit not affiliated with the Rabbinical Alliance or the United Synagogue. This approach closely follows the inclusionist policy of defining as within the fold all who have not formally joined the competing denomination. In truth, many famous present-day RCA rabbis began their careers in such mixed-seating pulpits, effected change over time, and ultimately rose to prominence in their movement. Clearly the history of Orthodox rabbis in less-than-Orthodox pulpits remains for future research.

122. Translated text of a Soloveitchik interview with the *Jewish Day*, November 19, 1954, quoted in Bernstein, p. 59.

123. We have noted that during Rabbi Jacob Joseph's unsuccessful career, his nemesis, Rabbi Segal, attracted followers from among Galician and Hungarian Jews who felt uncomfortable with the leadership of the Lithuanian Rabbi Joseph. They formed the association of the Congregation of Israel of Poland and Austria. Clearly the issue of ethnic subdivision within immigrant Orthodox Jewry remains to be examined beyond the limits of the present work.

124. See above for our discussion of East European rabbinic noncooperation in the area of kashruth.

125. Margolis was the author while still in Europe of *Agudat Erov* (Vilna, 1895), a commentary on the Passover Haggadah, *Shem Olam* (Vilna, 1901), a series of funeral orations, *Toras Gabriel* (Jerusalem, 1902), a commentary on Genesis and Exodus, and *Ginze Margaliot* (n.p., 190[?]), a commentary on the Book of Esther. In this country he published *Hiruzei Margoliot*, 2 vols. (1919). For Margolis's biography and bibliography, see Eisenstadt, pp. 240–241.

126. Margolis's account of his difficulties over kashruth with the Agudat ha-Rabbanim is recorded in his *Hiruzei Margoliot*. See pt. II, pp. 378, 381–385, 394–395, 400. See Gastwirth, pp. 118–122, for both sides of the story.

127. *Sefer Knesseth ha-Rabbanim*, vol. 2. (New York, 1924), pp. 22–23.

128. Ibid., pp. 44–45. Margolis was, of course, not the only outspoken critic of the schools Revel built and refashioned. Rothkoff points out that the founding of Yeshiva College as a bonafide liberal arts college particularly troubled a group called the Rabbinical Board of New York, which in January 1932 complained that Yeshiva was devoting too much time to secular studies and taking away from the hours of talmudic study. From within Yeshiva, complaints were often heard from *roshei yeshiva* that funds which should have gone to RIETS were being diverted to the less-talmudic Teachers Institute and to the "secular" college. To be sure, many Agudat ha-Rabbanim members, as we have noted, had their own difficulties with the directions RIETS took. But they stayed within RIETS as its ordaining body.

129. Volume 1 of *Sefer Knesseth* consists primarily of letters of support for the organization drafted by individual rabbis, reprinted articles on organizational conventions from the Orthodox New York newspapers, the *Yiddishes Tageblatt* and the *Morgen Zhurnal*, and the resolutions and speeches made and given at Knesseth conventions during the early 1920's. (It seems as if the

Knesseth was defunct by the end of that decade.) The sources note in passing that 135 members affiliated as of 1921. Of these, forty-three names and thirty-six addresses of rabbis can be derived from the text. Not surprisingly, all the rabbis about whom we have information served in communities where Agudat ha-Rabbanim members resided and in proportion to the opponents' settlement patterns. A natural basis for rabbinical competition thus seemingly existed. Of the thirty-six for whom we have addresses, thirteen were New York– or Brooklyn-based, fourteen lived along the Baltimore-Boston seaboard, and seven in Boston or environs alone. (It should be remembered that Margolis was a chief rabbi in Boston prior to moving to New York.) Three others resided in Cincinnati, and St. Louis, Kansas City, Omaha, and Montreal were home for the others. It also should be noted that six Knesseth members appeared as Agudat ha-Rabbanim affiliates in the latter's 1929 *Sefer ha-Yovel*. These sources give one the impression that the Knesseth was at best a loose confederation. Members may have held varying degrees of commitment to it and opposition to the Agudat ha-Rabbanim. We have noted the similarities in the groups' platforms. When the Knesseth died, it was probably not a large step "back" into the Agudat ha-Rabbanim's fold.

The looseness of the organization even on the ideological level can be seen with reference to its approach to Zionism. Although Margolis, as late as 1922, still opposed Zionism theoretically, the organization he led took a somewhat different stance. Although refusing to mention Zionism by name, instead referring to the "government in Eretz Yisrael," it did, in 1920, indicate support for the settlers in Palestine. Of course, it also strongly urged that the Torah leaders of Eretz Yisrael introduce into the *new yishuv* "their understanding of Judaism and culture." Unqualified support was understandably pledged to the pre-1881 Orthodox community of the *old yishuv*. This position is very much akin to the stance taken by the Agudath Israel in the 1930's and 1940's, which we will discuss below. Knesseth members explicitly stated that with fellow Jews in trouble in the Ukraine, in Soviet lands, and with American laws soon to restrict Jewish immigration to these shores, "we have no other hope for our people than to help build up our Holy Land in which our unfortunate brothers shall find their resting place." Of course, they opposed Zionist political aims. See *Sefer Knesseth*, vol. 1, pp. 9, 21.

Finally, membership in the Knesseth ha-Rabbanim may be related, interestingly enough, to the rise of Prohibition legislation in the United States. Under Internal Revenue Commission regulations, to be allowed to utilize wines for sacramental purposes, a rabbi had to show that he was a member of a recognized rabbinical body. Illegal kosher wine "peddling," of course, often became an abuse of this system. In any event, the Knesseth gave rabbis a home base for legal or possibly illegal wine handling. See *Sefer Knesseth*, pp. 74–76. Clearly Rabbi Gabriel Wolf Margolis in his multifarious activities is worthy of much more intensive study beyond the present effort.

130. Helmreich, *The World of the Yeshiva* (New York, 1982), p. 24. It should be noted that even in its European-style infancy RIETS always offered some basics in secular studies.

131. Belkin's participation in this school warrants fuller explication. It was certainly an institution quite unlike the university he would later lead. Helmreich notes two basic sources on the life and career of Levenberg, "Rabbi Yehuda Heschel Levenberg," *Olameinu*, January 1975, pp. 14–15, and Isaac Ever, *Harav Yehuda Heschel Levenberg: Zayn Leben und Kamf* (Cleveland, 1939).

132. Helmreich, pp. 26–37. Significantly, when Mesivta Torah Vodaas was founded in 1917 in the acculturated, middle-class Williamsburg, Brooklyn, neighborhood, the school's curriculum was quite modern and American. Classes were conducted in English and Hebrew, and Talmud was not the cornerstone of study. Rabbi Mendlowitz transformed the yeshiva almost overnight, modeling it after the Hungarian yeshivot of his youth. See Alexander Gross, "Shraga Feivel Mendlowitz," in *Men of the Spirit*, ed. Leo Jung (New York, 1964), pp. 533–561, for a

discussion of this rabbi's career, including his activities in the founding of Torah Umesorah (National Society of Hebrew Day Schools) in 1944. Yeshiva Rabbi Chaim Berlin began as an elementary yeshiva in 1906. It did not rise to advanced status until the leadership era of Rabbi Hutner, ca. 1940.

133. Israel Meir Ha-Kohen Kagan, *Niddehei Yisrael* (Warsaw, 1894), pp. 129–130, quoted in Rakeffet-Rothkoff, p. 18.

134. Helmreich, pp. 39–44. For a hagiographic biographical sketch of Rabbi Bloch, see Chaim Dov Keller, "He Brought Telshe to Cleveland," in *The Torah World: A Treasury of Biographical Sketches*, ed. Nisson Wolpin (New York, 1982), pp. 262–276. For a similar treatment of Rabbi Kotler, see Shaul Kagan, "From Kletzk to Lakewood," in ibid., pp. 184–205. *The Torah World* is a collection of interesting short biographies of yeshiva-world luminaries culled from the pages of the *Jewish Observer*, the voice of the Agudath Israel in America. They give the reader of sense both of that group's understanding of history and of its reverence for its leaders.
The Mirrer Yeshiva (U.S., 1946) and the Kamenetz Yeshiva (U.S., 1960), both in Brooklyn, are other examples of refugee yeshivas. Rabbi Eliezer Yehudah Finkel and his son-in-law, Rabbi Chaim Leib Shmuelevitz, were the leading figures in the migration of the yeshiva community from Mir, Poland, to Shanghai, China, where it remained through 1945, when part of the school settled in Jerusalem. Rabbi Abraham Kalmanowitz, who preceded them to America, brought the rest of the yeshiva to Brooklyn. See on that episode, Eliyahu Meir Klugman, "Rosh Yeshivah in Mir-Poland, Mir-Shanghai and Mir-Jerusalem," and Chaim Shapiro, "The Last of Its Kind," in *The Torah World*, pp. 239–261. Rabbi Reuvain Grozovsky was a prime mover in the settlement of a Kamenetz community in America before taking a post at Mesivta Torah Vodaas. See his biography by Nisson Wolpin, "From Kamenetz to America" ibid., pp. 206–222. Helmreich notes three other ideologically similar "advanced yeshivas in America," Brooklyn's Beth ha-Talmud Rabbinical College, the Talmudical Academy of Philadelphia, and the transformed Rabbi Jacob Joseph Yeshiva. The latter institution, a long-time elementary yeshiva, acquired refugee rabbis in the late 1940's–1950's, earning it that elevated status. See Helmreich, pp. 48–49.

135. *EJ*, vol. 7, cols. 1399–1400; Ernst J. Bodenheimer with Nosson Scherman, "The Rav of Frankfurt, U.S.A.," in *The Torah World*, pp. 223–238; Charles Liebman, "Orthodoxy in American Jewish Life," *AJYB*, 1965, pp. 67–85; Israel Rubin, *Satmar: An Island in the City* (New York, 1972), pp. 39–42; Solomon Poll, *The Hasidic Community of Williamsburg* (New York, 1962), pp. 27–31. Clearly neither these books nor the present study begin to elucidate the multiplicity of differences among the various Hasidic sects in America. Our emphasis here has been solely on the commonalities of institutional structure and of allegiance to the figure of a *rebbe*/leader.
The placement of the Breuer community, for the purposes of this study, in the category of leader-oriented sects is based primarily on their its members' sense of allegiance to the late Dr. Breuer and now to his successor, Rabbi Shimon Schwab, although the followers of these two men would never apply the Hasidic term "rebbe," with all its quasi-mystical connotations, to them. And, of course, Breuer people take a theoretical attitude toward the permissibility of secular studies quite different from that of Hasidim. Indeed one of the major thrusts of Hirschian philosophy was a belief in the possibility of synthesizing Western knowledge with Jewish tradition. That should at first glance have made the Breuer people quite comfortable with their Yeshiva University neighbors in Washington Heights. See on Hirschian philosophy and practice in twentieth-century Germany, Herman Schwab, *History of Orthodox Jewry in Germany* (London, 1950).
And yet, as Liebman pointed out almost a generation ago, Hirschians in America have tended to align themselves with the Lithuanian yeshiva world. Liebman argued in 1965, and to be sure

these observations need updating, that the "Breuer community finds itself increasingly over-whelmed by the fervor of the yeshiva world" (including its negative attitude toward secular education). See Liebman, p. 72. It is also noteworthy from a bibliographic perspective that Rabbi Breuer's biography is included in *The Torah World* collection.

136. The denigration of RIETS's approach and curriculum by refugee-yeshiva rabbis dates back to before the war, when in 1938 Rabbi Elchanan Wasserman, then head of the Polish Baranowicz Yeshiva, visited the United States and publicly praised Mesivta Torah Vodaas while refusing to set foot in RIETS. Three years earlier, Rabbi Kotler, also on tour of America, refused a similar invitation from Revel. See Rothkoff, pp. 155–156. In 1950, at its second American convention, the Agudath Israel designated Mesivta Torah Vodaas, with Silver's acquiescence, its number-one funds beneficiary ahead of Yeshiva University. See Rakeffet-Rothkoff, p. 272. And in 1944, the Igud ha-Rabbanim was formed. This organization, made up primarily of graduates of the more traditional yeshivot in America, challenged the RCA/Yeshiva University and Agudat ha-Rabbanim association. See Liebman, pp. 75–76. Of course, one of the greatest targets of yeshiva-world acrimony has always been Rabbi Joseph Soloveitchik. Though no one has ever questioned his scholarship or Orthodoxy, refugee-yeshiva people have clearly not been comfort-able with his approach toward RIETS and modernity in general. Liebman notes a graphic illus-tration of how Soloveitchik is viewed by others. In 1962, at Rabbi Kotler's funeral, Soloveitchik was not called upon to eulogize his fellow Torah giant, while men like the Satmar Rebbe and Rabbi Moses Feinstein were both accorded that high honor and obligation. See Liebman, p. 85.

137. For an important recent study of the conflict between the Mizrachi and Agudath Israel during wartime and post–World War I Poland, see Ezra Mendelsohn, *Zionism in Poland: The Formative Years 1915–1926* (New Haven and London, 1981), pp. 24–25, 56–57. He notes there the Agudath Israel's "basically pre-modern Jewish identity" and its perception that religious Zionists were making it possible for the masses to "abandon their Judaism and still, in their own minds at least, remain Jews." For the Agudah's evaluation of its own history, see Joseph Frieder-man, "A Concise History of Agudah Israel," in *Yaacov Rosenheim Memorial Volume* (New York, 1968), pp. 1–66.

138. Rakeffet-Rothkoff, pp. 157–162. For more on the Agudath Israel's position on Zionism in theory and practice and the rise of the Yishuv, see Isaac Breuer, *Das Judische Nationalheim* (Frankfurt am Main, 1925), Yaacov Rosenheim, *Agudist World-Position* (New York, 1941), and Agudas Israel World Organization, *The Jewish People and Palestine* (London, 1947).

139. Rakeffet-Rothkoff, pp. 155–165.

140. Ibid., pp. 175–183.

141. Ibid., p. 290. In reality, however, Rabbi Kotler's Yiddish-only exhortation remained only a theoretical statement. Torah Umesorah, the National Society for Hebrew Day Schools, found-ed in 1944 by Rabbi Mendlowitz and headed by Rabbi Kotler until his death in 1962, which has done much to promote day schools and elementary-level yeshivot throughout the United States, has always adopted a multilingual (Hebrew, English, and Yiddish) approach to Jewish educa-tional instruction. In essence, Kotler too had to recognize certain limitations in establishing Torah education beyond the particular immigrant youth constituency. See Liebman, pp. 72–73. And for a history of that educational movement , see Doniel Zvi Kramer, "The History and Impact of Torah Umesorah and Hebrew Day Schools in America" (Ph.D. diss., Bernard Revel Graduate School, Yeshiva University, 1976).

142. Rakeffet-Rothkoff, pp. 140–142. Silver once referred to these new leaders as "zealots" and deplored their "zealotry."

143. Ibid., pp. 292–295.

144. Bernstein, pp. 141–156, discusses the disputes within and without the RCA over the ban

and the options which presented themselves for response.

145. Helmreich, pp. 233–235. The Hebrew Theological College too had been influenced by Aaron Soloveitchik, younger brother of the Rov, who in 1966 left RIETS and headed up the HTC. For more than a decade he strengthened that institution's rabbinical department, and most significantly, as Liebman found out, "Reb Aharon has resisted pressures . . . to urge students to accept positions in synagogues with mixed pews in the hope of instituting *mehizot* later on." See Liebman. "The Training of American Rabbis," *AJYB*, 1968, pp. 25–26. However, in the late 1970's, he left HTC to found the Brisker Yeshiva of Chicago.

For an example of present-day RIETS reverence for men like Rabbi David Lifshitz, see Noah Goldstein, "HaRav Dovid Lifshitz, Shlita," in the publication of the RIETS Rabbinic Alumni *Chavrusa*, April 1982, p. 4.

146. The traditions of Mendes or a De Sola Pool of both serving a Sephardic Orthodox congregation and becoming involved in broader communal affairs is continued today on a less publicized basis by Rabbis Louis Gerstein and Marc Angel from the home-base of Shearith Israel in New York. There are, however, other Sephardic rabbis who serve congregations outside the metropolis. The men who minister in New Rochelle, New Jersey, Houston, San Francisco, Los Angeles, and the recent Syrian immigrant community in Brooklyn stay clear of larger organizational ties. They serve immigrants who came here either before World War I or after World War II. These men, trained at Yeshiva University, stay clear of all existing Ashkenazic rabbinic combines. Their feeling is that in joining such organizations they would lose their distinctive Sephardic heritage and with it their popularity in their own ethnic community. They also have their own immigrant rabbis to contend with. For more on this understudied Jewish group, including its denominational orientation, see Marc Angel's "The Sephardim of the United States: An Exploratory Story," *AJYB*, 1973, pp. 77–138.

147. *Intermountain Jewish News*, February 24, 1956, as quoted from Bernstein, p. 145.

148. *EJ*, vol. 11, col. 1581; vol. 13, col. 1494; vol. 14, col. 935. See also I. J. Karpman, *Who's Who in World Jewry* (Tel Aviv, 1978), p. 619 and passim. Clearly the military chaplaincy forces the Orthodox rabbi to interact daily and ceremonially with Jews of all denominations. A subject which demands further investigation is to what degree RIETS more than other yeshiva men volunteered for this somewhat religiously problematic service during wartime as well as beyond. The role of the chaplain in world conflict, including the area of difficulties with civilian and military authorities in protecting Jews, also should be examined. Toward that end, see Emanuel Rackman, "Mah Lamadu Anu Rabbanei ha-Tzava," *Talpioth*, April 1947, pp. 273–278.

It should also be emphasized strongly that when it came to saving Jews from Nazism or dealing with problems of refugees in general, the RCA rabbis had no monopoly upon concern and activity. During World War I, the Agudat ha-Rabbanim was in the forefront of the Central Relief Committee, which helped the displaced Jews of Eastern Europe. And though they placed a particular emphasis on helping Orthodox Jews, they helped all of their brethren and *cooperated* with American nontraditional groups. The same also can be said about the activities of the Agudath Israel and the refugee scholars in the establishment of the Vaad Ha-Hatzala, which tried to rescue Jews from Nazism and which also cooperated in relief and rescue efforts. See on this subject Rakeffet-Rothkoff, pp. 186–215, and Efraim Zuroff, "Rescue Priority and Fund Raising as Issues During the Holocaust: A Case Study of the Relations between the Vaad Ha-Hatzala and the Joint, 1939–1941," *AJH*, March 1979, pp. 305–327. The significant difference between their approach and that of the Americanized rabbis is that during the acute crisis the latter worked very often *within* existing interdenominational organizations and continued their support in calmer days. The differences here are very much akin to the differences between the attitudes of the Mizrachi and the Agudath Israel toward Palestine and Israel in the post-1930 era.

149. It is important to here note a very different type of split within Orthodox rabbinic ranks over attitudes toward activities outside the purely religious realm. In the 1960's, Rabbi Meir Kahane, a Brooklyn-based rabbi, founded the Jewish Defense League. That organization challenged the RCA establishment rabbis and their less-traditional partners in interdenominational, umbrella organizations over their perceived "soft" policies toward meeting the challenge of Russian Jewry. For more on Kahane as rabbi, leader, and *rebbe*, see Janet Dolgin, *Jewish Identity and the JDL* (Princeton, N.J., 1977).

150. Although the three men noted here and now Berman are the most famous American Orthodox cooperators, they are by no means unique. A perusal of the *AJYB* and other sources over the last two generations indicates that RIETS/RCA men like Gilbert Klaperman, Sol Roth, and Frederick Hollander have all been presidents of the New York Board of Rabbis. Interestingly, the present executive director of that group is Paul Hiat, a RIETS/RCA man. Orthodox presidents of the SCA beyond the first generation of Goldstein, De Sola Pool, and Lookstein include Joseph Karasick, Theodore Adams, and Walter Wurzberger. Of course, innumerable RCA men have served as presidents of local boards of rabbis.

151. Anne Lapidus Lerner, "Who Has Not Made Me a Man: The Movement for Equal Rights for Women in American Jewry," *AJH*, 1977, pp. 3–38; Charlotte Baum, Paula Hyman, and Michel Sonya, *The Jewish Woman in America* (New York, 1976).

152. The debate within the American Orthodox rabbinate over women's role can be followed to some extent through the pages of *Tradition*, an RCA publication, and other contemporary journals. See, for example, Saul Berman, "The Status of Women in Halachic Judaism," *Tradition*, Fall 1973, pp. 5–28; Michael Chernick, "The Halachic Process—Growth and Change," *Sh'ma*, April 1976, pp. 92–94; A. M. Silver, "May Women Be Taught Bible, Mishnah and Talmud," *Tradition*, Summer 1978, pp. 74–83; R. P. Bulka, "Women's Role: Some Ultimate Concerns," *Tradition*, Spring 1979, pp. 27–37; Emanuel Rackman, "The Principle of Polarity," *Judaism*, Winter 1980, pp. 9–11; Avraham Weiss, "Women and Sifrei Torah," *Tradition*, Summer 1982, pp. 106–118; Saul Berman and Shulamith Magnus, "Orthodoxy Responds to Feminist Ferment," *Response*, Spring 1981, pp. 5–18. See also the *Jewish Press*, December 10, 1982, p. 3, for the Agudat ha-Rabbanim's condemnation of women's services.

153. "Norman Lamm," *Current Biography*, 1978, pp. 27–30.

154. *Jewish Week–American Examiner*, July 3–16, 1981; *Young Israel Viewpoint*, September 1982; *Jewish Week–American Examiner*, October 4, 1981, p. 3; "Yeshiva University President Urges Orthodox Community to Broaden Its Horizons," undated press release, Union of Orthodox Jewish Congregations of America; Norman Lamm, "Modern Orthodoxy Identity Crisis," *Jewish Life*, May–June 1969, p. 7, quoted in Helmreich, p. 320. See also *New York Times*, September 25, 1982, p. 6, for an account of a meeting between Lamm and leaders of the other denominations to discuss a unified American Jewish voice on the issues surrounding the 1982 Israel-PLO Lebanese war.

The Conservative Rabbi—"Dissatisfied But Not Unhappy"

Abraham J. Karp

This essay on the Conservative rabbinate deals with its birth and early growth in the first two decades of the current century, followed by an account of how the rabbis established a functional definition of their vocation in the period between the world wars, and concludes with an examination of the twin tensions which affected the rabbis' perception of self and vocation: the tension of serving a movement which lacked a defined ideology and was marked by an ambivalent attitude toward Jewish law; and the tensions inherent in a vocation which is both a calling and a profession.

For this study the definition of rabbi is limited to *congregational rabbi*, though the Rabbinical Assembly's roster lists many academicians and communal servants, a good number of marked distinction. It does not deal with the Conservative rabbi as a national figure, though such names as Mordecai M. Kaplan, Jacob Kohn, Elias Solomon, Louis Finkelstein, Solomon Goldman, Israel Goldstein, Simon Greenberg, Morris Adler, Max Arzt, and Arthur I. Hertzberg come to mind; nor does it discuss the contribution of the Conservative rabbinate to Jewish learning and religious thought through such men as Louis Epstein, Milton Steinberg, Max Kadushin, Robert Gordis, Jacob B. Agus, Ben Zion Bokser, Isaac Klein, Harold M. Schulweis, and Samuel H. Dresner, congregational rabbis all, who have produced an impressive corpus of literature.

In a word, the theme of the essay limits itself to the Conservative rabbinate as a vocation serving the cause of Judaism and the Jew through spiritual leadership within the congregation: the challenges faced, the tensions perceived, and the responses to them.

Because it deals with an articulate body of men, and because it dwells on how they perceived the demands and the anomalies of their vocation, wherever possible their words are cited rather than paraphrased.

Rabbi Sabato Morais
(1823-1897)

Rabbi Solomon Schechter
(1847-1915)

Professor Louis Ginzberg
(1873-1953)

Rabbi Solomon Goldman
(1893-1953)
Courtesy Jewish Theological Seminary of America

Rabbi Simon Greenberg
(born 1901)
Courtesy Jewish Theological Seminary of America

Rabbi Louis Finkelstein
(born 1895)
Courtesy Jewish Theological Seminary of America

Rabbi Israel Goldstein
(born 1896)
Courtesy Jewish Theological Seminary of America

Rabbi Charles Eliezer Hillel Kauvar
(1879-1971)

Rabbi Israel Levinthal
(1888-1982)
Courtesy Jewish Theological Seminary of America

Rabbi Gerson D. Cohen
(born 1924)
chancellor, Jewish Theological Seminary of America

Rabbi Mordecai M. Kaplan
(1881-1983)

Rabbi Isaac Klein
(1905-1979)
Courtesy Jewish Theological Seminary of America

Class of 1926
Jewish Theological Seminary
of America
Courtesy Jewish Theological Seminary of America

Preface: A Conservative Congregation Seeks a Rabbi—1976

In 1976, a leading Conservative congregation was in the process of seeking a rabbi. Its rabbinic search committee, as the chairman reported, recognized that the procedure "is not easy and the responsibility is tremendous. Upon the decision of a relatively small group of people will depend the religious health of many."[1] It therefore undertook a "program of self-education," the first step of which was the drawing up of twelve characteristics "which might be important in a rabbi." The congregation had been founded in 1915 by a group of ten men who left the leading Orthodox synagogue to form a Conservative congregation which they felt would better serve their spiritual needs as acculturated American Jews, placing its emphasis on family worship and the religious education of their children. In sixty years, the congregation had been served by six graduates of the Jewish Theological Seminary, so that the characteristics which were chosen for a "Rabbinic Profile" were descriptive of what a Conservative congregation had come to expect of its rabbi.

The dozen points were:

1. *Scholarship:* depth of knowledge on Jewish matters.
2. *Youth:* appeal to and personal relationships with this group of the congregation.
3. *Pastoral activities:* fulfillment of duties such as counseling, hospital visits, and *shiva* calls.
4. *Sermons:* ability in both sermons and public speaking on other occasions (such as weddings, funerals, etc.), both speaking ability and content of message.
5. *Wife-supportive:* attitude of wife whether she is supportive of his rabbinical role. This includes an understanding of the time requirements of his position and the demands on his personal life because of his leadership position.
6. *Experience* in being the primary professional in a congregation with a wide scope of activities such as school, youth, adult education, sisterhood, etc.
7. *Educator:* skill as an educator or teacher in a classroom situation having more than ten students.
8. *Executive leadership:* possession of qualities needed in dealing with both staff and laity.

9. *Programming skills*, creativity, originality of ideas in programming, and ability to function as a resource person.
10. *Community involvement*, in both the Jewish and general community.
11. *Wife's involvement* in congregational activities such as sisterhood, adult education, attendance at services, etc.
12. *Importance of age:* a question raised relative to some of the other listed characteristics, assuming the rabbi is between thirty-five and fifty years old.

The characteristics are listed in descending order of importance, but their very listing as considerations by the search committee indicate them to be the legitimate expectations which a Conservative congregation may have of its rabbi: that he be scholar, pastor, youth worker, preacher, educator, executive, and creative program initiator; and that he have had the wisdom (and good fortune) to have married a woman who would share him with the congregational family and aid him in his work.

Roots of the Conservative Rabbinate

Conservative Judaism has three main institutional components. The oldest of these is the Jewish Theological Seminary of America, located in New York City, which trains its rabbis, teachers, and cantors. The thousand-odd Conservative congregations in the United States are organized in the United Synagogue of America. The movement's rabbis comprise the membership of the Rabbinical Assembly of America.

The Jewish Theological Seminary Association was organized in 1886 for "the preservation in America of the knowledge and practice of historical Judaism," and its Seminary was formally opened on January 2, 1887. It was reorganized in 1902 under its present name. The United Synagogue of America was founded in 1913, Dr. Solomon Schechter, president of the JTSA, serving as its first president (1902–1915). An Alumni Association of the Jewish Theological Seminary was organized in 1901. In 1918 it took on the more adequately descriptive name The Rabbinical Assembly of the Jewish Theological Seminary. In the 1930's, in recognition of the growing number of non-JTSA graduates on its lists, and in order to establish its position of institutional independence and parity in the triad of Conservative Judaism, it changed the designation from "of the Jewish Theological Seminary" to "of America."

As early as 1866 Jonas Bondi, rabbi, publisher, and editor, noted that there had developed in American Jewish religious life a "golden middle way" which was termed "orthodox" by the left and "reformed" by the right, and which was apparently making such progress that it is "hated on both sides."[2] He identified this movement with "positive historical Judaism . . . [which] contains all the ideas of the development of Judaism."[3] James Parton also noted the tripartite division of American Israel, but as he described it, "Perhaps one third of the Jews are still orthodox, another third neglect religion except on the greatest days of the religious year . . . another third are in various stages of Reform."[4]

W. M. Rosenblatt observed the threefold division in 1872: "I shall call the first the Radicals and the others the Orthodox; and between the two are what I shall term the Conservatives."[5] As an avowed assimilationist, he consigned "Dr. Wise of Cincinnati, Dr. Lilienthal of the same city . . . Dr. Huebsch of the Bohemian Synagogue in New York . . . [and] Dr. Mielziner of Norfolk Street Synagogue" to the Conservatives.

Three religious tendencies, not yet movements, existed in the late sixties and seventies of the nineteenth century, the composition of each determined by the religious outlook of the perceiver. Thus Simon Wolf, after worshipping in Rodef Shalom, Philadelphia, during the High Holy Days of 1869, was surprised that its rabbi, Dr. Marcus Jastrow, was called Orthodox: "To say that the Rev. Jastrow is Orthodox was doing him a great injustice, for a minister who is in favor of a temple, an organ, pews . . . cannot be considered as reflecting the ideas of the past."[6] Mr. Wolf would fully agree with the unanimous designation of Jastrow's Philadelphia colleague, the Reverend Sabato Morais of K. K. Mikveh Israel, as Orthodox. Yet in the early 1870's Morais put forth this plan for the ritual and liturgy of the American synagogue:

> The badge we all should have proudly worn is that of "American Jews" . . . (not Portuguese and German, Polish and Hollander) . . . signifying that the circumstances which had given origin to marked differences in the ritual had ceased to exist, and that the necessity for reconstructing another . . . more

conformable to our changed condition had arrived. . . .

The demand is for a simpler prayer-book. . . . Expurge, then, what relates to the ordinances followed by the ancients in the performances of sacrificial rites; strike out what belongs to Mishnic and Talmudic lore . . . avoid, as far as practical, the reiterating of supplication, confession or sacred song . . . compare long-established Rituals . . . select what is more chaste in style, more exalting in ideas. . . . Then endeavor to fill up a portion of the space made empty by the expurgatory process with compositions suited to our existing wants, the print-ed and unedited writings of our philosophers and poets can supply a vast deal, the learning of our modern Rabbis may also be of service.⁷

Morais, expounding a centrist position, was attacked from both sides. Reform leaders criticized his meekness, the Orthodox his devia-tion from tradition. But what he proposed was the way to be pursued by those neither Orthodox nor Reform; what he laid out was the direction for Conservative Judaism. Already in the 1870's and more pronouncedly in the 1880's, some leading rabbis identified as Reform or Orthodox were becoming increasingly uncomfortable in Reform and Orthodoxy. The former, Rabbis Marcus Jastrow, Benjamin Szold, Alexander Kohut, and Aaron Wise, would not associate themselves with the thrust to Radical Reform as indicated by the platform adopted at the Philadelphia Conference in 1869 and even more so by the Pittsburgh Platform of 1885. Rabbis Sabato Morais, H. Pereira Mendes, Henry Schneeberger, and Bernard Drachman were not at home in the East European Orthodoxy which was then establishing itself as the "true" traditional Judaism, nor could the immigrant com-munity accept them as their *rabbonim*. The religious radicalization of Reform and the growing insularity of Orthodoxy brought those with centrist tendencies together. Those from the right brought with them a commitment to Jewish law and its ritual and the synagogal mode of westernized traditional Jews, decorum, the sermon, the use of the ver-nacular; those from the left, an ideology expressive of the Positive-Historical Judaism of Zechariah Frankel, principal of the Jewish The-ological Seminary at Breslau, of which Solomon Schechter wrote:

The historical school has never, to my knowledge, offered to the world a theological program of its own. . . . On the whole, its attitude toward religion may be defined as an enlightened skepticism combined with a staunch conser-vatism which is not even wholly devoid of a certain mystical touch. . . . It is not the mere revealed Bible that is of first importance to the Jew, but the Bible as it repeats itself in history . . . as it is interpreted in Tradition. . . . Since the interpretation of Scripture or the Secondary Meaning is mainly the product of changing historical influences it follows that the centre of authority is actually removed from the Bible and placed in some *living body*, which, by reason of its being in touch with the ideal aspirations and the religious needs of the age, is best able to determine the nature of the Second Meaning.

It would follow then that what was needed in America was a body of individuals possessed of a knowledge of the total Jewish historical experience, committed to its traditions, and conversant with the needs of the age. The mandate to both the traditionalists and those of the historical school was clear: the establishment of a rabbinical seminary to train such a rabbinate.

In 1886 Judah D. Eisenstein, a leader of the Orthodox East European Jewish immigrant community, wrote in the *New Yorker Yiddische Zeitung* on "The Founding of the Seminary."

> Judaism in America is divided into three factions or parties: Orthodox, Conservative and Radical. . . . Those who are called Conservative, or "middle of the roaders," wish to go in both directions. . . . The Conservative, like the radical, has no authority, since he does not rely on the *Shulhan Aruch* except for a small fraction of his ministry. . . .
> There is a world of difference between the Radical and Conservative students; the Torah that the Radical studies was superficial in comparison with the Torah of a Conservative rabbinical student. To the Radical, secular knowledge is paramount. . . . The Conservative . . . looks upon Hebrew literature as of first importance and constantly immerses himself in it.[8]

Eisenstein's characterization of the Conservative student was not description but mandate. Unless the students of the proposed Conservative Seminary, he warns, are taught by teachers who are strictly observant, unless the studies are conducted with "covered heads" and are in strict accord with the *Shulhan Aruch*, and unless their training begins at an early age and continues in a Jewish all-day school in which the language of instruction is English but the secular studies are accorded a secondary position, "there will be no difference between the seminary which they contemplate establishing and the College in Cincinnati." Eisenstein had little faith in the new Seminary and became a leader in the enterprise of bringing a chief rabbi for New York's Orthodox Jewish community a year after the Seminary was established.[9] Two years earlier nineteen rabbis had met in conference in Pittsburgh, adopting a platform for Reform Judaism. In the year be-

1886, the Jewish Theological Seminary was established. In the space of three years the three tendencies within American Judaism had become institutionalized as religious movements.

The Jewish Theological Seminary of America

The Conservative rabbinate in America had its inception in the vestry room of Congregation Shearith Israel, New York, on Monday, January 3, 1887. On that day the preparatory class of the newly founded Jewish Theological Seminary of America held its first session. "Ten pupils were enrolled in the class," the Honorable Joseph Blumenthal, president of the Jewish Theological Seminary Association, reported to its first biennial convention, "and the tuition was for time imparted by the various members of the Advisory Board. This arrangement was, however, in the nature of things, only temporary, and on the first of February the class was placed in charge of Rev. B. Drachman as preceptor."[10] He further reported to the thirty-one delegates, representing twenty-four congregations in New York, Philadelphia, Baltimore, New Haven, Pittsburgh, Galveston, and San Francisco, that:

> During the year many applications for admission to the Seminary were received from students whose attainments were in advance of the studies pursued in the preparatory class. . . . The services of Dr. G. Lieberman were secured as preceptor, and the junior class organized. . . . The pupils of both classes . . . ten in the preparatory class, and four in the junior class . . . are prosecuting their studies diligently and earnestly, and are giving promise that our most ardent anticipations will be realized.[11]

The composition of both the Advisory Board of Ministers and the "conservatives entitled to representation" point to the coalition nature of the constitutency which founded the Jewish Theological Seminary as a

> seminary where the Bible shall be impartially taught and rabbinical literature faithfully expounded, and more especially where youths, desirous of entering the ministry, may be thoroughly grounded in Jewish knowledge and inspired by the precept and the example of their instructors with the love of the Hebrew language, and a spirit of fidelity and devotion of the Jewish law.[12]

Of the rabbis, five—Sabato Morais (president of the faculty), Henry P. Mendes, Bernard Drachman, Henry W. Schneeberger, and Abraham P. Mendes—were traditionalists who comfortably termed themselves Orthodox; and five—Alexander Kohut, Marcus Jastrow, Henry S. Jacobs, Frederick De Sola Mendes, and Aaron Wise—had broken with traditional Judaism and were considered by their congregations and themselves as adherents of Historical Judaism at the border (which side of the border is open to dispute) of Reform Judaism.[13] The congregations ranged all the way from the Beth Hamedrash Hagadol of New York, the first and leading East European Orthodox synagogue,[14] to the Sefardi Shearith Israel of New York, officially Orthodox, formally traditional, to Ahawath Chesed, Rodef Sholom and Shaarey Tefila of New York, then and now in the Reform camp. Of the founding congregations only B'nai Jeshurun of New York and Chizuk Amuno of Baltimore have been and are today Conservative congregations.

What influenced these disparate individuals and congregations to join together to establish a new seminary?

The immediate impetus came from a recognition of the radical nature of American Reform expressed in the platform adopted by the nineteen leading Reform rabbis who met in Pittsburgh in 1885. That Dr. Isaac M. Wise, president of Hebrew Union College, presided at this conference led to the realization that the existing seminary, the Hebrew Union College, which had from its inception indicated respect for, if not adherence to, traditional Judaism,[15] had now turned to Radical Reform. What better proof of this than the total disregard of kashrut at the banquet celebrating the first ordination exercises of the College. The shellfish served was not only an affront to Jewish tradition, but also a betrayal of the traditional Jews who had served the College, Sabato Morais among them.[16] Such a seminary would not produce a rabbinate which would be "reverent, thoughtful, and ready to lend its aid to the moral elevation of millions among our co-religionists who do need refining influences and a soul-inspiring example,"[17] as Morais expressed it to Kaufmann Kohler. Nor did Morais think that the needful co-religionists could do it for themselves. Responding to an inquiring reporter of the *New York Herald* about Rabbi Jacob Joseph of Vilna, who was being brought to serve as chief rabbi of the Association of the American Orthodox Congregations, he stated: "I never before heard of Rabbi Joseph. I am familiar with the manner in which the Hebrews in the place whence he comes are educated, and I know he is not a cultured man. He does not possess the knowledge nor the literary attainments which a rabbi should possess."[18]

The coalition was based on a dissociation from both Radical Reform and East European Orthodoxy. The former was dangerous to Judaism, the latter inimical to America. The rapidly growing American Jewish community would need rabbis who would be true to the traditions of Judaism and fully at home in the culture of America. The new seminary was founded to fashion such a rabbinate.

Of the ten students in the preparatory class, four had been born in New York, three in Hungary, and three in Russia. Those born in New York and two from Hungary were attending City College of New York; the others, recent arrivals, were in public school. Their average age was fifteen. All four in the junior class—aged seventeen, nineteen, twenty-five, and twenty-seven—had recently arrived from Russia and were still in public school. Of the fourteen students only one remained till ordination, Joseph Herman Hertz, who rose to the position of Chief Rabbi of the British Empire. One reason for the wide defection was the nature of the rabbinic positions that awaited a Seminary-ordained rabbi, described by Joseph Blumental in his presidential address:

> This . . . is more urgent than the training of silver-tongued and golden-priced orators for city pulpits. In little places where the congregations are supported by only a handful of members, but one congregational officer can be afforded, and that is usually and natually a *chazan*. We hope to give these places in one person a reader and as well—a preacher.[19]

If the spirits of prospective rabbis were cast down by the candid appraisal of Blumenthal, they should have been stirred by the challenge of Morais:

> Well-meaning, but unwise orthodoxy, tells us that by keeping altogether aloof from "Reformers" . . . we will guard our children from the effects of teaching subversive of Holy Writ. . . . Isolation is an impossibility. It would be inadvisable if it were possible. . . .
> This is the laboratory in which we try to mould the minds of men who will thus mightily battle for the religion hallowed by the suffering of ages. . . . By the

the moral force of our disciples, synagogues will be stripped of meretricious garments, and will put on the vesture given by Ezra and the Sages; pulpits now converted into a nursery for the propagation of heresies, will become strongholds of the written and oral law.[20]

Of the members of the Advisory Board of Ministers (to which Rabbis Benjamin Szold and Aaron Bettelheim were added), not one was succeeded by a graduate of the Seminary he had helped found and maintain. It is surprising that the Seminary survived into the twentieth century. It lacked the ingredients which gave life and strength to its elder sister institution, Hebrew Union College: a natural constituency, an ideology which served the felt needs of that constituency, and a charismatic, energetic leader.

The German-Jewish immigrant community had established its synagogues in the middle of the nineteenth century as sanctuaries of the faith and portals to America. In an America which accepted the synagogue as a component of the American religious landscape and the rabbi as colleague to the minister, synagogues were built and maintained and rabbis elected and respected as an expression of civic pride and responsibility. In the last decades of the century the Hebrew Union College was needed to provide English-speaking rabbis for the second generation of German Jews, which had rapidly Americanized and was well along a total emancipatory process. The Pittsburgh Platform, with its expression of broad religious universalism, its rejection of a ritual which insulates and religious observance which isolates, gave ideological underpinning and religious sanction to national, cultural, and religious assimilation. Isaac Mayer Wise, who intuited the felt needs of that community and had the imagination, skills, and energy to fashion institutions to meet them, succeeded in a quarter of a century in enlisting almost every major congregation in America in the Union of American Hebrew Congregations. They then provided ready pulpits for graduates of his Hebrew Union College. The Seminary could provide neither constituency nor ideology nor a charismatic leader.

The group which would become its natural constituency, composed of acculturated East European immigrants and their children, had not yet come into being. The immigrants came, transplanted their *shtiblach*, and appointed cantors and traditionally ordained rabbis who eked out a living largely through kashrut supervision. English-

speaking rabbis were viewed as a threat to the sanctity of the synagogue, which was a fortress against an America bent on the destruction of the ancestral faith. Judaism could only be preserved through
hermetic insulation which assured the continuity of the language, the
ritual, and the synagogue ways and mores of the Old World. These
had been tried and tested. They had survived and saved. Why change
them now? The Seminary and the rabbis it produced or was about to
produce would expose Judaism and the faithful Jews to influences
which would destroy both, the leaders of the East European religious
community inveighed.

Nor did the Seminary have the appropriate leaders to appeal to the
East European immigrant, who would hardly respond to a Sefardi
hazzan or a Central European–trained moderate Reform rabbi. As for
ideology—the lack thereof was an embarrassment then, as it would be
for a long time to come. Morais felt the need to refer to this at the
opening of his Report of the President of the Faculty in 1888: "The
opponents of the Jewish Theological Seminary still clamor for a definition of that purpose, ignoring the fact that the institution has set it
forth unequivocally." But the definition which he offered was one that
would hardly lure gifted young men into its student body, or congregations into its ranks.

Morais recognized the need for a charismatic leader, and as early as
1890 he chose the man. Dr. Solomon Solis-Cohen of Philadelphia reported that "in the year 1890, I had the privilege of bearing a message
from Sabato Morais and his colleagues of the Jewish Theological Seminary . . . asking Schechter to consider the possibility of joining the
teaching staff of that institution."[21]

For a dozen years thereafter, sporadic attempts were made, largely
by a group of intellectual Jews in Philadelphia, to bring Dr. Solomon
Schechter to America. Cyrus Adler, Judge Mayer Sulzberger, and Solomon Solis-Cohen corresponded with him, and brought him for a series
of lectures at the newly established Gratz College in 1895. With the
passing of Alexander Kohut in 1894 and Sabato Morais in 1897, the
Seminary was left with neither an intellectual leader nor an administrative head. Bernard Drachman, as dean of faculty, aided by the Rabbinic Advisory Board, carried on as best he could, but the Seminary
was neither an institution of higher learning nor a functioning rabbinic seminary. By the end of the century it had produced less than a

minyan of graduates. The rabbinic board was interested in it as an institution for the training of an American rabbinate; the Philadelphia lay leaders looked to it as a potential center of Jewish scholarship. To them Schechter was the one person who could accomplish both. His scholarly reputation was solid, based on East European grounding in traditional studies, and training in the scientific method in two West European institutes of higher learning in Vienna and Berlin. He was now a reader in rabbinics at Cambridge University, turning out scholarly works in a readable elegant English, and what was more, he was a man of great energy and unmistakable charisma.

The Schechter Era

It was during the incumbency of Solomon Schechter as president of the Jewish Theological Seminary, 1902–1915, that the Conservative rabbinate took shape and became a factor in the religious life of American Jewry. In 1901, when the Alumni Association of the Jewish Theological Seminary was organized, there were only fifteen graduates and former students who were considered eligible for membership.[22] By 1916, the Alumni Association's membership had grown to sixty-one rabbis occupying pulpits or engaged in associated activities. One could go clear across the continent and find Conservative rabbis in New York, Boston, Syracuse, Rochester, Buffalo, Toledo, Columbus, Detroit, Chicago, Minneapolis, Sioux City, Denver, and Spokane, and returning by a more southern route, meet them in Dallas and Beaumont, Texas, in Kansas City and Joplin, Missouri, in Montgomery, Alabama, in Louisville, Greensboro, Pittsburgh, Altoona, Baltimore, and Newark. Colleagues in Kingston, Jamaica, in Montreal and Hamilton, Canada, and in the seat of Chief Rabbi of the United Hebrew Congregations of the British Empire gave the association an international constituency

Prior to coming to America, Schechter had viewed the presidency of the Seminary as an opportunity for "founding a school on a scientific basis."[23] "In your country," he wrote to Sulzberger, "I can hope to 'make school' and to leave students which may prove useful to the cause of Judaism as well as that of Jewish scholarship."[24] Equally important, he realized, was to make the Seminary an institution for the training of a scholarly rabbinate. In his Inaugural Address, he outlined a broad program:

> We all agree that the office of a Jewish minister is to teach Judaism; he should accordingly receive such a training as to enable him to say: "I regard nothing Jewish as foreign to me." He should know everything Jewish—Bible, Talmud, Midrash, Liturgy, Jewish ethics and Jewish philosophy; Jewish history and Jewish mysticism, and even Jewish folklore.[25]

In what must have been an oblique critique of the rabbis whom the other seminary was ordaining, he stated: "It is hardly necessary to remark that the Jewish ministry and Jewish scholarship are not irreconcilable. The usefulness of a minister does not increase in an *inverse ratio* to his knowledge."[26]

What we also find here is the intimation that in the modern rabbinate, alas, that formula is often true—the demands of the rabbinate leave little time and energy for scholarship. It is a prejudice which was present in all Jewish institutions of higher learning, East European *yeshivot (oder a lamdon, oder a rov)* and Western seminaries equally. It persisted in the Seminary which Schechter built, in large measure because of the scholarly distinction of the faculty he appointed.

The course of study reflected Schechter's pledge to draw up "the curriculum of the studies for the classes, in such a way as to include in it almost every branch of Jewish literature."

1. *The Bible* . . . grammar of Hebrew and Biblical Aramaic . . . a thorough acquaintance with the ancient and modern commentaries . . . Biblical Archaeology.
2. *Talmud of Babylon and Jerusalem* . . . taught on philological and critical lines . . . the Mekilta, Sifri and Sifra, the Midrash Rabba . . . Codes of Maimonides, R. Jacob b. Asher, R. Joseph Caro, R. Abraham Danzig. . . .
3. *Jewish History and the History of Jewish Literature.* . . .
4. *Theology and Catechism* . . . Jewish philosophy and ethics, the Jewish liturgies. . . .
5. *Homiletics, including a proper training in Elocution and Pastoral Work* . . . the initiation of the student in the profession of teaching . . . visiting the poor, ministering to the sick and dying . . . preparation for the practical part of the minister's vocation.

Hazanuth . . . optional with the students of the Senior Class.

The requirements for ordination called for the successful completion of four years of postgraduate studies, and the admission requirements, in addition to "the Degree of Bachelor of Arts . . . from a university or college of good standing," included knowledge of the Hebrew language, the ability to translate and interpret at sight any portion of the Pentateuch and stated selections from the books of Judges, Isaiah, the Psalms, and Daniel, most of the *Seder Moed* of the Mishnah, the first thirteen pages of *Gemara, Berakoth*, and a general acquaintance with the prayerbook and Jewish history.

Schechter asked for more than a learned clergy (which the requirements listed above were fashioned to provide): he called for a rabbinate committed to the disciplines of Judaism, but open to its multifaceted ideological composition.

> Judaism demands control over all your actions, and interferes even with your menu. It sanctifies the seasons and regulates your history. . . . It teaches that disobedience is the strength of sin. It insists upon the observance both of the spirit and of the letter.

And yet,

> You must not think that our intention is to convert this school of learning into a drill ground where young men will be forced into a certain groove of thinking, or, rather not thinking; and after being equipped with a few devotional texts, and supplied with certain catchwords, will be let loose upon an unsuspecting public to proclaim their own virtues and the infallibility of their masters. . . . I would consider my work . . . a complete failure if this institution would not in the future produce such extremes as on the one side a roving mystic who would denounce me as a sober Philistine; on the other side, an advanced critic, who would rail at me as a narrow minded fanatic, while a third devotee of strict orthodoxy would raise protest against any critical views I may entertain.[27]

Schechter thus drew what became the hallmark of the Conservative rabbinate, commitment to the disciplines of Judaism and wide latitude for one's theological beliefs and ideological stance. He thus laid the foundation for the ideological diversity which has marked the Conservative rabbinate, bound together more by institutional loyalty than ideological agreement. This diversity became evident in the different kinds of pulpits which the rabbis occupied, and in the beginnings of an ideological cleavage between colleagues which recreated the diversity in thought and practice that had marked the group of rabbis who joined to found the Seminary in 1886.

Schechter's expectation that the Seminary would produce religious diversity was fulfilled in his own lifetime. Mordecai M. Kaplan, Charles I. Hoffman, Jacob Kohn, and Eugene Kohn were among the first of the "advanced critics" which the Seminary produced in good numbers, and C. E. Hillel Kauvar and Herman Abramowitz were among the early graduates who called themselves Orthodox.

Seminary-ordained Paul Chertoff was rabbi of Congregation Beth Israel, Rochester, New York, an Orthodox synagogue, which had separate seating of men and women, fully traditional Sabbath and weekday services, a cantor facing the ark, an all-male choir. It was the chief support of the Vaad Hakashrut, and recognized as its rabbinic authority the Orthodox "Chief Rabbi" Solomon Sadowsky. Contemporary and colleague Herman H. Rubenovitz introduced the use of the organ and a mixed choir to his conservative congregation, Mishkan Tefila, Boston.

What did the Seminary graduate face? Newly ordained Rabbi Herman H. Rubenovitz describes what he found:

> I arrived in Boston in the fall of 1910. . . . Assimilation was rampant, and its leading exponent was . . . the Rabbi of Reform Temple Israel, the wealthiest and most socially prominent Jewish congregation in New England. Hebrew had been practically eliminated from its service . . . the traditional Sabbath had been made secondary to the Sunday service. Even intermarriage between Jew and gentile was openly advocated. But what was even more menacing to the future of Judaism hereabouts, was the fact that by far the greater part of the Sunday morning Congregation which Rabbi Charles Fleischer[28] addressed, was made up of the sons and daughters of orthodox Jewish parents. The Orthodox . . . synagogue worship . . . was, with few exceptions, utterly devoid of decorum, and its spiritual quality all too often lost in noise and confusion . . . alienated the youth. When . . . these young people purchased seats for the High Holidays, they saw little of the interior of the synagogue, but instead mostly congregated on the sidewalk outside. . . . Religious instruction of the boys—the girls were completely neglected—was conducted in dark and dingy vestries, or by itinerant *rabbis* . . . teaching the Bar Mitzvah chant and the Kaddish prayer. Little congregations sprang up like mushrooms. . . . Every other day the community was rocked by some new scandal connected with the administration of *Kashrut*.[29]

Rubenovitz saw the Jews of Boston as "hopelessly divided into two hostile camps . . . a stagnant Orthodoxy on the one hand and a militant, radical Reform Judaism on the other." His was a "long and bitter struggle to establish the Conservative view. I not only had to overcome the inertia in my own congregation, the very human tendency to cling to the old familiar ways, but I also had to face the denunciations of those in the Orthodox camp who branded me a heretic and reformer."[30]

The natural constituency for the Conservative rabbi were the sons and daughters of the East European immigrant community, some of whom Rubenovitz saw either filling the pews at the Sunday services of the Reform temple or socializing in front of the Orthodox synagogues on the holiest days, but with the majority turning away from all religious mooring. Rubenovitz reminisced: "Wherever I went I appealed to the younger generation to accept a new synthesis of tradition and modern spirit; to provide well-housed and properly graded Hebrew schools; to participate actively in the upbuilding of Zion; to create a comprehensive program of adult education."[31]

Rabbi Rubenovitz remained at Mishkan Tefila for the remainder of his life and saw it become the leading Conservative congregation in New England. More typical of the challenges facing a Seminary graduate in the early years of the twentieth century was the tenure of Rabbi Paul Chertoff at Congregation Beth Israel.

Founded in 1874 as an Orthodox synagogue for Rochester's growing community of East European immigrants, it was forced by its younger, more acculturated members to engage Seminary-ordained Nathan Blechman in 1906 as "Preacher and Teacher." The title rabbi was reserved by the congregation for the communal Orthodox rabbi, and they referred to their "preacher" as "our Rev. Dr. Blechman."[32] He was succeeded by Dr. Jacob Lauterbach, and in 1911, Seminary-ordained Paul Chertoff was elected to serve as preacher "to deliver lectures and teach in daily school at a salary of $1,200, for one year trial by a vote of 35–16."[33] Preaching duties were divided between Rabbi Chertoff and the Orthodox communal *rov*, Solomon Sadowsky. "The Preacher will lecture the first day of Rosh Hashanah and after Musaf on Yom Kippur in English: Rabbi Sadowsky will deliver a sermon on the second day of Rosh Hashanah and Shabbat Shuva in Yiddish," the minutes of the congregation's board of directors specify.[34] The Conservative congregational rabbi was designated "Preacher" or "Reverend"; he was not accorded the rabbinic status which was reserved only for the Orthodox communal *rov*.

Nor was this the major problem facing the young rabbi. The congregation had assumed a double burden of financial support, its traditional participation in maintaining a communal *rov*, and the salary of its own preacher. Before the year was over, the board, though recognizing the need for a "Preacher and Teacher," claimed that the congregation did not have sufficient income to pay his salary. It requested the board of education (largely comprising younger members) to do what it had done in the past, i.e., to solicit special pledges beyond the regular dues with which to pay the salary of the preacher. Rabbi Chertoff had apparently done a splendid job in organizing and running the congregational schools, so the money was raised and the preacher reelected, but this time by the close margin of 29–23.[35] The congregation was in constant financial difficulties, and it was split by the issue of priority of *rov* vs. preacher, which was but an indication of a more deeply rooted division between adherence to Orthodoxy and a growing tendency toward Conservative Judaism, especially among the younger members. Rabbi Chertoff encouraged the latter, a group of whom left in 1915 to organize a Conservative congregation, Beth El. The best young leaders gone, Rabbi Chertoff left a year later.

During his tenure he instituted a broad program of education through the congregational schools and youth clubs, and turned the congregation toward the newly organized United Synagogue of America.[36]

As indicated by the case of Rabbi Chertoff, many of the early graduates of the Seminary were faced with the problem of serving in congregations which did not accord them full rabbinic status (whether in title or in fact) and which were almost always in financial straits as well as ideological conflict. Clearly, what was needed, a growing number of rabbis felt, was a national organization of like-minded congregations which would recognize the rabbinic status of Seminary ordination, help strengthen the individual congregations through programmatic aid, and help fashion the ideological stance of Conservative Judaism.

In the fall of 1909, Rabbi Rubenovitz suggested to Rabbi Charles I. Hoffman, president of the Alumni Association of the Jewish Theological Seminary, that the graduates of the Seminary take the lead "in the establishment of a union of conservative forces in America." At its annual meeting the Alumni Association, after a "lively discussion," voted unanimously to sponsor the launching of "a Union of Conservative Congregations." Some of the purposes of such a union would be "to print an inexpensive prayerbook; to prevent the isolated man [i.e., rabbi] from being swallowed up; to prevent the isolated synagogue from being swallowed up; to see that our views are fairly represented in the Jewish press; to have a regular traveling representation; to have a Sabbath observance department."[37] The leaders of the Alumni Association urged that the organization be a union of *Conservative* congregations, but the more traditionally oriented rabbis and the leaders of the Seminary insisted that it be directed, as Cyrus Adler expressed it, to "the 1600 congregations remaining outside the fold of Reform." Dr. Schechter urged that, traditionalist and liberal forces having joined to found the Seminary, the same should obtain in establishing the union of congregations, which took the name of the United Synagogue of America.[38] "This United Synagogue," he stated at the founding convention, "has not been called into life with any purpose of creating a new division." He spoke of "this Conservative, or if you prefer to call it, this Orthodox tendency."[39] The rabbis of liberal orientation, though unhappy with Schechter's stance, accepted it as a needed compromise for the time. The traditionalist rabbis could continue to call themselves Orthodox. The ferment within the congregations could continue, and the rabbis would be at the vortex of forces within their congregations, pulling to the right or to the left. It made their daily lives all the more difficult, but it afforded them the opportunity to exert great influence on the direction which their congregations would take. A rabbi of deep ideological commitment possessed of leadership abilities could be a "spiritual leader" (as rabbis came to be called) of considerable significance.

The Conservative rabbi in the first decades of the century perceived himself as standing in confrontation with Orthodoxy, whether he was a liberal like Rabbi Rubenovitz, in conflict with members of his congregation opposed to his program of changes in synagogue ritual, or a traditionalist like Rabbi Chertoff, chafing at the denial of rabbinic status by the Orthodox communal *rov* and his followers. Schechter saw differently. To him the confrontation was with Reform, which asserted "that the destruction of the Law is its fulfilment." The danger to the Conservative rabbi lay not in combative congregants or imperious rabbis; the danger lay in themselves, in their perception of what the rabbinate demanded and in what constituted success in the calling. He feared that the Conservative rabbi would be tempted to emulate his visibly successful Reform colleague. In jeopardy were the quintessential qualities which the rabbinate as a calling demanded: scholarship, sacrifice, humility, and authenticity.

"It is hardly necessary to remark," he noted in his Inaugural Address in 1902, "that the Jewish ministry and Jewish scholarship are not irreconcilable." He observed, however, that in the American rabbinate scholarship and success were not synonymous, so he urged his graduating students six years later, "It would not even injure the Rabbi if he should from time to time engage in some scientific work, publishing occasionally a learned article."[40] He inveighed against "the Rabbi who will use his freedom of interpretation to explain the laws regarding the Sabbath in such a way that they should not interfere with his own pleasures and comfort."[41] In obvious reference to Reform's "mission idea" he asked:

> We constantly speak of ourselves as a nation of priests and a people with a mission. . . . Where are our Parishes profiting from our priestly calling? And where are the converts giving evidence of our missionary activity? . . . We want teachers for our own youth. . . . We want students who will continue the work of the old Yeshibot in a new country . . . with more scientific discipline.[42]

"The office of rabbi," he reminded his students-disciples, "means service, not mastery and dominion. . . . Humility . . . the very calling of Moses . . . is the suppression of our ego, which does not know when it shines."[43] And lest the pulpit become empty of Jewish content, as he had observed in the temples about him, he warned, "Do not deceive yourself that you will help Judaism much by becoming exponents of topics belonging more to the Lyceum than to the synagogue."[44] Only when the synagogue retains its distinctiveness will its message contain authenticity. And commenting on the "successful" rabbis about him, Schechter stated, "It is not the highest praise for a rabbi that he is invited to preach in some church, or that he has succeeded in procuring some high ecclesiastic or statesman to preach in the synagogue. . . . It does not help Judaism. . . . It rather reflects upon our sense of religious delicacy, upon our confidence in our own cause, or even self-respect."[45]

Schechter was impressed by the native ability of his students but looked with some trepidation at their driving ambition. He saw the day when they would be the spiritual heads of congregations of size and influence, when they would be looked to as spokesmen for authentic Judaism. He looked to that day with soaring hope and sober concern.

The "Between Wars" Era

Schechter had charged the Conservative rabbinate with the task "to organize new congregations and to raise the old ones from the sloth of indifference and the vice of strife into which they have fallen."[46] The generation of rabbis which issued from what was now called "Schechter's Seminary"[47] now set itself to this task. In the process the rabbis fashioned a new synogogue for America, differing substantially both from the radical Reform temple and from the East European shul.

Both temple and shul were responses to the melting-pot image of America, which the immigrant understood as permitting religious expression but demanding cultural and ethnic assimilation. Reform synagogue and rabbi had yielded to such an America, temples taking on aspects of the "American" Protestant church, such as Sunday worship in the vernacular sans headcovering or *tallit*, and the rabbi becoming preeminently a pastor and preacher like his Protestant colleague. Orthodoxy withdrew from such an America, insulating itself from its influences in *shtiblach* where Hebrew was the sole language of worship and Yiddish the language of discourse, with rabbis striving valiantly to retain the East European pattern of the rabbinate, the communal *rov* as scholar, judge, and ritual arbiter. The Conservative rabbi, who in his ministry associated with both Reform and Orthodoxy, felt called upon to assume the rabbinic obligations delineated by both.

The post–World War I American scene was marked by a turning from the melting-pot image to that of cultural pluralism. Within the American rabbinate, the Conservative rabbis became its most pronounced adherents, and Dr. Mordecai M. Kaplan its most influential ideologist. He and his colleagues structured their synagogues to meet the needs of an American Jewry which defined its Jewishness in the broadest terms—cultural, religious, ethnic—but which recognized that the climate of America would most readily and comfortably accept its institutionalization as a religious community, with the synagogue as its central institution.

The challenge and opportunity for Conservative Judaism in the Midwest is described by Cleveland-born Rabbi Abraham Burstein:

> In the great midwest section . . . there are over a million Jews. . . . Fully three-quarters are of decidedly conservative sympathies in matters Jewish. Yet they have been largely beyond the reach of any united Jewish influence that stresses that type of Judaism to which they would prefer to be faithful. Either they have been beyond the reach of any influence at all, or they have succumbed to a denatured kind of Judaism which is but a temporary halt in the process of assimilation. In the large centers there have existed the same faults that have beset traditional Judaism everywhere in this country. . . . Customs retained by immigrant groups have driven our young far from the observances of their elders.[48]

The pages of the *United Synagogue Recorder* for the years 1921–1929 contain numerous descriptions of the activities of the Conservative synagogues in communities large and small. They range from daily services to Sabbath and holiday worship to schools, youth clubs, adult education, forums, dramatic groups, athletic activities, and more.

As Schechter demanded, new congregations were established and old altered, the rabbi serving as initiator, as maintainer, and, when and where necessary, as reviver, as the following reports indicate. In the spring of 1923

> Temple Israel, of Scranton [Pa.], is one of the newest synagogues in the United States . . . founded only one year and a half ago by the leading Jews of Scranton. . . . The first service held was the High Holy days in 1921 under the leadership of Rabbi A. H. Kohn who received the call to take charge of building up this new conservative synagogue. . . . Under the ministry of Rabbi Kohn [Temple Israel] has made very rapid progress . . . and has already won a reputation among the conservative Jewish synagogues of U.S.A. . . . Services are held three times daily, and on Sabbaths, festivals and holidays you always find a large congregation of worshippers. At the late Friday night Services . . . visiting speakers from New York were delighted to find such a large turn-out considering the location of the Temple, being in the non-Jewish section of the city. . . .
>
> The following are the activities built up by the untiring efforts of the Rabbi:
> 1. *Educational.* A Hebrew School . . . over 100 children attending daily. . . . The religious school meets every Sunday morning and the children are taught the elements of Jewish ethics, ceremonies and Jewish history.
> 2. *Social and Communal Activities.* Boy Scout Troop . . . second leading troop in the city. . . . Girl Scout Troup . . . carried away all the prizes for scout work. . . . Both troops go to summer camp. . . .
> 3. *The Ham-Zam-Rim Society* . . . the musical glee club of the Junior congre-

gation . . . only boys of musical and vocal talents are accepted. . . .
4. *The Zadik-Zadik Club* of the Junior Auxiliary look after the social programs. . . .
5. *Junior Menorah Society* high school boys and girls meets weekly for discussion . . . and papers are read by members. . . .
6. *The Progress Club*, consists of older sons and daughters of members . . . organized by the Rabbi. . . . They are now beginning to function more Jewishly.

A Bible class has been organized by the Rabbi, which is patronized by a good number of the Sisterhood.

Temple Israel has already outgrown its seating capacity and a building committee has been appointed . . . for the construction of a new temple.[49]

Far more challenging was the enterprise of turning Anshe Emet into the Cleveland Jewish Center. "Like a good many Jewish congregations in America," Martha Marks reported, "it was founded some fifty-five years ago [i.e., 1870] by a number of men who wanted a minyan." A quarter of a century later, when Anshe Emet built its synagogue, the bimah was removed from the center and the curtain from the gallery. Later it merged with another synagogue, extending a call to Rabbi Solomon Goldman, who was serving a Conservative congregation in Cleveland. He set about turning the center Conservative, the first step of which was to allow men and women to sit together in the synagogue. Twelve members brought the congregation to court, accusing its rabbi of seeking to introduce Conservative Judaism, "which is detrimental to and disruptive of orthodox Judaism." The congregation had overextended itself and had to pay off a debt of $175,000 besides meeting an annual budget of $90,000, a large sum in 1925. The aforementioned chronicler reported: "It is unfortunate that hundreds of well-to-do families in the vicinity of the Center, who have benefited from the Center—sent the children to the Athletic Department . . . come to all services . . . were satisfied to allow the 'rich men of the Jewish Center' to bear the burden."

The chief burden in such situations, and they seem to have been endemic to the emerging Conservative congregations, was borne by the rabbi. He had to keep the congregation viable, financially and programmatically, and to bear the brunt of defamation by those who accused him of being a "destroyer of Judaism." Goldman's great talents and boundless energy could cope with it all.

A gifted orator, he attracted record congregations to the late Friday night, Sabbath, and holiday services. He found it necessary to press upon his congregation the importance of decorum. "Worship without decorum is unworthy of an intelligent congregation," declared a card signed by the rabbi, given to each entering worshipper. He emphasized education, and could point to a Hebrew school of six hundred and a religious school of one thousand. "The High School was founded by Rabbi Goldman three years ago," the chronicler reported, "and we feel amply rewarded for all the efforts that we have put into it." At that time the rabbi also founded the Center Forum, featuring leading lecturers. Despite the warning of Dr. Schechter, the platform was given to such as H. A. Overstreet, Bruce Bliven, Sherwood Anderson, and Norman Thomas. Apparently apologetically it was stated that "an effort is made to make this program Jewish."

Courses in the Bible, the Hebrew language, Jewish history, philosophy, religion, etc., were offered, with the promise, "For next year a much more elaborate program is planned to include a number of secular courses, which will be given by members of college faculties." Among the fifty-nine clubs meeting in the building, one, the Deoth Club, is singled out for "particular mention." "It is a group of young men, college graduates, most of them Phi Beta Kappas from Harvard, Columbia, Ohio State, Michigan and Western Reserve meeting fortnightly under the leadership of Rabbi Goldman for the study of civilization."

The center hosted "one of the finest congregational libraries in the country" and ambitious programs of social and athletic activities. The building was used by many organizations, and the chronicler boasted especially that all important Zionist meetings were held there. And she emphasized that Rabbi Goldman had from the start attempted to involve gifted young men and young women in the work of the institution.

> The Center Forum is headed by a Michigan and Columbia graduate. . . . The Religious School is under the leadership of . . . a Harvard B.A. and LL.B., Phi Beta Kappa, possessor of several prizes in English and Menorah prize. . . . The principal of the High School . . . is a B.A. and M.S. Phi Beta Kappa from Harvard.[50]

Those financing the Seminary hoped that the Seminary's graduates would "civilize" and Americanize the sons and daughters of the East

European immigrants.[51] The graduates of the Seminary aspired to educate Jewishly and attract to synagogue activities the most gifted of them, and thus to demonstrate that the Jewish cultural heritage could capture the interest of the most academically accomplished. The Conservative rabbis' allegiance to Positive-Historical Judaism was rooted in the conviction that the historical Jewish spiritual experience was of more than historical interest. They felt obligated to prove that to educated young Jews, upon whom the future of the Jewish community in America depended, the Jewish heritage, sympathetically absorbed and understood, could offer meaning and direction in life. The Conservative rabbi apparently needed constant self-reassurance that the Judaism he espoused was not only deep in roots but promising in flower. Hence the inordinate emphasis on Jewish education by the Conservative rabbinate, education of self and of those about them, and the ongoing agonizing search for a coherent ideology.

More typical than the experience of Rabbi Solomon Goldman was that of Rabbi Harry R. Goldberger at the Sinai Israel Congregation, Steubenville, Ohio.

> Since the arrival of our worthy rabbi, much work was accomplished for the cause of Judaism in our community.... Friday evening services ... are attended by many young and old. . . . The children of the city attend every Saturday morning their own services at which the Rabbi delivers a sermon.
>
> The Hebrew School meets every day, and about seventy-five children are receiving a modern Hebrew education conducted by the Rabbi. The Sunday School has an attendance of one hundred and thirty children. . . . A play was presented Purim at the local High School by Young Judean Club under the supervision of the Rabbi. . . . The Bible Class for adults owes much to our Rabbi. . . . Our women are always ready to help our Rabbi in all his undertakings.[52]

Most rabbis found that most of their time and energy had to be given to the management of struggling synagogues rather than to intellectual creativity. And this is what the board of the Seminary seems to have expected of them. The appointment in 1924 of Dr. Cyrus Adler as president of the Seminary, rather than a leading Jewish scholar, seems to have signaled this. Much as the Seminary graduates might have disliked the managerial role, they recognized its need. No long-established, well-endowed, socially prestigious congregations were their lot. They had to create or recreate young, frail, struggling synagogues, fill their membership rolls, establish their schools, create their activities, secure their budgets, build their buildings, and worry lest the leaders of the congregation decide that a new building needed a new rabbi.

Rabbi Ralph Simon described his five-year tenure at Rodef Sholom, Johnstown, Pennsylvania, his first congregation:

> This congregation was a traditional Orthodox synagogue which was founded by East European immigrants about the year 1885. I was the first Seminary rabbi to serve them. . . . the decision to invite a Conservative rabbi came as a result of the insistence of a younger group who correctly believed that the next generation would join the Reform temple unless the synagogue was modernized. The older generation was suspicious of innovations. . . . The rabbi had to walk a narrow line in order to remain on good terms with the elders as well as to satisfy the rebellious young people. . . . Very few changes [were made] in the Sabbath and holidays Synagogue service. It was only in Friday evening late service that changes could be made, since the leaders of the older group did not attend and did not recognize it as an authentic service. The major changes were sermons in English, insistence on decorum and interpretation of the liturgy. One activity which won the elders over to a trust in the new rabbi was the formation of a Talmud study group.
>
> The major area of change was in the cultural and social program. All the activities envisioned in the synagogue-center program of Dr. Kaplan were introduced. Adult education classes were organized. A good Hebrew school was conducted. There was an active Men's Club, Sisterhood and Youth Group. There were frequent programs of music, a new choir, dramatic presentations and guest speakers.
>
> The unique aspect of the new Conservative rabbi was his multifaceted role. He was the preacher, pastor, teacher, executive and communal figure. . . . One activity of the rabbi was received with great approval by practically the entire Jewish community. He began to appear before church and civic groups who welcomed an erudite Jewish spokesman. As the rabbi became popular with the non-Jewish community, his popularity increased with the Jewish community.[53]

Rabbi Jacob Kraft spoke of his duties as rabbi in the Beth Shalom Congregation, Wilmington, Delaware, in the 1930's:

> This rabbi acted as a *kol bo* [all-purpose functionary], taking charge of the services, preaching weekly, explaining Torah portion on Sabbath morning. He supervised the school, taught, took care of assemblies, visited the sick several times a week, the hospitals, visited the home during *shivah* period and conducted services, taught some converts to Judaism (about 3 or so during the 30's) etc., etc.[54]

What kept rabbinic morale alive was the recognition that "managing" a synagogue called for a high order of creativity. What they were fashioning was something that had not been, and whatever they added to the institution they served was an act of creativity. They also knew that what they were engaged in was of signal importance. The future of the Jewish community, American Israel, was in their trust. For many, Dr. Mordecai M. Kaplan provided an ideology which was for the moment satisfying and for the future promising. And more, he set the example, when he created the Jewish Center, his own congregation, of what a modern American synagogue should be.

Others, attracted to the Seminary by a faculty unequaled in the realm of Jewish learning, found spiritual support for their traditionalist tendencies in the towering scholarship of Professor Louis Ginzberg, who served as a living example of the salutory results of the wedding of traditionalist commitments to Western critical modes of scholarship. To the Seminary student, Ginzberg was the "absolute fullest embodiment of the totality of Jewish learning in all history,"[55] while Kaplan provided the challenge and stimulation of discovering (to use his own favored phrase) a new "universe of discourse." Rabbi Eli Bohnen recalled: "His influence was great; I came from an orthodox background and he opened a new world for me."[56] Rabbi Elias Charry concurs: "He taught us not to be afraid to think, to question, and to reconsider. He was a hard taskmaster and we responded by opening up a new area of concern. Dr. Kaplan was indeed a crusader, an activist, an innovator."[57]

Ginzberg provided his students, the rabbis, with solid roots; Kaplan gave them wings. The roots provided mooring in an uncertain and sometimes hostile environment; the wings permitted them to soar above the ordinary, the commonplace, the everyday managerial routine.

The majority of Seminary graduates during this period were European-born, but almost all were graduates of American universities. Of the three graduates in 1923, one was American-born, a graduate of Columbia. The others were born in Russia and Hungary, came to America at an early age, and received their degrees from New York University and CCNY. In 1925, the graduates numbered seventeen, of whom four were American-born. Seven had received their degrees at CCNY, two at Columbia, two at Penn, the others at Rutgers, NYU, Chicago, Haverford, Boston, and Wurttemberg universities; and they set forth to serve congregations in Houston, Lincoln, Fall River, Phila-delphia, Allentown, Wilmington, Staten Island, Binghamton, Stam-ford, the Bronx, Sioux City, Waterbury, and Toronto. One "returned to Germany to enter the rabbinate there." The number of graduates in 1928 fell to eight, of whom three were American-born, and six had received their degrees at CCNY.[58]

By that year membership in the Rabbinical Assembly had grown to 203. Its membership was a diverse group of rabbis. Herbert S. Gold-stein served the Orthodox Institutional Synagogue, while his Manhat-tan neighbor, Israel Goldstein, served Congregation B'nai Jeshurun, at that time just this side of Reform; in Philadelphia, Leon H. Elmaleh, serving Mikveh Israel, which clung to its full Sefardi tradition, was colleague to Max D. Klein, whose Adath Jeshurun had long since departed from traditionalism in liturgy and congregational ritual; and in Chicago RA member Morris Teller served the fully traditional B'nai Bezalel, while RA member Gerson B. Levi was rabbi of a Reform congregation, Temple Isaiah-Israel.

Such was the ideological division within the Rabbinical Assembly that Rabbi Louis Finkelstein, president-elect, felt impelled to present a paper on "The Things That Unite Us," citing the conception of God and attitudes toward Torah, changes in ceremonial, Israel, Palestine, the Hebrew language, and the Seminary. The discussion which fol-lowed indicated that some of the "things" suggested as unifying actu-ally divided, the Rabbinical Assembly retaining the dual components of traditionalists and progressives in the Conservative rabbinate. But there were, of course, basic "similarities and likenesses" in the mem-bers of the Conservative rabbinate, the most pronounced of which was that, in the words of Rabbi Finkelstein, "Through [the Seminary] we became not only comrades in arms, but also brothers . . . we are all of us Seminary men."[59] The tie that bound was not so much ideological as institutional, which is what Dr. Schechter had anticipated when he took the helm of the Seminary and the movement.

As the 1920's came to an end, the Rabbinical Assembly's concerns included Jewish life in America and in other parts of the world, chal-lenges facing Conservative Judaism, and problems plaguing the Con-servative rabbi.[60] The more candid discussions, those between friends and colleagues touching on a rabbi's concerns, fears, hopes, aspira-tions, frustrations, rarely get recorded. It is to the credit of Rabbi

Philip R. Alstat that he spoke publicly at the 1929 conference what most rabbis would state only in private conversations. It is worth quoting at length.

> Of what avail is it to discuss the relationship of "Traditional Judaism and Modern Life . . . " or to analyze the "Spiritual Elements in Judaism," or to ascertain the "Abiding value of the Belief in Resurrection" unless the exponents of Judaism are invested with dignity and armed with authority? The rich "all-right-nickes" inwardly despise the rabbi because he is poor in worldly goods and economic security. . . . How much respect can they have for the authority of their spiritual leader whose position is precarious, whose bread and butter they control, whose brief tenure of office and fear of the annual re-election make him the football of contending factions, an impotent creature whom they can bully, intimidate and abuse with impunity? The Jewish intellectuals . . . despise the rabbi because, they charge, he is poor intellectually and spiritually, that he has no message for them . . . no solution for any of our vexing problems . . . that he is not a thinker or spiritual leader, but a maker of empty phrases. . . .
>
> The Yiddish-speaking orthodoxy also despises the modern rabbi . . . because in their opinion, he is poor in Jewish scholarship and is poor in unquestioning loyalty to the letter of the Shulchan Aruch. All of them together agree that he is poor in sincerity of principle and constancy of policy, except in his coarse opportunism . . . and in his unsatiable hunger and vulgar striving for publicity. . . .
>
> The rabbi's advice is rarely listened to in the councils of the congregation. . . . His views are not sought by lay leaders of Jewish education and philanthropy. . . . When I tried to persuade the promising sons of wealthy traditional Jews to enter the Jewish ministry, I was rewarded for my efforts with polite scorn. The parents, remembering how they regarded and treated their own rabbi, resented the suggestion that their sons voluntarily condemn themselves to lifelong martyrdom.[61]

Rabbi Alstat's views stemmed, as he states, from his experiences and observations in New York City. The situation was better outside the metropolis. Rabbis Herman Abramowitz in Montreal, C. E. Hillel Kauvar in Denver, Charles I. Hoffman in Newark, Herman H. Rubenovitz and Louis Epstein in Boston, Abraham Hershman in Detroit, Abraham A. Neuman and Simon Greenberg in Philadelphia, Solomon Goldman in Chicago, Abraham E. Halpern in St. Louis, Louis Feinberg in Cincinnati, David Aronson in Minneapolis, Gershon Hadas in Kansas City, Max Arzt in Scranton, Louis Levitsky in Wilkes-Barre, and Morris Silverman in Hartford were men of prominence and influence in their communities. And in New York City itself Rabbis Mordecai M. Kaplan, Israel Levinthal, Elias L. Solomon, Israel Goldstein, and Louis Finkelstein were rabbinic personalities whose advice was listened to and whose views were sought by lay leaders.

When the Rabbinical Assembly[62] met for its fortieth annual convention, held in Detroit in June 1940, its membership had grown to 282, an increase of about 40 percent during the preceding decade. Its placement committee reported that forty placements had been made during the year, that the committee was in negotiation with thirty-three other positions, but that thirty-three members were without positions, six of whom "are this year's graduates." The committee on Jewish law had considered such questions as the legality of the use of an organ at Sabbath and festival services; whether it is permissible to eat cooked vegetables and broiled fish in nonkosher restaurants; the Jewish attitude toward autopsies; the validity of civil marriages; the attitude toward birth control; the legality of burying a person in a crypt or mausoleum; whether a physician may act as a *mohel*; and the question of relief for the *agunah* (a woman whose husband has disappeared or abandoned her without having granted her a Jewish divorce), a problem which has agitated the assembly throughout its existence. There were also reports by the committees on adult education, elementary education, social justice, and the Seminary campaign; and statements on chaplaincy, interrabbinical cooperation, Jewish students, activities, Palestine, and the pension fund.[63]

The Rabbinical Assembly had become a functioning professional organization, operating on the volunteer labors of its members, on a total annual budget of $4,430. For the first time it had ventured beyond the eastern seaboard to dispel, in the words of its president, Rabbi Max Arzt, "the mistaken impression that Conservative Judaism is, in the main, an Eastern movement limiting its influence to the Hudson River Valley."[64]

The convention's theme was the rabbinate itself, and introspective self-examination. Rabbi Morris Adler of host Congregation Shaare Zedek reminded his colleagues:

> As our teacher, the late Professor Davidson, once pointed out, whereas in our day of specialization every profession has contracted the area of its intensive study and operation, the office of the rabbi has, on the contrary, assumed new and multiple duties. . . . He is, or is expected to be, at once scholar, teacher, priest, pastor, preacher, administrator, communal-leader, social worker and ambassador of good-will. To him come many and diverse appeals for assist-

ance, for counsel, for . . . leadership. . . . In the brief span of a fortnight a rabbi, to give a concrete example, has been approached on behalf of the Yiddish Scientific Institute, the Zionist Organization, the publication of a Biblical encyclopedia, a B'nai B'rith project, the Federation of Polish Jews and the Agudath Israel. Nor is the appeal exclusively for financial aid. The rabbi is urged to take part in the leadership of these numerous causes.[65]

Adler argued that the rabbi cannot remain aloof from "the multitudinous manifestations of Jewish life in the community" nor "from the social and cultural movements of American society. . . . In the desire to preserve the character and strength of the synagogue [the rabbi] must seek to guide, to channel and inform with something of his spirit, the streams of Jewish life that course outside of the synagogue."[66]

A discussion of "The Rabbi and the Inter-faith Movement" discloses differing views on the value and effectiveness of specific facets of the enterprise, but there is full agreement that a rabbi is not free to desist from participation in it. Papers and discussions on the relationship between synagogues and Jewish community centers, the conflicts between them, and "the function of the rabbi in such institutions," "Preaching Modern Religion," "Vitalizing Public Worship," "Religion and the Home"—all elaborate on Morris Adler's description of the gamut of rabbinic duties. Dr. Mordecai Kaplan urged a broadening of the functional definition of the modern American rabbi.

> It will not be possible for the rabbi, whose official duties bind him to the synagogue, to keep up with the growing needs of Jewish life. . . . The principle of division of labor would have to be applied to the function of the rabbi. Some rabbis would serve congregations, others would specialize in educational work, and still others in the various types of communal endeavor. . . . It will be necessary for men with a rabbinic training and outlook to serve in administrative capacities in every phase of Jewish activity. . . . *When Jewish institutions come to prefer as administrators those who have had an intensive Jewish training, the entire trend of Jewish life will be transformed from one of decline to one of ascent.*[67]

The convention was met in a world at war. As American Jewish spiritual leaders, its members unanimously adopted a statement, which they had printed and widely circulated.

> These are days when all thoughtful minds and sensitive hearts are burdened by the overwhelming present tragedy and its terrifying implications for the

future. . . . Millions of men, women, and children have lost either life, sanity, or home. . . . We . . . avoid the sinful error of disassociating ourselves from any share in the responsibility for our present woes. . . . We were all too willing to compromise with evil and to benefit from the spoils which its deprivations could put at our disposal. . . . We condemned only with our lips the rape of Ethiopia, China, Austria and Czechoslovakia and the cold-blooded, systematic annihilation of almost a million Jews in Central Europe. . . . We believe that every necessary measure should at once be taken to defend our country from its enemies both within and without. . . .

The greatest tragedy of all would be if we, in our hysterical haste to resist the enemy, would use his weapons of persecution, injustice, oppression, and group hatreds. . . . The extent and depth of the calamity which has overtaken all of our brethren on the European continent cannot be exaggerated. . . . Thank God that we in this land are a numerous community enjoying the blessings of freedom and equality. . . . American Israel is today the "head of the household" of Israel . . . to save what can be saved . . . and to protect what can be protected. . . . The community in Palestine must be given increasing support. . . . Those who can be saved . . . from the hate surrounding them on the European continent must be saved.[68]

As Jews, as Americans, as sensitive spiritual leaders, the rabbis returned to their communities fired by these words of contrition, concern, and resolve. As Conservative rabbis to whom congregation after congregation had turned because of the implied promise that it was they and the Judaism they espoused which would secure the coming generation for the ancestral faith, the words which disturbed and challenged them most were these by Rabbi Louis Katzoff:

A survey was made by the American Council on Education in 1938 on the activities and attitudes of the youth of America. In this volume called "Youth Tell Their Story" a chapter is devoted to the religious attitudes of youth, and it was amazing to discover the strong attachment of Christian youth to the church in contrast to our Jewish youth. Whereas 85% of the Catholic youth and 65% of the Protestant youth attend their church services at least once a month, only 15% of our Jewish youth come to the synagogue that often.[69]

In "The Land of the Three Great Faiths"

In his address at the first postwar commencement exercises of the Jewish Theological Seminary,[70] Judge Simon H. Rifkind observed that, whereas in Europe the rabbis were the products of the community they served, in America the community is shaped by the rabbis who serve it. The newly ordained rabbis accepted the judge's observation as issuing a challenge and pointing to an opportunity.[71] A new American Jewish community would be fashioned in the decades ahead, and the rabbis would be its architects. As *Conservative* rabbis their anticipation was even more pronounced, because Conservative Judaism seemed uniquely positioned to avail itself of the cultural and religious climate of postwar America.

Its definition of Judaism as "the evolving religious civilization of the Jewish people"[72] fit in well with culturally pluralistic America turning toward "ethnic assimilation and religious differentiation." The emphasis on "civilization" pleased those (mainly of the older generation) still clinging to cultural pluralism; the underscoring of "religious" as the core feature of the civilization attracted those (mainly of the younger generation) who preferred an imaging of America as "The Land of the Three Great Faiths,"[73] for it lifted America's Jews from minority status to one-third of America.

The Conservative synagogue, which by the late 1930's had become a "synagogue center" offering religious, cultural, and social programming "for every member of every family," was the institution most appropriate for the rapidly growing suburban communities. Its mode of worship was the one which the returning serviceman had experienced in the armed forces, and it was most readily acceptable to young families coming from a wide variety of religious (or nonreligious) backgrounds. As the religious movement which had had the longest and strongest identification with Zionism,[74] the movement and its congregations benefited most from American Jewry's turning toward Zionism and its identification with the State of Israel.

Almost the entire generation of young Conservative rabbis served as chaplains in the armed forces. They returned from the wars with heightened knowledge of the spiritual and existential needs of the young Jews they had served, who would form the bulk of the membership of their synagogues, and they looked forward to a continued relationship in civilian life not unlike the officer–enlisted man relationship they had enjoyed in the army. For the veterans and their wives, new immigrants to suburbia, the synagogue served the function which it had a century earlier performed for the West European Jewish immigrants to America, as the institution which would aid their integration into their new environment. It was to be their tie to the old and portal to the new. But unlike the synagogue of the second half of the nineteenth century, which responded to the real or imagined demands of melting-pot America—ethnic and cultural assimilation—the synagogue of mid-twentieth-century America responded to the mandate of cultural pluralism to retain, maintain, and expand ethnic and cultural distinctiveness. The suburban synagogue saw as its role to provide a "total Jewish experience" to its members, while relating itself to its neighboring churches as partners in concern for the spiritual, moral, and ethical life of the community and the nation.

At the first postwar convention of the Rabbinical Assembly, the rabbis turned their attention to Conservative Judaism and Zionism: "The Rabbinical Assembly reaffirms its support of the ideal of a Jewish commonwealth in Palestine . . . a democratic state in which the Jews, by virtue of their numbers, will never be in danger of losing their political or social rights";[75] to personal guidance by the rabbi: "I would like to underscore the function of counseling as one of the most essential in the rabbinate. Unfortunately, neither the Seminary nor the Rabbinical Assembly . . . have given any real treatment to the entire field";[76] to the rabbi as preacher: "The synagogue was primarily a schoolhouse, where the congregants received instruction";[77] to the rabbi in education: "Our schools will be failures if we do not produce God-fearing human beings, God-fearing Jews";[78] to "the manner in which the rabbi can fortify the democratic way of life through interfaith activity";[79] and to the rabbi as administrator: "the Rabbi today is more than scholar and teacher, pastor and preacher, communal worker and civic leader. . . . All the congregational activities such as Sisterhood, the Brotherhood, the Alumni, the Youth Groups, the School, the Parents-Teachers Association, the Study Courses, the discussion groups, the literary and dramatic units, the lecture and Forum Programs, are all placed, and rightly so, under his general charge and direction. He has to organize and inspire them, guide them, regulate them and manage them."[80]

There was little hesitation about what the rabbi's work would be, and little apprehension about any untoward difficulties. The Conservative rabbi felt himself in a situation of great promise for the movement and his rabbinic career. The membership of the Rabbinical Assembly had risen to 389, and the Seminary was able to choose its students from a large pool of applicants.

The sharing of rabbinic experiences at the 1949 convention provides us with a view of the rabbinate in the small and large communities—their labors, achievements, and problems. Thus Rabbi Louis Levitsky of Wilkes-Barre and Newark reports:

> When I was in a smaller community, I was an integral part of every Jewish agency. I served on every board, attended every meeting, and exercised very directly whatever influence I possessed on every activity: fund raising, policy, Talmud Torah, women's organizations, etc. . . . In this large community . . . I soon learned to restrict my active participation to the Jewish Education Association and to the Jewish Community Center. . . . In this large community, I find it possible to make of the synagogue the center of genuine spiritual fellowship. . . . A large community affords the rabbi the opportunity of influencing and directing a large number of people to serve the great variety of causes—local, national, and overseas.[81]

Rabbi Elliot Burstein, on his experience in San Francisco:

> In the larger community one could easily expend all his energies on outside activities . . . but the results are not worth it. To keep our own congregations going and growing is a full-time job in itself. . . . To assure a consistently large Friday evening attendance, we have discovered that all that is necessary is to invite a different local organization or group to sponsor the service.[82]

Rabbi Eli A. Bohnen of Providence, Rhode Island:

> Our sermons must be planned in such a way that we shall always be a channel through which the wisdom of our sages may reach the congregation. . . . the burden of what I was saying had most meaning when it was not I, but the sages of Israel, who were really speaking. . . .
> I have found no satisfaction to equal that which comes through teaching adults. . . .
> If the rabbi can . . . appear not only as a friend, but as a *Jewish* friend, he will feel that the time and effort expended on pastoral visiting are indeed worth while. . . . I have found that the person consulting me accepts what I have to offer with greater confidence when I can point out that what I am saying comes from the vast experience of Judaism.[83]

Rabbi S. Gershon Levi argues that "a direct, personal relationship to the school of his synagogue is the duty, rather than the option, of every rabbi. . . . He should observe classroom teaching . . . make a practice of having pupils visit his study for short chats."[84]

"The rabbi in the small comunity can be as busy as in the larger community," Rabbi Reuben J. Magil of Harrisburg, Pennsylvania, a community of 3,500 Jews, maintains, "and his activities are far more fruitful in terms of Jewish spiritual achievement." His congregation, Temple Beth El, holds services daily, morning and evening, Sabbaths and holidays, conducts Hebrew and Sunday schools, and has the usual gamut of congregational activities. The rabbi has had to be innovative and creative in maintaining and fostering all. Thus, to help assure a minyan each morning, breakfast is served after the service, but still members need to be drafted by the brotherhood's minyan committee. The Saturday morning service has an abridged *musaf*; the introduction of the triennial cycle for the Torah reading is being considered; and the junior congregation is brought in for the *musaf* service. The Confirmation service was moved to Sunday or Friday evening because "businessmen would not leave their business on Shavuot morning." Simhat Torah was revived by the introduction of a consecration service for children beginning their Hebrew studies. To assure a respectable attendance at the Megillah reading, a "sort of supper and carnival, the Annual Family party," is to be introduced. And, again, for an increase in attendance, the Hebrew school graduation has been moved from Sunday to the final "Friday evening sermon service."

The raising of the Confirmation age from thirteen and one-half to fourteen and one-half was accomplished only after a "gruelling battle," and the same seems to be in store for the phasing out of the Sunday school in favor of the three-day Hebrew school. Rabbi Eliezer A. Levi reported that in his Youngstown, Ohio, congregation, when all children aged eight and up had to attend weekday Hebrew school rather than Sunday school, "in the first two years of operation of this system, we had about 90 resignations from the congregation who joined the Reform congregation up the street whose rabbi campaigned on the platform, 'Come one day a week to us, and they will be just as good Jews.' "[85]

Rabbi Magil further reports that he greets each member as he leaves the Friday evening services, that the rabbi is expected to remain at weddings and other *simchas* "to participate in the festivities as an honored member of the family," that the small-town rabbi must be a member of at least one service club and "he must be ready to speak in and out of season at community functions."[86]

And there is a soul-searching uneasiness in the discussion, suggesting that some rabbis suspect that their great busyness and their creative innovations to bolster attendance—breakfasts after services, Oneg Shabbat collations, and the rest—keep them from addressing the question whether all of this is advancing Judaism, fashioning the "God-fearing Jews" Simon Greenberg seeks. Rabbi Hyman Rabinowitz, who fashioned an exemplary Jewish community in Sioux City, Iowa, commented with humor on the "creative innovations," and questioned in seriousness, "In Sioux City, we found that the best attendance we have is on Yom Kippur. . . . I don't know what you call good attendance or bad attendance, but after you get the people into the synagogue, how do you get them to pray? . . . Even the English readings are so mechanical and so dull . . . there is no emotional response at all. . . . How can you make them pray?"[87]

The area of greatest congregational growth was in the suburbs of the major cities. Rabbi Max Gelb of White Plains, New York, saw his congregation grow fourfold. "I have had to adjust myself to a new congregation . . . every few years."[88] What is more disturbing to him is the impress of the suburban environment. "The pull of the Christian environment is very powerful. Every Christmas presents a crisis in our school. There are scores of homes in which children experience a Christmas tree and parent arguing with the rabbi whether it is a national or religious holiday."

No less a problem are the secular forces which "tend to secularize your activities even within the congregation—the emphasis on the social."[89] For many years the congregation was housed in a very small building which limited its activities. Now a section of a new building has been completed, "costing to date about a half million dollars. That took years of effort, and the rabbi was very much involved in it . . . neglecting some very important duties." Now that the new building is completed, making possible the extension of the program of congregational activities "to introduce the many aspects of a cultural and religious nature which I find essential," Rabbi Gelb finds that the solution of the old problem has created a new one. "The leadership thinks . . . of the new building fund . . . and it is difficult to get them to accept the budget for personnel."[90] This was a plaint heard again and again in the 1950's and 1960's, the period in which American Jewry was smitten, as a wit had it, with an "edifice complex." This particularly was heard from Conservative rabbis, since the great majority of congregations organized in the suburbs were Conservative. Many reported that the same people who labored with devotion and contributed with great generosity to the building of the synagogue facilities suddenly became depleted of time, energy, and interest when it came to use them. It was far easier to build a synagogue than to fill it with worshippers.

A survey on synagogue attendance in Conservative congregations in 1950[91] disclosed that of two hundred congregations queried, 95 percent scheduled late Friday night services, and that in the great majority of congregations it was considered the main Sabbath service; over half the services were attended by less than one hundred worshippers, and only 10 percent had an attendance of over three hundred.[92] As for Sabbath morning services, only 11 percent claimed two hundred or more worshippers, 57 percent reporting only fifty. Only 20 percent of the members of congregational boards, i.e., the lay leaders of the congregations, attended services regularly.[93] The survey's evaluation of Friday night services: "The Friday night service is in the majority of our congregations the main service of the week. Attendance at this main service is at an appalling disproportion with the congregational membership."[94] Of the Sabbath morning service: "It appears that a Saturday morning service has fallen into widespread neglect or even has been given up as a lost cause—except of course in those congregations where the main service is held on Saturday morning."[95]

One can readily imagine what such lack of response did to the morale of rabbis who declared the synagogue central to Judaism and the Sabbath service central to the synagogue. What may have been even more devastating to rabbinic morale was the survey's disclosure that, in the opinion of congregational lay leaders, the "interest in religion which is manifested by young people" was: great, 8 percent; moderate, 30 percent; small, 48 percent; none, 2 percent; no answer, 12 percent. But most rabbis must have agreed with the survey's comment: "It is a highly optimistic indication that only 2% are reported as having no interest whatever. It is obvious the interest is there in varying degrees and remains to be intensified and cultivated."[96]

"Must have agreed" because there was remarkably little defection from the Conservative rabbinate to other pursuits. But there was constant self-criticism and complaints against others: either a lashing out against the laity or an agonizing critique of one's own failure to live up to the highest mandates of the calling, or both. Rabbi Sidney Riback turns on both laity and rabbinate in criticism and warning: "The tendency of the laity nowadays is to distort the rabbi into their own image . . . whether he is a 'swell or regular guy.' . . . The deplorable part of it is . . . that the rabbi often succumbs."[97]

Rabbi Max Davidson in his president's message at the 1952 RA convention pleaded for his constituency:

> I have referred on several other occasions to the helplessness and dependence of many of our rabbis. . . .
>
> We minister to people most of whom fully believe that they are wiser than we, better than we, certainly richer than we.
>
> When rabbis have attempted, e.g. to promote Sabbath observances, or to campaign for Friday night closings, they were not fully supported by the laymen. . . . When rabbis attempted to protect Jewish self interest and dignity, or their rights as American citizens in communities and schools with Christmas and Easter celebrations, they were not wholeheartedly supported by their congregations . . . community councils . . . defence agencies.[98]

The criticism was generally self-targeted. They called upon themselves and their colleagues to remain true to the mandate imposed by their ordination as "Rabbi, Teacher and Preacher,"[99] with the last two words as descriptive of the functions of the office, and the function of the preacher understood to be not to exhort but to educate. Robert Gordis reminded his colleagues in 1947, "I cannot conceive of any more drastic decline than for the rabbi to cease being a teacher and to become an ecclesiastical functionary. . . . Nor is it much better for the rabbi to be a mere spellbinder."[100] But as we have noted, the cited descriptions of the rabbi's activities pointed to his role as a functionary. No rabbi missed the opportunity to proclaim his love of teaching and the importance of the enterprise, but most also complained that the call of other duties left little time and energy for the scholarship and preparation that effective teaching demanded.

The rabbis would rather be in the prophetic tradition than in the priestly, but Rabbi Nathan Barack outlined the dilemma: "On the one hand, tremendous responsibility and opportunity to inspire faith in God and His way of life, but with hardship and even loss of bread as a possible price; on the other hand, retention of our comforts, but with failure to come to grips with the moral crisis facing us, and thus failing in our leadership."[101]

Sociologist Marshall Sklare and theologian Arthur Cohen pointed to factors in the training and role expectations of the Conservative rabbi which are at the root of much of the unease with self and disaffection with the calling. Sklare observes that the Seminary's curriculum, "centered about the study of the Jewish legalistic system," would be appropriate for the training of rabbis who would be serving congregations made up of observant Jews, but is not relevant to the actual situation in most Conservative congregations, as illustrated by the following comment by a typical Conservative rabbi: "I receive practically no inquiries about ritual or legal problems. Only on one holiday do people ask me a few questions—that's Passover. A death in the family may also provoke a query or two."[102] Moreover, Sklare notes, such a course of study is deficient in preparing the student for the multifaceted demands of his rabbinic office. It will leave him forever dissatisfied with those rabbinic functions which are not in the realm of halachah, and disdainful of congregants whose attachment to Judaism is an amalgam of culture, folkways, sentiments, ethnicity—the majority of his congregation. The emphasis on halachah in his rabbinic training apotheosizes a rabbinate of authority. How can a rabbi respect himself as a rabbi in a world in which, as Sklare puts it, "The sanction of a rabbi is no longer required for the correct practice of Judaism"?[103]

Rabbi Morris Adler spoke of the problem to his colleagues at the 1948 convention:

> I need not tell you how untypical is the attitude of the professors toward American Jewish life . . . and, I am sorry to say, towards the graduates of the Seminary. How much of a gap there is between the way in which we approach our problems and speak as if we possess authority, and the kind of feeling that prevails among the revered scholars who were and are our teachers.[104]

The fact that the Seminary professors were truly revered—most admired, some loved—by the graduates exacerbated the situation. It made the rabbis ask more seriously, "For whom and for what do I labor?"

Arthur Cohen speaks of "the desperate situation of the American rabbinate."[105] He does so with sympathy and offers "understanding and counsel." The seminaries offer "little formal assistance to rabbinical students in search of spiritual direction." The Jewish Theological Seminary has never resolved the paradox of being an "academy for higher Jewish learning . . . which must therefore encourage independence of inquiry and freedom of research," and a rabbinical school, which "needs, therefore, to be committed to a definite point of view." It is then left to the rabbis to work out the "issue of ideology and commitment." But the rabbis' "efforts to create an authentic community of responsive and serious Jews is handicapped when the rabbi is burdened with enormous congregations, an insufficiency of staff, a tremendous physical plant to manage, frequently uncooperative boards . . . and when the rabbi is to be lecturer, book reviewer, ambassador of good will . . . pastor on call, educator . . . and lastly . . . to be what he has chosen to be: a student and teacher of Torah."[106]

What the rabbi *must* do and what he has *chosen* to be stand in wide divergence. In fact, the former militates against the latter. The rabbi needs the reassurance by colleagues and observers that he labors under this "handicap." His spirits would be bolstered, his morale uplifted if his revered teachers would indicate their sympathetic understanding.

Sympathy and understanding bring but a temporary respite. The underlying unease persists. Now and again it was brought to the surface, and it hurt most when this was done by thoughtful, sympathetic friends. In 1955 it was Marshall Sklare's *Conservative Judaism,* a sociological study "which showed that what the rabbis think and say does not matter much to their congregation; the rabbis had known this all along, but to see it in print, documented and established, was chilling."[107] This was recalled by Milton Himmelfarb three years later, and he asked in exasperation:

> How are we to explain the Conservative rabbis' readiness to put up with the inconsistencies, contradictions, and ambiguities they have to live with? These things hurt. One of the ways in which the rabbis try to soothe the hurt, unavailing but revealing, is to change congregations; the Conservative rabbinate is a restless body of men. . . . The average Conservative rabbi dislikes his job and dislikes the intellectual muddle.[108]

His characterization of the rabbis as restless men is documented and underscored by Sklare, who wrote: "It is highly significant that during one year 40% of the rabbis who held Conservative pulpits applied to the placement commission of the RA for recommendations for new positions."[109]

Restlessness in the rabbinate is not confined to the Conservative rabbinate or to twentieth-century America. While many European rabbis in previous centuries held one or two rabbinic positions during their lifetime, a goodly number, through personal preference or due to conditions beyond their control, were "restless," as were some leading American rabbis of the nineteenth century, e.g., Bernard Illowy, who served six congregations, and Isidor Kalisch, who from 1850 to 1875 served in eight communities.

The "restlessness" of the European rabbis was due in large measure to political upheavals and communal strife, and the moving about of the American rabbis was often occasioned by the rapidly expanding and changing American Jewish community and the confrontations within the community between traditionalist and Reform elements. Similar circumstances made for the high mobility in the postwar Conservative rabbinate. The generation of younger rabbis had been uprooted by the war, taken from their pulpits into the chaplaincy. When they returned to their congregations, both had changed. Though sometimes the adjustment was smooth and easy, often it presented problems, and the rabbi sought relocation. Many new congregations being organized in the suburbs sought rabbis, and their newness offered the challenge and opportunity that young men sought. Established congregations underwent a change in membership and leadership as young war veterans affiliated, and thus at times made either the rabbi or the congregation or both uneasy and desirous of change. It was a time of flux in the American social and economic structure, a time when change seemed right and good. By 1960, as Rabbi Albert Gordon reminded his colleagues at the Rabbinical Assembly convention, "three million of America's Jews now live in the suburbs."[110] America's Conservative rabbis were following America's Jews to the greener grass of the suburbs. In that year, though Brooklyn's one million Jews made it by far the largest Jewish community, only thirty of the RA's 750 members were there, while the new communities of Long Island had already attracted sixty-eight. It is not at all surprising that a decade earlier, as the transition from urban to suburban life was taking place, two-fifths of the Conservative rabbis were seeking relocation. It should also be noted that a significant number of Conservative rabbis have served in but one or two congregations during their entire ministry.

What is more significant than the "internal, inner movement" of the Conservative rabbinate has been its stability as a profession. Professor

Eli Ginzberg of Columbia University, a leading authority on manpower, reported at the same convention on a series of studies he had conducted on the manpower problems of Conservative Judaism. By 1957, the Seminary had produced 615 rabbis, of whom only 6 percent were in fields unrelated to the rabbinate. "I know of no other profession, save medicine," said Ginzberg, "where the losses to other fields are so low. If you graduate from the Seminary you remain a rabbi."[111]

Milton Himmelfarb had asked "Why?" Why enter the rabbinate, why remain in it? The first and simplest answer was the socioeconomic one. Shortly before the war, in a study of applicants for the rabbinate, ministry, and priesthood in New York City, Ginzberg found that applicants for rabbinical training at the Seminary "came overwhelmingly from the lower economic groups, primarily from the more recent immigrant groups."[112] Men may have been entering the Conservative rabbinate for social mobility and economic opportunity. The rabbi, upon assuming office, entered the social class of the lay leaders of the congregation, and was accorded a position in the Jewish community which was reserved for the wealthy and distinguished. The income of a rabbi was generally higher than that of salaried professionals in education or social service, and though tenure in an individual congregation was not secure, the abundance of available positions in Conservative congregations (except during the Depression years) offered a high degree of job security within the profession. It was the rare Conservative rabbi who was without a job. Some may have been attracted to the Conservative rabbinate because of a prevalent perception in the Orthodox immigrant community of the economic well-being of Reform and Conservative rabbis, a perception bolstered by the accusations leveled by Orthodox rabbis that their heterodox colleagues had been "seduced by the Golden Calf."

The motivation to enter and the decision to remain in the rabbinate went beyond that. Beyond the desire to make a living and to gain social status and a measure of power was the drive to fashion a significant life. The rabbinate offered the opportunity to serve the Jewish people, not so much individual Jews as the *Jewish people*, and American Jewry, which was destined to become the leading Jewish community in the world. This prospect had lured Schechter to America, and it was this which attracted many students to his Seminary.

Motivations are hard to discern. What weight can be given to the public claims of spiritual motivation by one who knows that spirituality is expected, even demanded, of him? Look then to the lives of the rabbis, to the careers of those who were not touched by fame or good fortune, but who eked out a meager livelihood as rabbis in small congregations in small towns almost devoid of Jewishness, in positions lacking security, fair game for congregational petty politicians, lacking the communal stature of Reform colleagues or the respect accorded the Orthodox *rov*, measuring accomplishment by a daily minyan co-opted, a Bar Mitzvah Haftarah well-read by a young man they would rarely later see, and all the many "inconsistencies, contradictions and ambiguities." Yet they persisted, going from job to job, hopeful but realistic.

At a Seminary-sponsored conference on the moral implications of the rabbinate, in September 1962,[113] rabbis examined with creditable candor the ethical problems which the rabbinate imposes, and the spiritual dangers[114] which inhere in the office.[115] Rabbi Stephen Schwarzschild spoke of the anguish and the glory of a calling which is incompatible with its worldly environment, and as if in answer to Himmelfarb's query, he said:

> We know of ourselves that we are steeped in sin, beset by doubts and frustrations, and mired in fruitless gropings. We know that the Jewish people is more "hard-necked and narrow of spirit" than ever. We know that we have taken on the fight against an entire world which is profoundly pagan. . . . Why then do you want to be a rabbi? You don't, but for the life of you, "here I stand, I can do no other."[116]

Simon Greenberg proclaimed a more direct and functionally usefuled answer—a justification of the calling.

> Despite all of the shortcomings of the rabbinate, however, it stands today . . . between the hope for a possible renaissance of Judaism in America and the certainty of its utter deterioration. . . . Within world Jewry today the rabbinate is the only group in a position of leadership which treats the masses of our people, not primarily as donors or recipients of philanthropy, but as bearers of a great tradition. . . . The rabbi must be ready to talk with them, not only from the pulpit or from behind the teacher's desk, but at weddings and funerals, at Bar Mitzvah parties and at the sick bed, at Israel Bond rallies and at Federation dinners. And let him not be ashamed to admit and even announce . . . that he is a thousandfold more anxious to talk to them than they are to listen to him.

Greenberg knew full well that the role the rabbi is most satisfied with, indeed glories in, is that of teacher. Very well, he argued, wherever one who wants to instruct and one who needs instruction meet, that place can be a classroom. To make it so is "both his glory and his burden."[117] He continued:

> A rabbi should be dissatisfied but not unhappy. He dare not ever be satisfied with his achievements. . . . Unhappiness . . . reflects a lack of appreciation of the blessings of devoting his life to the teaching of Torah and the service of God.[118]

Dissatisfaction in the Conservative rabbinate was not so much with self and career as with the "inconsistencies, contradictions, and ambiguities" in Conservative Judaism. Defining Judaism as "the evolving religious civilization of the Jewish people" provides a felicitious characterization, but it cannot serve as the unifying ideology which the movement has seemingly been seeking from its inception. Already in 1911 Dr. Friedlaender wrote of "the difficulty in regard to formulating the definite theological credo of Conservative Judaism in distinction from Orthodox Judaism . . . and in distinction from Reform." He suggested that "at the present time . . . a general agreement as to practical work"[119] would be wisdom. And the Conservative rabbi in 1960 knew that what united the movement now as then was not a definite theological credo, but "a general agreement as to practical work."

In 1927, when Finkelstein put forth his "The Things That Unite Us," Eugene Kohn responded that "we should not delude ourselves into imagining a consensus of opinion if none exists."[120] Two years later Dr. Kaplan commented on three position papers presented to the Rabbinical Assembly:

> The mere fact that there can be three such different views as expressed by Doctor Finkelstein, Rabbi Drob, and Rabbi Eugene Kohn, and that we can still work together is evidence of the greatness of Shalom. . . . Doctor Finkelstein is equidistant between Rabbi Drob and Rabbi Eugene Kohn.[121]

The old two-pronged ideological coalition within the movement had now become three, and Kaplan seemed to welcome it. This tripartite division was accepted and institutionalized in the 1950's, when the presidency of the Rabbinical Assembly, by common agreement, went seriatim to a leftist, a centrist, and a rightist, until the far more numerous centrists realized that undue weight of influence was being accorded to the right and to the left. But the legitimacy of diversity continued to be held sacred and useful. At the 1980 convention, both a leftist, Reconstructionist Rabbi Alan W. Miller, and a rightist, Rabbi Wilfred Shuchat, presented papers on "Toward a Philosophy of Conservative Judaism."[122]

The "contradictions" and "ambiguities" which hurt were in the realm of the functional life within the movement. It had posited its commitment to halachah, to the observance of the Sabbath and kashrut, but all Conservative rabbis knew that in their congregations, the observant Jew was the exception—in many congregations, the rare lonely exception. The rabbi may also have felt apprehensive at the gap which had developed within the Conservative rabbinate on the question of halachah, which had come to a head at the 1958 convention, and in the frustrations experienced by law committees in confronting Jewish law from a Conservative stance, described by Rabbi Max J. Routtenberg at the 1960 convention.

Rabbis Jack Cohen, Jacob Agus, and Isaac Klein presented papers on "Theoretical Evolution of Jewish Law," from the left, centrist, and rightist positions respectively. Rabbi Cohen recommended that the Rabbinical Assembly "declare publicly that ritual can no longer be a matter of law" and that synagogue members be "encouraged to participate in an effort to develop standards for the entire congregation."[123] He thus advocated that "standards" replace laws, and that laymen, learned or unlearned, committed or uncommitted to ritual observance, have a hand in the formulation of the standards. Rabbi Klein reacted: "Rabbi Cohen's paper is a philosophy of *halachah* to do away with *halachah*. . . . I cannot react to Rabbi Cohen, we do not stand on the same ground. We have no common platform."[124]

On the question of Jewish law, the Rabbinical Assembly had become divided between adherents to a halachic Judaism and espousers of a nonhalachic Judaism. Rabbi Agus attempted to weld both viewpoints—halachah and standards—into an integrated whole, and Rabbi Ben Zion Bokser argued that "there is a greater measure of agreement among us," and the differences are a matter of emphasis; but the basic divergence on the question of the authoritative nature of halachah, which had long existed, had now openly and sharply been delineated.

Conservative Judaism had been committed to Jewish law, and to the proposition that within the legal system itself there exists the mechanism for adjustment, change, and development of the law. A Committee on the Interpretation of Jewish Law, established by the United Synagogue in 1917, was presided over by Professor Louis Ginzberg, who was recognized as the one and sole authority. Its decisions were few and cautious. By 1927, the Rabbinical Assembly felt secure enough to exert its rabbinic authority by establishing its own Committee on Jewish Law, which replaced the former but was little more venturesome than its predecessor. Both committees adhered to the principle of dealing with the law solely through the instrumentalities provided by the law.

With the expansion of the movement and in response to a growing segment of the assembly urging a liberalization of the process to afford greater freedom to adjust and develop, the Rabbinical Assembly, at its 1948 convention, defeated a motion that the committee "hold itself bound by the authority of Jewish law and within the frame of Jewish law," and formed a new Committee on Jewish Law and Standards whose membership would represent the "varied and varying points of view of the Rabbinical Assembly."[125] Its first chairman, Rabbi Morris Adler, explained its purpose to the 1948 convention of the United Synagogue:

> We must face the truth that we have been halting between fear and danger; fear of the Orthodox and the danger of Reform. We have set our watches by their timepieces. The time has come for our emergence from the valley of indecision. We must move forward to a stage in which Conservative Judaism revolves about an axis of positive and unambiguous affirmations. This will require a measure of boldness and vision on our part which, as a movement, I am sorry to say, we have not thus far manifested.[126]

In 1960 most Conservative rabbis felt that a good measure of boldness had been manifested in the dozen years past and that more and greater was in store for the future. Not too many felt the "hurt" discerned by Milton Himmelfarb, not in the late fifties and early sixties, when Conservative Judaism was thought by its rabbis to be the religious movement most vital, most creative, and if not yet the most numerous, soon to become so.

The Sixties and the Seventies

Most Conservative rabbis were far too busy to spare the time needed to turn dissatisfaction into unhappiness. Consider the schedule of one serving a large congregation in the Northeast in the year 1962.

Preacher. Two sermons weekly at the late Friday evening and the Sabbath morning services, as well as at all holiday services.

Teacher. Mondays: men's club downtown study group, at noon. Subject: "The Living Talmud."

Tuesdays: Confirmation class and post-Confirmation class. Subjects: "Conservative Judaism"; "History of Religions."

Wednesdays: Three six-week semesters of Adult Education Institute, two courses each session. Subjects: "The Legacy of Solomon Schechter—Conservative Judaism"; "The Wisdom Literature of the Bible."

Saturdays: Talmud study group, the tractate *Berakhot.* Monthly young-marrieds discussion group; Jewish current events discussion groups at Sunday morning postminyan breakfasts; biweekly Sabbath-afternoon LTF study group.

Administrator. The congregation dedicated its new synagogue building in June 1962 after four years of planning, fund raising, and building, in all of which the rabbi participated. Attended meetings of congregational board, ritual committee, school committee, adult education committee. Conducted weekly staff meetings. Wrote weekly column for congregational bulletin.

Ecclesiastical functionary. Officiated at forty-two weddings and thirty-nine funerals, all in the congregational family. Premarital interviews; attendance at wedding receptions; visited with bereaved families before funeral; officiated at one or more services at mourners' home conducting a study session. Attended daily morning services on Sunday, Monday, and Thursday mornings. Officiated at unveilings, *Brit Milah,* and *mezuzah* ceremonies in new homes.

Jewish community activities. On boards of Jewish Community Federation, Jewish Family Service, Israel Bonds, Day School, Vaad Ha-kashrut.

Community activities. Member, Mayor's Advisory Board; Committee on Religion and Race; boards of Association for the United Nations, Friends of the Public Library.

National activities. Member Executive Council, Rabbinical Assembly; Editorial Board, *Conservative Judaism*; Rabbinic Cabinet, Jewish Theological Seminary; Executive Council, American Jewish Historical Society; Publications Committee, Jewish Publication Society.

Lecturer. Weekly radio program, *From a Rabbi's Study.* Lectured to ten local Jewish and Christian groups; and in three Florida and two New England communities for the Jewish Theological Seminary. Delivered one scholarly paper at annual meeting of a scholarly society.

Pastor. In answer to the question, "When you were at the Seminary what did you think you would be doing as a rabbi, and how has it actually worked out?" the rabbi wrote in the congregational bulletin:

> In most areas I anticipated the demands of the calling. True, Dr. Mordecai M. Kaplan, Professor of Homiletics, warned us that one sermon every two weeks is as much as any man can properly do, yet I preach four times as many. I knew that I would be devoting my time to teaching, congregational planning, community activities and too little time to study and writing. That was all expected.
>
> What was unexpected was the time and emotional energy that a rabbi today is called upon to give to counselling. There are weeks when half the time is spent with people who have problems. One cannot help but become emotionally involved, and when you see your rabbi with a sad burdened look, or seemingly distracted, or even impatient, know that there are heavy problems on his frail shoulders.
>
> Problems there are of every kind: intermarriage, divorce, separation, children who do not behave and parents who are bewildered; a man needing employment, and a woman who doesn't know what to do with her time and herself; a family beset by a serious illness and a couple who are "eating each other up."
>
> Often, all that is needed is a sympathetic ear, or a bit of compassionate advice; sometimes the problems are rooted in deep psychological disorientation. Too often, the rabbi seems to hear the implied challenge, "Solve my problem or you have failed as our rabbi."
>
> I expect this, for what is more fraught with danger and personal pain than counselling. I expect it, and I accept it for the compensations are very many. What greater reward can life offer than the privilege to serve. To ease the pain of one heart, to straighten out one youngster, to keep one family together.[127]

The American rabbi had become an extraordinarily "busy man," particularly the Conservative rabbi, who felt impelled to match the activities of his colleagues, Orthodox and Reform. The Orthodox rabbi preached on Saturday morning, the Reform on Friday, the Conservative on both, for only in his congregation were both "major" services. The Orthodox rabbi dealt with *B'nai Mitzvah*, the Reform with Confirmands, the Conservative with both. The Conservative rabbi would meet his Orthodox colleague at meetings of the day school and the Vaad ha-kashrut, but not the Reform, whom he would see at meetings of the ministerial association and the committee on religion and race, both of which were outside the realm of interest of the Orthodox. The Conservative rabbi needed to work all the harder to retain his status in the institutions serving the most "parochial" Jewish interests, where the credibility of his Orthodox colleague was not in question, and had to strive all the harder for his acceptance as a significant participant in interfaith activities, in which his Reform colleague had long been the recognized spokesman for the Jewish community. He strove harder to invite counseling opportunities, for he found in these the vocational satisfaction which the Orthodox rabbi found in his self-appointed role of "defender of the faith," and the Reform rabbi experienced in his role as "ambassador to the community."

The 1950's and 1960's were the "glory days" of the American rabbinate. Religion was esteemed in America as a significant force whose influence was growing,[128] and the Jews, as Maurice Samuel observed, were "like everyone else, except more so." The synagogue was universally recognized as the preeminent institution of the Jewish community, and rabbis were accorded respect and exerted influence. Particularly impressive during these decades was the growth of Conservative Judaism. Marshall Sklare, who wrote the classic study of the movement in the early 1950's,[129] took another look in the early 1970's and reported:[130]

> Conservative Judaism has flourished during the past two decades. . . . The trend to Conservatism is particularly evident in the cities of substantial Jewish population . . . a noticeable increase in the number of Conservative synagogues, as well as a sharp rise in membership of those synagogues. . . . Reform and Orthodoxy have come to look to Conservative models in fashioning their own religious institutions.[131]

He noted that Conservative Judaism had become the "favored religious self-designation of the American Jew" and that the movement had achieved "primacy on the American Jewish religious scene"; its synagogues have become, particularly in suburban areas in the East, "the leading congregations in their communities," and there has emerged "a sense of constituting a movement—a sense of a shared Conservatism on the part of the Conservative laity."

Sklare concluded that "these developments appear to portend a brilliant future for Conservatism." But, he noted, "Despite brilliant achievements and excellent prospects for future growth, the morale of the Conservative movement is on the decline. . . . Doubts about the movement are most frequently expressed by the rabbis."

He cited an excerpt from Rabbi Max J. Routtenberg's Presidential Address at the 1965 convention of the Rabbinical Assembly:

> During these past decades we have grown, we have prospered, we have become a powerful religious establishment. I am, however, haunted by the fear that somewhere along the way we have become lost; our direction is not clear, and the many promises we made to ourselves and our people have not been fulfilled. We are in danger of not having anything significant to say to our congregants, to the best of our youth, to all those who are seeking a dynamic adventurous faith that can elicit sacrifice and that can transform lives.[132]

One cause for the crisis of morale in the Conservative rabbinate, Sklare suggested, was its misreading of the future of Orthodoxy in America. Routtenberg spoke of why he and friends at the yeshivah "decided to make the break and become Conservative." It was because they despaired that Orthodoxy could hold the next generation of Jews to Judaism. "We loved the Jewish people and its heritage," and seeing "both threatened we set out to save them," through Conservative Judaism, the wave of the future. But the unanticipated resurgence of Orthodoxy—the growth in the number of yeshivot, the establishment of Orthodox congregations in middle- and upper-class areas, the attractiveness of Orthodoxy to a small but significant number of serious, cultured Jews of Conservative and Reform background, and its triumphalist elan—brought into question the old self-justification for turning to Conservatism: to secure the future generations for Judaism. "The ground was prepared," Sklare wrote, "for the development of a kind of Conservative *anomie*."

> The problem was particularly aggravated in the case of one segment of the Conservative elite—the rabbis. Many rabbis had deep sympathy with Jewish traditionalism. Thus on the one hand they admired and identified with the Orthodox advance. But on the other hand they were filled with dismay and hostility toward this totally unexpected development.[133]

Another cause for the crisis in morale, especially among the rabbis, was what Sklare termed "Conservatism's defeat on the ritual front which can be demonstrated in almost every area of Jewish observance." For documentation he cited that in "Conservative-dominated Providence, Rhode Island, only 12% of those who designate themselves as Conservative attend services once a week or more," and the attendance declined with every generation: 21 percent in the first, only 2 percent in the third. The same generational decline obtained in the observance of the Sabbath and kashrut. What was even more disturbing was to find that in the Har Zion Congregation, Philadelphia, which had long been considered the model Conservative congregation in the nation, Sabbath candles were lit in only 52 percent of the households, only 41 percent bought kosher meat, and only 33 percent used kosher dishes.[134] There was little confidence among Conservative rabbis that this erosion of observance among Conservative Jews was reversible. They remembered the great campaign for the revitalization of the Sabbath in the early 1950's with embarrassment. Hopes had been high, the cause noble, the campaign imaginative and painstaking, the results nil.

Conservatism, Sklare further noted, "has lost its older confidence of being in possession of a formula that can win the support of younger Jews. . . . Many Conservative young people not only lack Jewish culture, but they have been influenced by youth culture—some are card-carrying members of the Woodstock Nation, others are fellow travelers, and still others have inchoate sympathies with the counter-culture." We need add that the rabbis were accorded no small measure of blame for the "loss of our youth." When they implored their congregants to give them their children three days a week instead of one for religious instruction, did this not carry the promise of a generation of Jews loyal to their faith and to the Jewish community? Where was that promised generation now, what had become of it?

Four rabbis and an educator offered "Reactions to a Critique of the Conservative Movement," which the editor of *Conservative Judaism* titled "Morale and Commitment."[135]

There is general agreement with Sklare's critique, and agreement too that his critique is not general enough, that his strictures apply to Orthodoxy and Reform as well as to Conservative Judaism. Rabbi Stuart Rosenberg asks Sklare to view with favor the growth of Conservative membership, as it provides a larger number of Jews with "Jewish associationalism," which Sklare himself spoke of in positive terms, for it gives "the survivalist the time which he needs and the public which he requires in his attempt to change associational Jews to ideological Jews." What Rosenberg is saying, not so much to Sklare as to his colleagues in the Conservative rabbinate, is that they have been granted an historic opportunity. For reasons historical or sociological they have before them in their congregations Jews who have affiliated because they need the company of fellow Jews. Theirs is now the challenge to make such Jews feel the need for Judaism.

Gilbert Rosenthal's statement is both a confession of failure and a call to the convinced to "rally round the flag."

> We have been hardest hit ... because of the inherent problems of our movement and the innate flaws in our ideology. ...
> Despite our movement's official espousal of *mitzvot* ... the pattern of personal observance among the bulk of our congregants is barely distinguishable from that of their Reform neighbors. ... We have missed the boat in not making demands of our people. ... Ideologically, we have followed the outmoded and naive view of Schechter ... that we must make a virtue of nonpartisanship. ... In the process, we have so blurred the borders [between Conservatism and the other wings of Jewry] that we may have undermined our *raison d'etre.* ... He who seeks to be all things to all men, ends up being nothing to too many. ...
> The Conservative movement has done wonders. I believe it is the right approach to meaningful Jewish living and creative Jewish survival. Those of us who have committed our lives and talents to the movement must help it move forward into the future cognizant of its failings, but confident of its virtues, and convinced that we are serving God, Torah and Israel.[136]

Jordan S. Ofseyer delineates the special problem of a centrist position.

> Many of our people have joined our synagogues ... have become Conservative for reasons of compromise rather than conviction. Can we reasonably expect them to evince excitement or enthusiasm? ... Shall we then be surprised that there exists a crisis of morale? ... Should we expect anything but a decline in the level of observance when congregants are not asked to make any *a priori* commitment to mitzvot upon joining the Conservative Congregation? ... We desperately require a comprehensive Conservative guide to *halachah.*[137]

Mordecai Waxman argues that what Sklare observed is not a "failure of morale, but a heightening of discontent." No small cause for discontent is the common occurrence that after long years of laboring with his congregation, building its facilities, establishing and developing its school, the rabbi is suddenly faced with a changing neighborhood, a declining birthrate, a mobile population which may denude or radically change the composition of the congregation, so that he is left with the feeling "that he has been plowing water." This, which is but a minor point in Waxman's essay, is an insightful grasp of a major cause for discontent among rabbis, particularly Conservative rabbis of the post–World War II era. Because they had literally "built" their congregations, they became so identified with them that they would judge their vocational success by the current well-being of their particular institution, rather than by what they had been able to contribute to the furtherance of Judaism and the psychic and spiritual welfare of individual Jews—wherever they might now reside.

But the discontent was far deeper, the special discontent of the Conservative rabbi. In preparation for a paper delivered at a Seminary and Rabbinical Assembly conference on the rabbinate in 1970,[138] I solicited the views of a number of highly respected rabbis, specifically about their discontents as Conservative rabbis. A leading rabbi wrote:

> Worship services which consist of a repetition of words which most of the congregation cannot translate, and which are not in keeping any more with the modern rabbi's idea of God, raise serious questions in the mind of those of us who want to be honest. Part of the problem of the modern rabbi is that he has to push aside, continually, the disturbing self-questioning concerning the validity of prayers which border on magical incantations when their content is not understood, and which for him, who does understand them, have next to no relevance to his theology.[139]

Another wrote:

> We [the Conservative rabbis] alone stand for sanity, for a genuinely consistent combination of what is authentic and ancient on the one hand, and what today demands of us intellectually and practically.
>
> Now having saluted the flag, let me turn to the sadder side of the story. Both the Orthodox and the Reform have a significant following. We don't. How come? Simple enough. The Orthodox rabbi leads a congregation that substantially subscribes to Orthodoxy; lives by its laws or at least feels guilty for breaking them. On the Reform side, inasmuch as ritual and symbolic behavior is optional, theory and practice are again dovetailed; non-observance wedded to non-expectation. Ethical sensitivity is practiced, or at least courteously recognized as deserving to be practiced, by rabbi and layman alike. But with our-

selves? Whatever we say, there is a vast gap. We preach to congregants about *kashrut, Shabbat, halakhah* in general, knowing that the vast majority neither keeps them nor feel any compunctions over ignoring these rules. The fraud is open, mutually recognized, with all the implicit contempt and self-contempt it engenders. Sorry about the rough words, but they are true, I think. The frustration, with Jewry and oneself, is therefore sharper in our own guild than in the others.[140]

The year 1975, the seventy-fifth-anniversary year of the Rabbinical Assembly, was utilized by the Conservative rabbinate for self-appraisal. Rabbi Wolfe Kelman, who had served for almost a quarter of a century as the assembly's chief executive officer, urged an end to the unwarranted self-flagellation which had characterized such undertakings in the past. "I know of no other group in Jewish life," he told his colleagues in convention assembled, "which has developed such a tendency to believe the best about others and the worst about themselves." He was particularly exasperated by the "internal and external chorus of anxiety and despair"[141] which strangely had accompanied the spectacular growth and rich achievements of the movement. In but the past thirty years, the Rabbinical Assembly had grown from "approximately 300 rabbis serving primarily in Metropolitan synagogues to a membership of over one thousand, more than sixty percent of whom serve in Conservative synagogues . . . half [of which] had been founded during these thirty years."[142] And, he claimed, "no other group of committed Jewish professionals in recent Jewish history has been more successful in achieving those goals to which it has been *unequivocally* committed, such as the cause of Israel, the plight of Soviet Jewry, the civil rights movement (particularly when it was less ambiguous), the cause of Jewish education."[143] Kelman is, of course, aware of the lingering problems in the area of *halakhah*, in which "we have not as yet resolved all the ambiguities and contradictions," but "unlike other groups, we have at least grappled with them. . . . [But] the task of reconciling *halakhah* and a tradition which was shaped in the pre-technological civilization, cannot be resolved even by a generation as gifted as ours at problem-solving."[144] But it was specifically to resolve this problem that Conservative Judaism had called itself into being, and the Conservative rabbinate had promised to accomplish it.

Kelman's insistent call "to dwell on what we have achieved" and not constantly to proclaim what the Conservative rabbinate has failed to achieve or what "we are still trying to accomplish" has helped restore some balance to an account which had become distorted by an almost self-righteous publicly pronounced humility. His suggestion that the incessant self-criticism may be the result of "a depression which can afflict a person or a group, not when they are struggling but when they have achieved the goal" may be right on target. But "the agony and the anguish and the loneliness of the rabbis are very real," and affect even those most visibly successful, serving the movement's leading congregations. Rabbi Stanley Rabinowitz, the leading rabbinic personality in our nation's capital, president of the RA, spoke of "The Changing Rabbinate."[145]

> The expectations of the rabbi have changed. The rabbinic calling has been trivialized. A massive horde of ribbon-cutting ceremonies. . . . The image of the rabbi has changed. The pre-modern Jewish world defined the rabbi as a civil servant, who was a teacher and a sage. The contemporary synagogue defines him as an employee, who is a preacher and a pastor.[146] . . . The rabbi's authority in the synagogue today is only as strong as his hold on the people's affection.[147]

Rabbi Wilfred Shuchat, rabbi of Canada's leading congregation, elaborated on the theme.[148]

> The rabbi can be most popular with the masses of congregational members, but if he fails with the elite group (President, Officers and Board) he is ineffective in the congregation. Much of the rabbi's efforts [and sometimes those of his family] have to be oriented into [a] kind of public relations with all its many stresses. . . . He receives his entire salary from the congregation. . . .
> Many rabbis [most] receive an additional income from . . . weddings, funerals, etc. Very often this creates a customer-client relationship.
> The irony of the situation is that the higher salaried a man is, the greater his stake in these relationships and the deeper the tensions.[149]

What makes for even deeper tensions is not so much that he often has to cater to the elite group (other professions make similar demands), or that he is financially dependent on the congregation (it does, after all, pay his salary), but that "in many respects he is owned by them, their possession. A member of a congregation will say, 'he is *my* rabbi.' Very often unusual demands will be made by members because, 'he is *my* rabbi.' "[150]

Simon Greenberg's claim that the Conservative rabbi is dissatisfied but not unhappy was borne out by the contents of a symposium titled

"The Congregational Rabbi and the Conservative Synagogue," published in the Winter 1975 issue of *Conservative Judaism*.[151] Of the ten questions posed, the first two and the last two touch upon our subject.

1. How have your religious observance and your attitudes towards God, revelation and Jewish law altered since you were ordained?

2. What has given you most satisfaction in the congregational rabbinate? What has given you least?

9. How satisfactory are your relationships with other Jewish religious leaders and with the philanthropic and defense organizations functioning in your community?

10. Have you found that your position as a congregational rabbi has posed special problems with regard to your wife, your children and your home life?

The conductor of the symposium, Rabbi Stephen C. Lerner, sums up the responses to the first query.

> A significant number of participants averred that they had become more liberal both in attitude and in pattern of observance as a result of their contact with their congregants over a period of years. And many did not apologize for that admission but felt that they had developed a different kind of understanding that was unavailable to the schoolmen in the various seminaries at which they trained. . . . At the same time, another group of contributors moved to greater traditionalism, feeling that the real need was not for a rational faith but for the establishment of a more traditional pattern of living.[152]

A few responses:

> The critical point in my own pattern of observance came at the time the Responsum on the Sabbath was adopted by the Rabbinical Assembly Committee on Jewish Law and Standards in 1950. I favored the majority view [permitting riding to synagogue on the Sabbath] and since then I have been observing the Sabbath in keeping with the majority decision.[153]

> Since my ordination my religious observances have deepened. Once . . . I began to realize how few religious observances my congregants kept . . . [this] convinced me of the need to spend less time constructing super-sophisticated systems of Conservative Jewish thought and more time teaching my people Jewish behavioral skills.[154]

> When I was interviewed by the admissions committee of the Seminary, Dr. Kaplan asked me whether I was not worried that the *apikorsus* (non-belief) I

would learn at the Seminary would cause some problems. . . . I told him that all the *apikorsus* the Seminary could teach me I was already acquainted with. The difference was that in the yeshivah there was not a soul with whom I could discuss these problems.[155]

I eat dairy foods in restaurants and in congregants' homes. I do not ride on the Sabbath, partly so that I have a sense of Sabbath (after all, I spend the morning conducting instead of *davening*) and partly to retain credibility in the eyes of my more traditionally-minded congregants. It makes my radical theological and liturgical suggestions more acceptable. . . . My theology has changed more than my observance. I have seen so much tragedy, officiated at so many funerals, held the hands of so many suffering people that I can no longer affirm that all that happens on earth is somehow part of God's plan.[156]

I have moved toward a less rigid pattern of observance. . . . After leaving the Seminary I . . . began the process of selecting those aspects of Jewish tradition which have greater meaning for me. My attitude toward revelation has not altered, but my respect for Jewish law has considerably diminished.[157]

My observance has become more traditional, mainly due to my children, who attend an Orthodox yeshivah.[158]

In 1934 I came to a congregation determined to preach a doctrine of Judaism liberal about God, revelation, and Jewish law and observance because traditional Jews were unenlightened and would lose their children unless I enlightened them in these matters. During these forty years I have seen the American Jewish community become so secularized, assimilated, non-believing and non-practicing that I find myself pleading for an appreciation of and a return to Jewish values, faith in God, loyalty to tradition and the beauty and worth of observance for strengthening Jewish identity. I have turned around one hundred percent.[159]

There is fullest agreement, by both the older and younger men responding, with Agus's statement: "My greatest satisfaction in the rabbinate derives from the many opportunities to teach that are open to me." It is shared by Benjamin Englander, ordained in 1934, and Azriel Fellner, ordained thirty-three years later. "In more recent years," Elias Charry reports, "counselling has taken second place only to teaching." For some of the younger men it is even a greater source of personal and vocational satisfaction. Preaching is enjoyed more by the older, while among the younger, the opportunity to introduce congregants to the joys and meaningfulness of Jewish living, to turn *rites de passage* into moving religious experiences, is an achievement rich in reward. David H. Lincoln writes:

The main satisfaction lies in the possibility of touching people's lives and influencing them to a greater observance of Judaism as well as a wider Jewish awareness. As an Orthodox rabbi in my native England I was certainly not able to influence people in the same way as it is possible to do here.[160]

Among the chief sources for dissatisfaction are "my apparently ineffective efforts to make the congregation more observant"; "the feeling of emptiness and despair I experience when facing a congregation made up of the invited friends and relatives of the bar mitzvah family"; and "the traumatic experience of being hired and retained. I find it enormously difficult to face the prospect of a group of people voting on whether or not I have stroked them adequately."

The majority of men report that their relationship with colleagues Orthodox and Reform (with but rare exceptions) and with communal organizations are good. The word "excellent" is used often. But, as one rabbi reports, "major decision-making takes place in the councils of the Jewish Community Federation, where rabbis and synagogues are absent. The religious institutions are on the periphery."[161] Jacob B. Agus reports that his relations with noncongregational institutions in the community are very good, "but my greatest feelings of frustration are in the realization that the ideals and values of our sacred tradition are rarely honored in the community as a whole. The fund-raising activities of our institutions belie at times the ideals that we represent."[162]

The younger men complain about the deprivations members of a rabbinic family suffer. "My irregular hours require my wife and children's generous understanding."[163] "Shabbat is no Shabbat and the *hagim* are not *hagim* for me. . . . A rabbi's schedule raises havoc with my home life."[164] "It is difficult for the family of a rabbi."[165] Rabbi Albert L. Lewis, after twenty-seven years in the rabbinate, wrote:

It's the same problem that afflicts any professional who is not bound to a nine-to-five schedule. It affects physicians, attorneys, and men who are in top administrative positions in industry. . . . I do not regard the rabbinate as a job or a profession: I regard it as a calling. . . . I feel that when a congregant has a problem and calls upon me, I cannot refuse to listen. . . .

I'm always on duty on Shabbat. As a result, the congregation has become my children's surrogate family. This situation has great positive features but also negative ones. I am very fortunate that my wife . . . shares my desire to help Jews become more Jewish. . . . She has taken care of the home front and has utilized our home as an adjunct to the synagogue. . . . Yet this is a problem that has to be resolved, for it is loaded with tension.[166]

Isaac Klein spoke from more than forty years of rabbinic experience.

> Of course we had special problems but we met them squarely and no one in my family has any scars. On the contrary, they show the advantages of living and growing up in a *beit harav* (rabbinic home). . . . Your wife plays a very important role as does your children's opinion of you as a rabbi. . . . I have been fortunate that it has been my *rebbetzin* who managed it so that no harm . . . touched my family because of my rabbinate.[167]

Looking back at more than four decades in the same congregation, Armand E. Cohen sees the benefits which accrue through life in a rabbinic household.

> My wife and children have enjoyed many benefits from my position as a congregational rabbi . . . high standard of Jewish home life and practice . . . doors of opportunity opened in forming friendships and pleasant social experiences. . . .
>
> The need for my children to maintain a high standard of personal and Jewish conduct just because they are a rabbi's children has been an enrichment to their lives and not a penalty.[168]

The general tone of the symposium is one of personal and vocational satisfaction. There is a sober sense of personal shortcomings, limited accomplishments, nor is the chafing at unrealistic expectations and pettiness on the part of congregations wanting. There is healthy complaint against congregants, the movement, and self. But one hears only echoes of the heretofore pervasive rabbinic questioning of the worthwhileness of dedicating one's life to a cause in which there is so little response and a calling which can record so few lasting accomplishments. What is heard loud and clear is that the work engaged in is eminently worthwhile, and that the achievements, which at the moment seem nebulous and tenuous, add up to a life well spent in service of a cause greater than any man ("No other person has priority. Only Judaism does," a rabbi approvingly quotes his wife) and worthy of all men.

Why the change? Why such a sense of unease and lack of accomplishment in earlier decades, and the apparent feeling of achievement and satisfaction in the 1970's? The answer may lie in the functional redefinition of the office of the rabbi. Teaching continued to be listed as the highest priority, but counseling replaced preaching as next in order—and in time expended and gratification received it may well have risen to the top. This was particularly so for Conservative rabbis, the majority of whom served in relatively new, suburban congregations, which the high and constant mobility in the Jewish community filled with relocated nuclear families. In time of crisis, having no elder member of the family available, they turned to their rabbi for guidance or solace. For the rabbi such an occasion provided an opportunity for *imitatio dei* (God is described in midrashic literature as counseling the bereaved, etc.), vocational gratification, and service to the congregation. The focus of the rabbinic mandate was turning from preserving the faith to serving the person. The rabbinate was becoming less a religious calling and more a service profession. A calling must have dissatisfaction as a constant component; can its practitioner ever be satisfied that he has fulfilled even a discreet portion of its mandate? A profession is less demanding. It requires but high competence and serious devotion, and its achievements, dealing as it does with defined, hence limited, projects, can be noted and enjoyed. It may well be that rabbis turned from "preaching the faith" to counseling the individual because the former was fraught with frustration while the latter brought satisfaction.

Preservation of the faith had been both the promise and the program of Conservative Judaism. The Conservative rabbinate remained committed to it, but it had lost much of its earlier immediacy. The demands for a "coherent ideology" and a "ritual guide" became less insistent. Ad hoc decisions of the Committee on Law and Standards were deemed sufficient. The very lack of a Conservative creed and code made possible the change and growth in "attitudes to God and revelation," as well as in ritual observance, that so many symposium participants endorsed. It enabled rabbis to engage in creative experimentation in the liturgy and in the ritual, which they found exciting, effective, and a source of great vocational satisfaction. Younger rabbis asked for a comprehensive philosophy and a code of law; older colleagues advised that freedom for creativity, disciplined by commitment to the preservation of the structure, the content, and the spirit of the tradition, was the more authentic and healthier way. Thus, for example, Rabbi Martin I. Sandberg, while yet a student, proposed in 1973

> a massive effort . . . by the Seminary, the Rabbinical Assembly and the United
> Synagogue, to write out, in detail . . . a system . . . of laws and customs [which]
> would be mandatory throughout Conservative Judaism . . . and to *apply* it
> systematically to all areas of Jewish life.[169]

The same issue of the *Rabbinical Assembly Proceedings* that
published the young rabbi's proposal carried the "Report of the Blue
Ribbon Committee of the Rabbinical Assembly." In summary conclusion it argues the value of the diversity which the absence of a creed
and code permits.

> The differences of opinion in our midst, whose waves are constantly surging
> beneath the surface and which sometimes erupt in dissension, may be the sign of
> a healthy movement, for we embrace many opposites. It is no small thing for a
> movement to have developed diverse approaches and cultural heroes as diverse
> in temperament and ideology as Ginzberg and Kaplan, Lieberman and Heschel,
> Finkelstein and Cohen. It is to the credit of the movement that we encourage
> religious creativity without threatening excommunication, and diversity with-
> out falling victim to anarchy.[170]

The same Blue Ribbon report discloses that its survey found that
"many rabbis are not happy with the role that congregations have
assigned to them . . . feel overworked by a multitude of tasks which
only minimally contribute to the realization of their personal and professional goals . . . [which] leaves meager time and energy for what was
once regarded as the primary function of the rabbinate: teaching and
studying."[171] It speaks of "rabbinic burn out . . . a reversal of a process
that begins with high enthusiasm and dedication, but which ends in
depression and alienation."[172] In response to the self-posed question of
"what can the Rabbinical Assembly do to enhance the status of the
rabbi?" it cites such suggestions as an RA-sponsored educational program to rekindle the "burned-out" rabbi; courses in arbitration and
mediation, with congregations informed that their rabbis are qualified
to act in arbitration situations; more seminars at conventions to deal
with the problems of the rabbinate; "the RA should distribute short
releases for use in synagogue bulletins which would be written in such
a way as to strengthen the status of the rabbi . . . and issue certificates
of recognition for achievements in various fields . . . to enhance the
image of the individual rabbi."[173] It concludes that "there is no ready
solution to enhancing the status of the rabbi." If there is no solution,
there may, however, be guidance to the individual rabbi. It may be

found in the response of Immanuel Lubliner to the question in the above-mentioned symposium: "If you were given *carte blanche*, what changes would you want to see implemented in your synagogue's educational, religious, and youth programs?" Said Rabbi Lubliner, "Maybe all of us have *carte blanche* and we don't even know it."[174] If not *carte blanche*, then certainly wide opportunities to serve and to concentrate one's energies and talents on those aspects of the rabbinate which one considers most important and most vocationally and personally satisfying.

The Conservative rabbinate had, after all, truly remarkable achievements to its credit. It had in but eighty years grown from less than a minyan to twelve hundred in 1980, experiencing a fourfold increase in the last three decades. During those thirty years, over six hundred Orthodox and Reform rabbis applied for membership, while less than ten left the RA for other rabbinic associations.[175] Its attractiveness was apparent, its ability to win loyalty, impressive. It had become an international organization with ninety-four members in Israel, twenty-nine in Canada, eleven in Latin America, and seven in Europe. In the United States it had spread from border to border and sea to sea, counting one hundred members in California and fifty-one in Florida. (Only twenty-two now remained in Brooklyn and six in the Bronx.) It was serving the movement which had become the largest in numbers. Within the movement it had risen to a position of centrality.[176] It had given to American Jewish life some of its most gifted organizational and intellectual leaders, and within their respective communities Conservative rabbis left permanent monuments of communal, congregational, and educational achievements.

Yet discontent there was, due in the main to the twin tensions under which the Conservative rabbi lived: the Conservative tension of reconciling an ancient tradition and the modern world; and the rabbinic tension of his ministry as both a *calling* untempered by compromise and a *profession* demanding accommodation. He wanted to be the prophet, "to pull down and to uproot . . . to build, to plant" (Jeremiah 1:10); his congregation needed a priest to officiate at its rites, to celebrate and to console.

His conception of his office and its mandates was formed by the remembered roles and functions of his European predecessors: the East European *rov*, expert in the tradition, his office invested with authority by his ordination, his influence commensurate with his scholarship; the Hassidic *rebbe*, guide and counselor of his flock, deriving his authority from personal or inherited charisma; the West European *rabbiner*, the man of wide Jewish and secular culture, bridge to the outside world, introducing the Jew to the world and the world to Judaism; and the American Protestant minister, pastor, preacher, organizer, and missionary. The Conservative rabbi had to be all and more, for in the free and open society which was America, he had to win to Judaism each generation anew.

Memory became mandate, and the expectation of office became a burden which was heavy on the spirit but apparently never crushed the resolve. Defections were far fewer than in the ministry or priesthood, and the Seminary did not lack for students.

It was a different kind of student who was entering the Seminary in the 1970's. Martin N. Levin of the class of 1969 reports that of a class of thirty, only one of four had attended a day school through high school, and he was the only one of the thirty to have attended a yeshivah while in college. He found that his classmates were products of the Ramah camps and "turn-ons from Hillel." They were "virtually unfamiliar with the intensity of Jewish tradition, its complex web of law and custom, its texts, its iconoclastic heroes, its intense tradition and demanding values, until [they] reached the Seminary."[177] The rabbi who emerged from the Seminary in the 1970's, Levin claims, is going in the opposite direction from his senior colleague.

> His reach is toward tradition, his dream is to be immersed in Gemara. His fight is not with a parochial God challenged by higher, more universal ideals; it is with an anonymous purposeless modernity, carelessly strangling a cloudy God and a nearly forgotten tradition. And so instead of Rosenzweig, he reads the *Jewish Catalogue* and instead of a robe he is wrapped in a full-sized *tallis*. . . . He calls for *minyanim* and spontaneity. His adult education courses speak not of theology but of ritual, and he gives more "workshops" than lectures.[178]

Whether this "new piety" will remain strong, or whether it will be tempered by the experiences of the rabbi as he confronts and serves his secularized congregants, and what effect this confrontation will have on his morale, a future observer will need to record and analyze. What is happening to this generation of young rabbis is what happened to their predecessors. They are responding to what they perceive to be the

Jewish needs of their time. They will experiment with considerable creativity in serving these needs in the context of the possibilities afforded by the social and cultural atmosphere in America. They will feel dissatisfaction, they will experience frustration, and they will adapt and persist as their senior colleagues have done before them.

It is appropriate that it was Louis Finkelstein, the acknowledged head of the movement during its period of greatest growth, who best expressed the basic sentiments of the Conservative rabbi, those which sustained him when frustrations shook his morale and those which drove him when opportunity beckoned. They were spoken in 1927, when the Conservative rabbinate was beginning its ascent as a force in Jewish life.

> We are the only group in Israel who have a modern mind and a Jewish heart, prophetic passion and western science. It is because we have all these that we see Judaism so broadly. . . . And it is because we are alone in combining the two elements that we can make a rational religion, that we may rest convinced that, given due sacrifice and willingness on our part, the Judaism of the next generation will be saved by us. Certainly it can be saved by no other group. We have then before us both the highest of challenges and the greatest of opportunities.[179]

Abraham J. Karp is Professor of History and Religion and the Philip S. Bernstein Professor of Jewish Studies at the University of Rochester. His most recent book is *To Give Life: The UJA in the Shaping of the American Jewish Community, 1939–1978.*

Notes

1. Peter Z. Adelstein, "The Rabbinical Selection Process" (typescript, 1976). The author is grateful to Dr. Adelstein for permitting him its use.

2. *Hebrew Leader*, vol. 8, June 29, 1866, p. 4.

3. Ibid., vol. 9, February 8, 1867, p. 4.

4. James Parton, *Topics of the Times* (Boston, 1871), p. 311.

5. *Galaxie*, January 1872, p. 47.

6. *Jewish Times* 1, no. 34 (October 22, 1869): 5.

7. *Jewish Messenger*, vol. 38, November 12, 1875, p. 5; November 19, 1875, p. 4; November 26, 1875, p. 5; December 3, 1875, p. 5; December 10, 1875, p. 5. Quoted in Moshe Davis, *The Emergence of Conservative Judaism* (New York, 1963), pp. 163–165.

8. The article appears in Hebrew in his *Otzar Zichronotai* (New York, 1929), pp. 206–211. An English translation was published in *American Jewish Archives* 12, no. 2 (October 1960): 123–142.

9. See Abraham J. Karp, "New York Chooses a Chief Rabbi," *Publications of the American Jewish Historical Society* 44, no. 3 (March 1955): 129–198.

10. *Proceedings of the First Biennial Convention of the Jewish Theological Seminary Association held in New York on Sunday, March 11, 5648 (1888)* (New York, 1888), p. 6.

11. Ibid., pp. 6–7.

12. Ibid., p. 9. From the Preamble of the Constitution of the Jewish Theological Seminary Association, adopted at its founding convention, May 9, 1886

. 13. On the ideological orientation and identification of the rabbinic founders of the Jewish Theological Seminary, see Davis, *The Emergence of Conservative Judaism*; Charles S. Liebman, "Orthodoxy in Nineteenth Century America" *Tradition* 6, no. 2 (Spring-Summer 1968): 132–140; and Abraham J. Karp, "The Origins of Conservative Judaism" *Conservative Judaism* 14, no. 4 (Summer 1965): 33–48. See also the opening section of Jeffrey S. Gurock's "Resisters and Accommodators" in this volume.

14. On Beth Hamedrash Hagadol see Judah D. Eisenstein, "The History of the First Russian-American Jewish Congregation," *Publications of the American Jewish Historical Society* 9 (1901).

Although the Beth Hamedrash Hagadol is listed as one of the congregations entitled to representation at the first convention of the JTS Association, the listing of contributions (which entitled representation) does not include it. Its tie to the new Seminary was apparently through the person of Sender Jarmulowski, an East Side banker, who is listed as an incorporator of the JTSA (Davis, *The Emergence of Conservative Judaism*, pp. 386–387) as well as an incorporator of the Association of the American Orthodox Hebrew Congregations (Abraham J. Karp, "New York Chooses a Chief Rabbi," p. 189). Rabbi H. Pereira Mendes, minister of the Shearith Israel congregation, co-founder with Sabato Morais of the Seminary, had looked forward to support for the new Seminary from the growing East European immigrant community in New York. When the community chose instead to channel its funds and energies to the importation of a "Chief Rabbi," Mendes publicly expressed his displeasure with the lack of support for the Seminary. He argued that the money spent on importing rabbis was largely wasted, for only graduates of an American seminary, speaking the language of the land, would be able to appeal to the younger generation. "Will he be able to take up the encroaching steps of Reform in America?" he asked about Rabbi Jacob Joseph, who was being brought. "Do not give away to false hopes," he warned, "Those who come after you will be Americans, full-blooded Americans like your brethren in faith uptown" (*American Israelite*, March 30, 1888).

15. Vol. 1 of the *Proceedings of the Union of American Hebrew Congregations* (Cincinnati, 1879) opens with:

On October 10, 1872, Mr. Moritz Loth, President of Congregation Bene Yeshurun, of Cincinnati, Ohio, at a general meeting thereof, submitted his annual report, wherein he used the following language: ". . . we must have Rabbis who possess the ability to preach and expound eloquently the true text of our belief. Such Rabbis we can only have by educating them, and to educate them we must have a 'Jewish Theological Faculty.'

". . . I respectfully recommend . . . the calling of a general conference . . . with a view to form a union of congregations . . . to establish a 'Jewish Theological Faculty.' . . . to adopt a code of laws which are not to be invaded under the plausible phrase of reform, namely, that *Milah* shall never be abolished, that the Sabbath shall be observed on Saturday and never to be changed to any other day, that the Shechitah and the dietary laws shall not be disregarded. . . ."

"And it shall be a fixed rule that any Rabbi who, by his preaching or acts, advised the abolishment of the *Milah*, or to observe our Sabbath on Sunday, etc., has forfeited his right to preach before a Jewish congregation."

16. Morais had served as an outside examiner in 1878. See *Proceedings of the UAHC* 1 (1879): 385, 524, 603, 605.

17. S. Morais to K. Kohler, "*American Hebrew* 32 (September 2, 1887).

18. *New York Herald*, July 21, 1888.

19. *Proceedings of the First Biennial Convention of the JTSA*, p. 11.

20. Ibid., p. 20.

21. *Students' Annual, Jewish Theological Seminary of America, Schechter Memorial* (New York, 1916), p. 61.

22. Max J. Routtenberg, "The Rabbinical Assembly of America," *Proceedings of the Rabbinical Assembly of America* 24 (1960): 191.

23. Schechter to Mayer Sulzberger, May 9, 1897, Jewish Theological Seminary of America Library. For an account of Schechter's coming to America, see Abraham J. Karp, "Solomon Schechter Comes to America," *American Jewish Historical Quarterly* 53, no. 1 (September 1963).

24. Schechter to Sulzberger, June 26, 1898, JTSA Library.

25. Solomon Schechter, *Seminary Addresses* (Cincinnati, 1915), p. 19.

26. Ibid., p. 20.

27. Ibid., p. 22.

28. For the radical nature of Rabbi Fleischer's religious views, see Arthur Mann, *Growth and Achievement: Temple Israel* (Cambridge, 1954), pp. 63–83.

29. Herman H. Rubenovitz and Mignon L. Rubenovitz, *The Waking Heart* (Cambridge, 1967), pp. 27–28.

30. Ibid., p. 30

31. Ibid.

32. Abraham J. Karp, "From Hevra to Congregation: The Americanization of the Beth Israel Synagogue, Rochester, New York, 1874–1912" (typescript), chap. IV, p. 18.

33. Ibid., chap. VI, p. 40.

34. Minutes, Board of Directors' Meeting, September 19, 1911. In the possession of the author.

35. Rabbi Chertoff's *Congregation Beth Israel Hebrew School and Sunday School* ledger records thirty students (27 boys and 3 girls) in the Hebrew school; and thirty in the religious school (i.e., Sunday school), of whom four were boys. The rabbi is listed as "Rabbi and Principal of the School," and he taught the most advanced classes. Among the subjects listed were "Hebrew Translation and Writing," "Abbreviated Humash," "Jewish Biblical History and Religion," and, of course, "Elementary Reading." The school ledger is in the possession of the author.

36. In the *Report of the Second Annual Meeting of the United Synagogue* (New York, 1914), Rabbi Chertoff is listed as representing Congregation Beth Israel, Rochester, N. Y.

37. Rubenovitz and Rubenovitz, *The Waking Heart*, p. 46.

38. For the founding of the United Synagogue, see ibid., pp. 35–59, and Abraham J. Karp, *A History of the United Synagogue of America, 1913–1963* (New York, 1964).

39. Schechter, *Seminary Addresses*, p. 20.

40. Ibid., p. 131.

41. Ibid., p. 128.

42. Ibid., p. 223.

43. Ibid., p. 224.

44. Ibid., p. 226.

45. Ibid., pp. 227–228.

46. Ibid., pp. 223–224.

47. This designation, or simply "Schechter's," was the popular name for the Jewish Theological Seminary in the East European immigrant community until World War II.

48. *United Synagogue Recorder* 6, no. l (January 1926): 12.

49. Ibid. 3, no. 2 (April 1923): 14.

50. Ibid. 5, no. 3 (July 1925): 20–22.

51. Mordecai M. Kaplan with unconcealed disdain stated that the chief motivation of the American Jewish financial elite (almost all members of Reform Temple Emanu-El) for supporting the Seminary in the first decades of the century was "to establish a training school for American trained rabbis who might stem the proliferation of gangsterism on the Jewish East Side." Kaplan to Abraham J. Karp, April 12, 1963.

52. *United Synagogue Recorder* 3, no. 2 (April 1923): 13.

53. Ralph Simon to Gary Geller, February 1, 1978. The author is indebted to his student Gary Geller for permission to use material he gathered in preparation for an honors essay for the Religious Studies program at the University of Rochester, "The 'Second Generation' Seminary Rabbi—Fashioner of Conservative Judaism," April 1978.

54. Jacob Kraft to Gary Geller, February 22, 1978.

55. Israel M. Goldman to Gary Geller, January 24, 1978.

56. Eli A. Bohnen to Gary Geller, January 28, 1978.

57. Elias Charry to Gary Geller, February 18, 1978.

58. *United Synagogue Recorder* 3, no. 3 (July 1923): 3, 7; 5, no. 3 (July 1925): 9, 10; 8, no. 3 (July 1928): 14.

59. *Proceedings of the Twenty-seventh Annual Conference of the Rabbinical Assembly of the Jewish Theological Seminary in America, Asbury Park, N.J., July 5, 6, 7, 1927*, pp. 42 ff.

60. At the 1928 conference, Dr. Cyrus Adler and Rabbis Israel Goldstein, Alter F. Landesman, and Norman Salit joined in a symposium, "The Synagogue Today." Rabbis Solomon Grayzel, David Aronson, Jesse Bienenfeld, and Kurt Wilhelm reported "on the Status of Judaism in Leading Centers in Europe," and Rabbis Louis Epstein, Louis Finkelstein, and Simon Greenberg presented learned papers on "Annulment of Marriage in Jewish Law," "Can Maimonides Still Guide Us?" and "Aspects of Jewish Nationalism in the Bible."

A year later Rabbi Elias Margolis spoke on "The Influence of the Conservative Movement on American Judaism," Alexander J. Burnstein on "The Abiding Values of the Resurrection Belief," and Rabbis Isidor B. Hoffman, Eliot M. Burstein, and Philip A. Langh presented reports on "Status of Our Movement Among College Students; On the Pacific Coast; In the Middle West."

61. *Proceedings of the Twenty-ninth Annual Conference of the Rabbinical Assembly of the Jewish Theological Seminary of America, July 8–10, 1929*, pp. 115–117.

62. The full name was now Rabbinical Assembly of America. "Of the Jewish Theological Seminary" was abandoned because of the increasing number of members who had received ordination from other institutions.

63. *Proceedings of the Rabbinical Assembly of America, Fortieth Annual Convention at Detroit, Michigan, June 25–27, 1940*, 7 (n.p., n.d.).

64. Ibid., p. 69.

65. Ibid., pp. 89, 90.

66. Ibid., pp. 91, 92.

67. Ibid., pp. 288, 289.

68. Ibid., pp. 55–58.

69. Ibid., p. 296.

70. October 7, 1945.

71. So it seemed to the author and his classmates about to enter the American Conservative rabbinate.

72. The phrase is that of Mordecai M. Kaplan; the concept goes back to Rabbi Bernhard

Felsenthal and Dr. Israel Friedlaender.

73. Will Herberg's description of postwar America in his *Protestant-Catholic-Jew* (New York, 1955).

74. See Abraham J. Karp, "Reactions to Zionism and the State of Israel in the American Jewish Religious Community," *Journal of Jewish Sociology* 8, no. 2 (December 1966): 150–174.

75. *Forty-sixth Annual Convention, the Rabbinical Assembly of America, June 24–27, 1946,* pp. 13–14. From Resolution adopted by the Rabbinical Assembly.

76. Ibid., p. 22, Rabbi Leon S. Lang.

77. Ibid., p. 85, Rabbi Louis Feinberg.

78. Ibid., p. 124, Rabbi Simon Greenberg.

79. Ibid., pp. 121 ff.

80. Ibid., p. 187, Rabbi Israel M. Goldman.

81. *Proceedings of the Rabbinical Assembly of America, Forty-ninth Annual Convention, Kiamesha Lake, N.Y., June 20–23, 1949,* pp. 141, 149.

82. Ibid., p. 151.

83. Ibid., pp. 157–162.

84. Ibid., p. 163.

85. Ibid., p. 191.

86. Ibid., pp. 171, 172.

87. Ibid., pp. 202, 203.

88. Ibid., p. 179.

89. Ibid.

90. Ibid., pp. 178–180.

91. *National Survey United Synagogue of America,* 1950, conceived, planned, and directed by Dr. Emil Lehman, with the participation of the Bureau of Applied Social Research, Columbia University.

92. Ibid. "Charting Synagogue Attendance," pp. 8, 9. If anything, the figures, supplied by lay leaders or personnel of the congregation, tended to be overstated.

93. Ibid., p. 35.

94. Ibid., p. 10.

95. Ibid., p. 41.

96. *National Survey,* "Spotlight Youth Work," p. 18.

97. *Proceedings of the Rabbinical Assembly Convention,* 1949, p. 167.

98. *Proceedings of the Rabbinical Assembly Convention,* 1952, p. 111.

99. The formula of ordination of the Jewish Theological Seminary of America.

100. "The Role of the Rabbi Today," *Conservative Judaism* 3, no. 2 (February 1947): 21.

101. "Religious Leadership in Our Critical Age," *Conservative Judaism* 8, no. 4 (June 1952): 32.

102. Marshall Sklare, *Conservative Judaism: An American Religious Movement* (Glencoe, Ill., 1955), p. 177.

103. Ibid., p. 178.

104. Ibid., p. 190.

105. "The Seminary and the Modern Rabbi," *Conservative Judaism* 13, no. 3 (Spring 1959): 1 ff.

106. Ibid., p. 8.

107. Milton Himmelfarb, "The Thought of Conservative Rabbis" (a review of Mordecai Waxman's *Tradition and Change*), *Commentary,* December 1958, p. 540.

108. Ibid., p. 541.

109. Sklare, *Conservative Judaism*, p. 285, n. 50.

110. *Proceedings of the Rabbinical Assembly Convention, 1960*, p. 49.

111. Ibid., p. 21. 75 percent were in pulpits; 11 percent deceased; 8 percent in Jewish community work. A survey conducted by students in my seminar on the American rabbinate at the Jewish Theological Seminary, in 1971, disclosed that over 90 percent of the graduates of the 1960 decade were serving in the rabbinate or allied fields. During this time period Christian theological seminaries noted considerable lack of interest in the ministry or priesthood on the part of their students, and a serious defection from the vocation on the part of their graduates.

112. Ibid., p. 25.

113. *Conservative Judaism* 17, nos. 3–4 (Spring-Summer 1963): 39 ff.

114. Ethical problems confront the rabbinate as a *profession*, as they confront other professions, e.g., medicine, law. Spiritual dangers arise from the rabbinate as a *calling*. In *The Making of Ministers* (1964), p. viii, the editors, Keith R. Bridston and Dwight W. Culver, make the distinction between *clergyman*, "a sociological definition relating to the role of a particular individual in society, a description of the function of a special member of a religious institution," and *minister*, one engaged in "a holy calling."

115. *Conservative Judaism* 27, nos. 3–4 (Spring–Summer 1963). See "Character-Destroying Factors in the Rabbinate" by Robert Hammer, pp. 55 ff.

116. Ibid., p. 43.

117. Ibid., p. 74.

118. Ibid., p. 76.

119. Rubenovitz and Rubenovitz, *The Waking Heart*, p. 42.

120. *Proceedings of the Rabbinical Assembly Conference, 1927*, p. 54.

121. Ibid., p. 5.

122. *Proceedings of the Rabbinical Assembly Convention, 1980*, pp. 44–77, 78–93.

123. *Proceedings of the Rabbinical Assembly Convention, 1958*, p. 100.

124. Ibid., p. 108.

125. *Proceedings of the Rabbinical Assembly Convention, 1960*, p. 211.

126. Ibid., p. 215.

127. *Bulletin of Temple Beth El*, April 8, 1964, p. 2.

128. A Gallup Poll conducted in 1957 asked: At the present time do you think religion as a whole is increasing its influence on American life or losing influence? The answers: increasing, 69 percent; losing, 14 percent; no difference, 10 percent; no opinion, 7 percent.

129. *Conservative Judaism: An American Religious Movement* (Glencoe, Ill., 1955).

130. "Recent Developments in Conservative Judaism," *Midstream* 18, no. 1 (January 1972): 3–19.

131. Ibid., p. 3.

132. Ibid., p. 7. Quoted from *Rabbinical Assembly Proceedings* 29 (1965): 23.

133. Ibid., p. 10.

134. Ibid., pp. 13, 14.

135. *Conservative Judaism* 27, no. 1 (Fall 1972): 12–26.

136. Ibid., p. 19.

137. Ibid., p. 21.

138. Abraham J. Karp, "Rabbi, Congregation and the World They Live In," *Conservative Judaism* 26, no. 1 (Fall 1971): 25–40.

139. Letter to the author, April 2, 1970.

140. Letter to the author, April 23, 1970.

141. *Proceedings of the Rabbinical Assembly Seventy-fifth Annual Convention, April 20–24,*

1975, p. 15.

142. Ibid., p. 14.

143. Ibid., pp. 15–16.

144. Ibid., p. 16.

145. Ibid., pp. 51–60.

146. Ibid., p. 53.

147. Ibid., p. 55.

148. Ibid., "The Rabbi and His Family," pp. 177-181.

149. Ibid., p. 178.

150. Ibid.

151. The symposium, conducted by Rabbi Stephen C. Lerner, the editor of *Conservative Judaism*, records the responses to ten questions sent to a cross-section of the Rabbinical Assembly, congregational rabbis from the classes of 1934, 1941, 1948, 1954, 1960, 1967, and a few more-senior colleagues. Sixty questionnaires were distributed and twenty-eight responses were received. See *Conservative Judaism* 29, no. 2 (Winter 1975).

152. Ibid., p. 5.

153. Ibid., p. 9. Rabbi Jacob B. Agus, ordained 1935.

154. Ibid., p. 17. Rabbi Azriel Fellner, ordained 1967.

155. Ibid., p. 40. Rabbi Isaac Klein, ordained 1934.

156. Ibid., p. 52. Rabbi Harold S. Kushner, ordained 1960.

157. Ibid., pp. 76–77. Rabbi Fishel A. Pearlmutter, ordained 1960.

158. Ibid., p. 94. Rabbi Morton J. Waldman, ordained 1967.

159. Ibid., p. 14. Rabbi Armand Cohen, ordained 1934.

160. Ibid., p. 66.

161. Ibid., p. 37. The city thus described is Cleveland. A veteran rabbi of that community, who for over forty years headed one of its leading synagogues, confirms this situation. "My relationship with Federation," he reports, "is cordial, pleasant and cooperative although the rabbinic influence in general has declined in Federation" (ibid., p. 15).

162. Ibid., p. 10.

163. Ibid., p. 12.

164. Ibid., p. 24.

165. Ibid., p. 93.

166. Ibid., p. 65.

167. Ibid., p. 42.

168. Ibid., p. 15.

169. *Rabbinical Assembly Proceedings,* 1980, pp. 396–397.

170. Ibid., p. 286. The statement is taken almost verbatim from Harold M. Schulweis's "Survey, Statistics and Sectarian Salvation" (*Conservative Judaism* 33, no. 2 [Winter 1980]: 68), a sharp critique of "A Survey of the Conservative Movement and Some of Its Religious Attitudes," by Charles S. Liebman and Saul Shapiro.

171. Ibid., p. 277.

172. Ibid., p. 279.

173. Ibid., pp. 279–280.

174. *Conservative Judaism,* Winter 1975, p. 72.

175. *Rabbinical Assembly Proceedings,* 1980, p. 14.

176. During the first two decades of this century, the Conservative movement was dominated by the Seminary, because it was all the movement had. In the 1920's, until the Great Depression, centrality was accorded formally to the United Synagogue, the lay organization, but it was

dominated by the faculty and alumni of the Seminary. During the incumbency of Louis Finkel-stein, a charismatic and forceful leader, as president and chancellor of the Seminary (1940–1972), Seminary dominance was total. During the 1970's, the leadership of the movement was being assumed by the Rabbinical Assembly, which had experienced explosive growth, and which benefited from the strong leadership of Wolfe Kelman, who became the movement's spokesman to the media.

177. *Rabbinical Assembly Proceedings,* 1979, p. 115.

178. Ibid., p. 116.

179. "The Things That Unite Us," *Proceedings of the Twenty-seventh Annual Conference of the Rabbinical Assembly of the Jewish Theological Seminary, July 5–7, 1927,* p. 53.

The Changing and the Constant in the Reform Rabbinate

David Polish

The Reform rabbinate is such an all-encompassing topic that it cannot be treated thoroughly within the scope of a single article. Since ideas and ideology are central elements in the development of a religious denomination, the essay that follows will focus mainly on certain fundamental ideas that have engaged Reform rabbis since the very beginnings of the Reform movement. By following the evolution and application of these ideas from the Pittsburgh Platform of 1885 to the present day, it will be shown that some of the principles formulated by the early Reform rabbinate, however fixed they appeared at the time, and however much they seemed to govern the Reform stance in regard to various issues, were never accepted by all Reform rabbis. Indeed, contrary to the widespread general impression then and now, the movement's formative principles were not monolithic and instead represented a dialectic between a clearly dominant majority and an articulate minority or, at times, between balanced ideological adversaries.

This process of dialectic, which has shaped Reform and enabled it to grow, is of vital significance. Because of it, Reform has developed as a cohesive movement even though it now differs in many important respects from what the founders created. Today's Reform rabbis are, and see themselves as, the legitimate heirs of the movement's founders, yet the most cherished tenets of the early Reform rabbinate have been almost totally reversed. These tenets were the original basis of Reform, yet the movement has held together and flourished even though its rabbis have embraced much of what was originally opposed. While there still may be a political consensus, since the Reform rabbinate has converted from anti-Zionist to Zionist uniformity, the former religious consensus has been replaced by pluralism in the areas of liturgy, practice, and belief. Ironically, as shown by the deliberations attend-

Rabbi David Einhorn
(1809-1879)

Rabbi Bernhard Felsenthal
(1822-1908)

Rabbi Isaac Mayer Wise
(1819-1900)

Rabbi Kaufmann Kohler
(1843-1926)

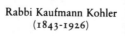

Rabbi Joseph Krauskopf
(1858-1923)

Rabbi Max Heller
(1860-1929)

Rabbi Emil G. Hirsch
(1852-1923)

Rabbi David Philipson
(1862-1949)

Rabbi Edward L. Israel
(1896-1941)

Rabbi James G. Heller
(1892-1976)

Rabbi Morris Lazaron
(1888-1979)

Rabbi Elmer Berger
(born 1900)

Rabbi Alfred Gottschalk
(born 1930)
president, Hebrew Union College-
Jewish Institute of Religion

Rabbi Abba Hillel Silver
(1893-1963)

Rabbi Judah L. Magnes
(1877-1948)

Rabbi Stephen S. Wise
(1874-1949)

ing the establishment of the Central Conference of American Rabbis, the national Reform rabbinical organization, the beginning of these transformations was implicit even at the beginning of the Reform movement itself.

The Central Conference of American Rabbis, today numbering about fourteen hundred members, has been one of the Reform movement's main arenas for dialectical confrontation. Founded in 1889, four years after the Pittsburgh Platform was drafted, it held its first annual convention in Cleveland in July 1890. Twenty-nine members were recorded as present. Among them were four who were listed as "Rabbis," fourteen as "Reverend Doctor," and eleven as "Reverend." (At the organizational meeting of the CCAR in Detroit on July 9 and 10, 1889, it was stipulated that among those eligible to join were "all autodidactic preachers and teachers of religion who have been for at least three successive years discharging those duties in any one Congregation.")[1] Six had come from the South (Atlanta, Memphis, Little Rock, Paducah, Nashville, Baltimore). The rest came largely from the Midwest (Peoria, Cincinnati, Detroit, Youngstown, Fort Wayne, Cleveland, Titusville, Pennsylvania; Chicago, Grand Rapids, St. Joseph, Missouri; St. Louis, Portsmouth, Ohio; Dayton, Ohio). The East was represented by Buffalo, Rochester, and Pittsburgh. Small towns and big towns were about evenly divided. The delegates to the convention included seven men who had attended the conference where the Pittsburgh Platform was drafted—Israel Aaron of Fort Wayne, A. Hahn of Cleveland, M. Machol of Cleveland, L. Mayer of Pittsburgh, David Philipson of Cincinnati, S. Sonneschein of St. Louis, and Isaac Mayer Wise of Cincinnati—but three important shapers of the Pittsburgh Platform—Kaufmann Kohler, Emil G. Hirsch, and Joseph Krauskopf—were absent. Of the twenty-nine who came to Cleveland, seven had been ordained since 1883, when the first class was graduated from the Hebrew Union College (HUC), founded eight years earlier. They were Philipson (1883), Grossman (1884), Schanfarber (1886), Calisch (1887), Guttmacher and Levi (1889), and Geismar (1890). Nine of those present in Cleveland were not to continue their membership in the CCAR.[2]

At the convention, the ideological foundations of the CCAR were established, presumably for the indeterminate future, by linking the body's future deliberations to prior rabbinical proceedings dating from 1844. At the preliminary organizing meeting in Detroit (July 9–10, 1889), it had been resolved "that the proceedings in all the modern Rabbinical Conferences from that held in Braunschweig in 1844, and including all like assemblages held since, shall be taken as a basis for the work of this Conference in an endeavor to maintain in unbroken historic succession the formulated expression of Jewish thought and life of each era."[3] In Cleveland, after a disagreement over "reasserting and publishing the Pittsburgh Platform in the Year Book," it was formally decided to "collect all the declarations of Reform that have been adopted by various Conferences, and record them in the Year Book."[4] Apparently as a compromise, it was decided to publish (but not reassert) all prior pronouncements. Nevertheless, a preamble to the pronouncements that appear in Volume 1 of the *CCAR Yearbook* reads, "In accordance with the motion passed at the Cleveland meeting the resolutions of past Reform Conferences, upon which as a basis this Conference builds, are herewith published as compiled, translated and abstracted by the Committee to whom the work was referred."[5]

This appears to have reinforced the Preamble to the Constitution of the CCAR, presented by David Philipson and adopted on July 14. The Preamble is, with minor changes, identical to the resolution passed in Detroit in 1889,[6] but the conference exceeded its own mandate by including "The Responses of the French Sanhedrin, 1807."[7] Following these, there appear the "Resolutions Adopted by the Braunschweig Conference, 1844"; "The Frankfort Rabbinical Convention, 1845"; "The Breslau Conference, 1846"; "Resolutions of the First Synod at Leipzig, 1869"; "The Second Synod of Augsburg, 1871"; "The Philadelphia Conference, November 3–6, 1869"; and "The Pittsburgh Conference, November 16–18, 1885."

The resolutions of the Braunschweig Conference, as compiled by L. Grossman and published in the *CCAR Yearbook*, are of special interest because most of the material refers to the Paris Sanhedrin, convened by Napoleon in March 1807. The responses of the French Jewish notables "are indorsed as in perfect keeping with the spirit and the precepts of the Israelitish faith." This includes the sanction of marriage between a Jew and a Christian woman, "if the State law permits that the children from such a marriage may be raised in the Jewish faith."[8]

It would appear that the founders of the CCAR regarded the Paris

Sanhedrin as a prototype of Reform if not explicitly Reform. But while the conference established prior Reform pronouncements as "a basis" for its future work, dissent in at least one area is recorded. While M. Faber and E. Schreiber wanted the principles of the Pittsburgh Platform to be "reasserted," M. Machol did not want them even "inserted." He then made the revealing comment that "at the time of their adoption I was opposed to some of them and am still opposed to them, and . . . there are members of this Conference who are likewise opposed to them."[9]

The immediate ideological precursor of the Pittsburgh Platform was the Philadelphia Conference, held in 1869. Among the thirteen in attendance were Kaufmann Kohler, L. Mayer, S. H. Sonneschein, M. Schlesinger, Isaac Mayer Wise, David Einhorn, and Bernhard Felsenthal. The first five were later to help write the Pittsburgh Platform. At Philadelphia, the following positions were taken: opposition to Jewish nationalism, support of the mission of Israel, abrogation of distinctive priestly rites and the idea of immortality, downgrading the use of Hebrew, equalizing the status of the woman at a marriage service, declaring divorce and the determination of the death of a missing spouse to be civil matters, and recognition of the Jewishness of the uncircumcised son of a Jewish mother. The first two statements in the Philadelphia Principles read:

1. The Messianic aim of Israel is not the restoration of the old Jewish state under a descendant of David, involving a second separation from the nations of the earth, but the union of all the children of God in confession of the unity of God, so as to realize the unity of all rational creatures and their call to moral sanctification.

2. We look upon the destruction of the second Jewish commonwealth not as a punishment for the sinfulness of Israel, but as a result of the divine purpose revealed to Abraham, which, as has become ever clearer in the course of the world's history, consists in the dispersion of the Jews to all parts of the earth, for the realization of their high-priestly mission, to lead the nations to the true knowledge and worship of God.

At Pittsburgh, nineteen men were present, including the five from the Philadelphia Conference, as well as Emil G. Hirsch, Joseph Krauskopf, David Philipson, and Michael Machol, but not including

Einhorn and Felsenthal. The platform they adopted is clearly linked to the Philadelphia pronouncement by the introductory passage, "In continuation of the work begun in Philadelphia, in 1869, [we] unite upon the following principles." The platform is an evocation of both the "consciousness of the indwelling God in man in all religions, and also the special mission of the Jewish people bearing "the Bible as the most potent instrument of religious and moral instruction." It seeks to extract the moral essence of Judaism, the "spirit of priestly holiness," from outmoded biblical and rabbinic rites and practices. It affirms Judaism as a "progressive religion" committed to the "postulates of reason." It envisions "the realization of the great Messianic hope for the establishment of the Kingdom of truth, justice and peace among all men," and therefore rejects Jewish nationalistic aspirations. It is committed "to solve . . . the problems presented by the contrasts and evils of the present organization of society." A dominant theme holding the platform together is the stress on modernity, as contrasted with the "primitive" past. The terms "modern," "modern times," "today," "our age," and "progressive" appear frequently in the text.

In addition to the principles, additional issues were addressed at Pittsburgh. Sunday services were declared compatible with "the spirit of Judaism"; a special mission to the Jewish poor was advocated in order "to bring these under the influence of moral and religious teaching"; and the question of brit milah was to be referred to the president of the conference, "since" the most competent rabbis no longer considered it "indispensable."

The reference to the "President of the Conference" refers to the Pittsburgh Conference and strongly suggests that it was envisioned as a continuing body, although this did not materialize.

As the Central Conference affirmed, the chain of Reform tradition, beginning with the Paris Sanhedrin and continuing beyond the Pittsburgh Platform, was incorporated into the newly created rabbinical body as the heir of the past. Yet it would appear that this was not achieved easily or unanimously, certainly as far as the Pittsburgh principles were concerned. The resolution brought in by M. Faber and E. Schreiber for reassertion and publication of the principles spoke for "a majority of your committee," which meant Faber and Schreiber. Michael Machol registered a minority report. It would seem that the sentiment against reaffirmation was sufficiently strong, at least at this session, to warrant an amendment that permitted publication only.[10] This would also appear to be at variance with a decision made on July 14, declaring all proceedings of prior conferences as "a basis" for the work of the Central Conference.[11] The action of July 14 apparently prevailed.

We do not know whether Machol represented others in his opposition, although he did make such a claim. In any case, his opposition is given added weight by his presence at the Pittsburgh Conference. We do not know precisely what he opposed at Pittsburgh, nor do we know whether others there joined him in his opposition. But we do know that Machol's rabbinical career at Anshe Chesed in Cleveland was marked by a conservative bent. In a congregation where the second days of festivals were discontinued, where an organ was installed and only a single Jew sang in the choir, he attempted, in 1891, to deflect the trend toward worship with uncovered heads.[12] Moreover, he once stated that it was "rather difficult to impress our age with the necessity of prayer, since we have commenced to reason in regard to its value . . . with the object in view to discard an obligation. . . . All our improved prayer books and all of our changes of the service will be of little avail,"[13] while on another occasion he wrote that: "for the man who clings to and represents the conservative party, religion is not merely a matter of mind and reason but also . . . an object of the heart. Conservatism . . . means not to ridicule the Bible, not to sneer at faith, not to destroy every ceremony, not to annihilate every Jewish peculiarity, not to dwell exclusively on the negative but to uphold the positive side of Judaism."[14]

The Issue of Jewish Nationalism

The Zionist issue is a paradigm of the process by which the CCAR was radically transformed. While the battle over Jewish nationalism represents only one component of the varied agenda of Reform, the issue was so pronounced, and exerted so compelling an influence on the movement, that hardly any other component has remained untouched.

The roots of anti-Zionism as a cardinal principle of Reform are to be found in Germany. In 1840, Rabbi Samuel Holdheim had said, "only if the Jew surrenders all particularistic national conceptions . . . can he be truly attached to his fatherland." David Philipson added, "From its very inception the new movement in Judaism has made a cardinal doctrine of this elimination of the nationalistic aspect."[15]

Certainly Reform Judaism was far more than a response to Jewish nationalism, but the importance of this factor cannot be denied. In this respect the seal adopted by the CCAR in 1889 is of great symbolic significance. Seven years earlier, as the delegates to the Cleveland Convention undoubtedly were aware, Russian Jews had founded BILU, the proto-Zionist organization that began the modern resettlement of Palestine. The group's name was an acronym for the first four words of the Hebrew text of Isaiah 2:5, *Bet Yaakov lechu v'nelcha* ("O house of Jacob, come ye and let us walk"), omitting the final words of the verse, *b'or Adonay* ("in the light of the Lord"). Seemingly as an answer to BILU's nationalism, the CCAR seal also utilizes Isaiah 2:5, but it says *Lechu v'nelcha b'or Adonay* ("Come ye and let us walk in the light of the Lord"), omitting the words *bet Yaakov* ("House of Jacob").

The origins of Reform anti-Zionism lay deep in the ensuing gatherings of the German rabbis. At the Frankfort Conference (July 15, 1845), a lengthy discussion took place during which a number of leading rabbis all agreed in varying idioms that the messianic aspirations for return to the Land of Israel were obsolete. "A longing for a separate Jewish State was born of oppression in the past. Such sentiment agrees no more with our modern state." It was therefore agreed that "the prayer for the return to the land of our forefathers and the restoration of a Jewish State shall be eliminated from our ritual."[16] At the Leipzig Conference (June 29–July 4, 1869), it was declared that

> the great historical mission of Israel as the banner bearer of truth and light must be strongly accentuated. Hence the national side of Israel has to be pushed into the background. The hope of the unification of the whole human family in truth, justice and peace should be emphasized. The hope that a Jewish monarchy in Palestine . . . will be re-established and all Israelites . . . return to the Promised Land has vanished entirely from our consciousness. The expression of such a hope in prayer would be a naked untruth.[17]

It would not be long before the waves of East European immigration to the United States would reverse major aspects of the Reform rabbinate's ideology. Indeed, internal ethnic tensions informed the early struggles of Reform. Xenophobia was not confined to late-nine-teenth-century American Protestantism. In 1897, Kaufmann Kohler obliquely suggested that by espousing Zionism, East European Jewry had become an instrument and a collaborator of anti-Semitism. Phi-lipson derided the "Orientalism" of Russian Jews. Four years later, Bernhard Felsenthal counterattacked. "Beware, . . . you with your reform notions will be swamped . . . in times approaching, when the immigration from Russia will swell still more. . . . Many others will . . . come ultimately to your Conference and vote there."[18] On this ethnic battleground, the currents of early Reform were to begin to change course.

The anti-Zionist position of German Reform, transmitted to the American Reform rabbinate, became part of the "basis" upon which American Reform was established. Yet an incident that occurred mid-way through the first convention of the CCAR suggests that even this issue was overtaken by controversy early on. On the evening of July 14, 1890, Dr. S. H. Sonneschein of St. Louis presented a paper on "Judaism in Its Relation to the Republic." Following the paper, the following resolution was presented by David Philipson, Max Lands-berg, and I. S. Moses:

> Although it has been stated time and again that the Jews are no longer a nation, and they form a religious community only, yet has this thought not been thoroughly appreciated by the community at large; we still hear of the "Jewish nation" and the "Hebrew people," and therefore this Conference feels called upon to declare once more that there is no Jewish nation now, only a Jewish religious body, and in accordance with this fact neither the name Hebrew nor Israelite, but the universal appellation Jew is applicable to the adherents of Judaism today.[19]

After extensive debate on the paper and the resolution, requiring that discussion be cut off, the resolution lost by a vote of 13 to 12. A motion for reconsideration carried, and "The question was then laid on the table till the next morning's session."[20] (According to the *American Israelite*, July 24, 1890, the vote was 14 to 11, with Philipson voting with the majority.) Neither the Sonneschein paper nor the dis-position of the disputed resolution is further alluded to in the *Year-*

book. The *American Israelite* recorded that "the motion was not called up again."[21]

It is noteworthy that at the next convention, held in Baltimore in 1891, Philipson delivered a paper on "Judaism and the Republican Form of Government," in which he said,

> There is no such thing as a Jewish nation or a Hebrew people; the Jewish nation ceased to exist eighteen hundred years ago. There is no Jewish nation now; we are Jews in religion only. Jew therefore is the proper name to be applied to us; Israelite is a misnomer because that is the name of an ancient nation that exists no more; so also is Hebrew a wrong appellation, for if it is the name of the people speaking the Hebrew language, it certainly can not be applied to the Jews, because the least of them understand, much less speak Hebrew.[22]

Despite the anti-Zionist chain of tradition and the sharp reminder in the Philipson resolution that "this Conference feels itself called upon to declare once more that there is no Jewish nation now," the anti-Zionist dogma apparently did not go unchallenged. After all, Bernhard Felsenthal and Max Heller (HUC, 1884) were avowed Zionists. This appears to be reflected also in an earlier gathering of the "First Conference of Southern Rabbis" (April 14, 1885), where reference was made to "the many false impressions" concerning the Pittsburgh principles, which the southern rabbis then reaffirmed.[23]   Another clue to the very early controversial nature of anti-Zionism is the abandonment by Bernhard Felsenthal of his anti-Zionist position. It has been noted that he had participated in the Philadelphia Conference, which began: "The Messianic aim of Israel is not the restoration of the old Jewish state . . . but the union of all men."[24] Felsenthal was absent at Pittsburgh. His turn to Zionism could have occurred before 1885.

The only first-hand report of what transpired at the Pittsburgh Conference is by David Philipson. Yet while he describes the preparations for the meeting and its stormy aftereffects within the non-Reform opposition, we are informed only that the sessions were "a love feast."[25] He also treats as quite incidental the two resolutions which were adopted after the platform—the desirability of Sunday services and the acceptability of noncircumcision for the son of a Jewish mother. These ostensibly minor matters were to become issues of consequence. But as for the Pittsburgh principles, we are left with the impression that their adoption came easily and by consensus. Nevertheless, internal evidence would indicate that a controversy took place, not only outside the Reform environs but within. The absence of a report on Philipson's lost and then tabled resolution, the clueless absence of Sonneschein's paper, and Philipson's reiteration of his resolution a year later raise intriguing questions. Had his resolution passed at its second reading, would he have repeated it so urgently without calling attention to the fact? All we know is that at the first convention of the CCAR, an antinationist resolution had lost.

Bernhard Felsenthal, Max Heller, and Professor Caspar Levias represent the original Zionist presence within the Reform movement. Felsenthal was the most active and vocal as well as the most interesting, having come to Zionism by way of the Philadelphia Conference.[26] In a letter to Theodor Herzl from Stephen Wise, there is a reference to "Rabbi Gustav Gottheil, the father of the Professor, and dear old Dr. Felsenthal of Chicago, the two venerable and beloved leaders of our Movement in this country."[27]

On October 26, 1897, writing to "Dear friend," Felsenthal stated,

> I am heart and soul sharing your views concerning Zionism. . . . I shall be exceedingly glad to learn that your endeavors in behalf of this great cause are crowned by success. I hope especially that some ways and means may be found to organize the various Zion societies in America in one great and influential body. Yesterday I wrote more at length to your dear father about this matter, and I would refer you to my letter I sent to the gentleman.[28]

Presumably this letter was sent to Richard Gottheil, with whom Felsenthal had an extensive correspondence. Writing to Felsenthal on May 27, 1898, Gottheil stated,

> As regards the representation of American Zionists at Basle, that is just the point at which we are working at the present. . . . I only wish that it were possible to persuade you to go, as I know of no one who could represent us better or more worthily than you. Is it really out of the question? I am only a stripling and a newcomer at your side; and I should be so glad for the whole American delegation to be headed by one who is known so far and wide as you are.[29]

Writing to Professor Gottheil again three years later, Felsenthal said,

> First let me . . . congratulate you and all the friends of the great philanthropic, aye, more than philanthropic cause of Zionism, that the Zionistic Movement, to create a legally secured home again for the myriads of homeless Israel has made such a mighty and blessed step forward within the last few days! God bless Herzl and his able co-workers![30]

Hardly had the Pittsburgh Platform been incorporated into the proceedings of the Central Conference when the confrontation over Zionism began to take shape, with the guiding principles of Pittsburgh both the banner and the target of the controversy. On January 25, 1915, Stephen Wise, writing to Morris Lazaron, his friend, confidant, and fellow-Zionist at the time, denounced the Pittsburgh Platform for its antinationalism, and was already proposing that it be rescinded. He accused Kohler and his co-worker Philipson of using the Hebrew Union College and the Central Conference as instruments for suppressing Jewish nationalism and intimidating the student body.[31]

The administration of Kaufmann Kohler as president of HUC was marked by bitter polemics and intrigue over the issue of Zionism, as is shown, for instance, by the following passage from Wise's letter to Lazaron:

> It was not his [Horace Kallen's] imagined agnosticism that moved Dr. Kohler and Dr. Philipson to deny him the possibility of speaking at the College chapel but the fact that he is a Zionist. You know of the frenzied and fanatical antipathy to Zionism which obtains, explicably enough, in the mind of Dr. Kohler though I confess quite inexplicably in the mind of a younger man such as Dr. Philipson in point of years. . . . The serious thing about the matter, my dear Lazaron, is, as you know, that the present attitude of the College, as it is embodied in the personality and leadership of Dr. Kohler and Dr. Philipson, is certain to do one of two things—either tyrannize the men, in that despite the other convictions, into the acceptance of the anti-Zionist position, or else do that which is most damaging to the souls of men who are to be teachers of truth and righteousness,—namely, brow-beat them into sullen and outward acquiescence with all the spirit-marring hypocrisy which that attitude implies.[32]

Long before the incident referred to in this letter, Max Margolis, a professor of biblical exegesis at the Hebrew Union College, was involved in a dispute that led to his leaving the College. It has been debated whether he left under pressure or was officially dismissed, but it is quite certain that the Zionist issue was at the heart of his ordeal. In 1916, writing to "my dear friend" (probably Max Heller) on College stationery, he stated,

> I . . . thank you most heartily . . . for your kind words in regard to my return to the College. I need not tell you that nothing but enthusiasm for the cause which the College stands for would have lured me away from a position of honor and I regret to say that my enthusiasm has been considerably chilled by the touch of reality as embodied in a head whose fitness for the position he occupies may seriously be doubted. I do not like on an occasion like this to go into details; at some future date, I shall gladly do so.[33]

In another letter to Max Heller, written several years earlier, Margolis stated,

> That your sympathies were with me in all this commotion I knew full well. . . . I am not so sure now that I shall consent to remain. With the present (mal)-administration there is no hope of a permanent peace. "Ayn adam dar in nachash b'kfifah achat" [One should not live together with a snake]. B[ernhard] B[ettmann] is supporting K[ohler] out of sheer fear of [Emil] Hirsch's big stick and I am preparing myself for leaving College. . . . I presume you know what is at the bottom of it all. The stand the College is taking against Zionism is dictated by a man who unable to secure the presidency for himself, is interested in keeping—you out of it. That is the sum and substance of the matter. . . . It is up to the alumni to decide whether the College should be handed over to the forces of radicalism–Hirsch et al.–or continue in the lines of I. M. Wise. . . . you are quite right that Radicalism must be fought. If Reform means what it meant up until now, denationalized Judaism and the dogma of the finality of the divinely ordained Diaspora, Zionism is incompatible therewith. According to [Prof. Gotthard] Deutsch the ultimate aim of Judaism is—absorption. It is this, taught by K. and the whole crowd that has forced me to declare myself. Beyond this I believe in Israel's mission myself. I furthermore know that at present we are all Diaspora Jews . . . but we Zionists recognized that though the Diaspora will still continue for a long while it cannot and must not be our ultimate aim. There must be created over against the Diaspora a Palestinian Jewry, a home for the Jewish people, not by any manner or means for all Jews—in other words the status ante seventy [i.e., the destruction of the Second Commonwealth] must be restored. This is the acharit v'tikvah [the ultimate hope; cf. Jer. 31:17].[34]

In still another letter, he wrote to Max Heller,

I realize the difficulty of establishing any standard whatever for the Hebrew Union College. . . . the possibility is of course open to them to draw up a body of negative doctrine. . . . I suppose the basis of such negative doctrine might be "political Zionism." What children they do make of themselves in setting up the strawman "political" knocking them down again. . . . it seems to me that your present position and Hirsch's present position are the same in principle. Each of you makes a personality the standard of action. The Reverend Dr. Hirsch making the present President his standard [and Heller making Isaac Mayer Wise his standard. D.P.]. Either the College remains what it was, a liberal institution, devoted to Jewish learning and the training of men who might form independent convictions . . . or it is once for all known as the Theological School of a petty sect in Judaism.[35]

On May 4, 1907, Margolis wrote to Max Heller,

It may interest you to know that of 42 returns from the alumni 28 were for me, 5 against me, the rest non-committal. Offenheimer and C. S. Levi stood out for me to the very last. But the Board was influenced by Philipson, and Bettmann played a dubious part. Two students have already withdrawn (Junior Class) and a third Junior contemplates withdrawing. He was told by Kohler that no sermon with Zionistic sentiments would be tolerated in the College chapel. The student body is in a commotion.[36]

Two months later, writing from Halle, Germany, Margolis told Heller,

The American Jewish papers have just arrived and I notice with great satisfaction that you have made Vice-President of the Conference. This action alone is ample evidence that the Conference as a body has not committed itself to an anti-Zionistic campaign. . . . let me hope that the Radicals will be held at bay. Large interests are at stake, and the future of Judaism must not be lightly thrown away.[37]

There may have been other factors at play. Michael Meyer cites "an oral tradition [which] . . . suggest[s] that Margolis at one point harbored the ambition of displacing Kohler as President."[38]

In a letter to Max Heller dated April 30, 1907, written on the stationery of the Federation of American Zionists, Judah Magnes stated,

Tonight is the meeting of the Board of Governors of the College, when

Margolis' fate will be determined upon. I suppose there can be but one outcome, inasmuch . . . as the question is practically one of a choice of president or
professor. . . . I am afraid that you will have to add a name to those which you
mention as being responsible for the situation, namely that of the former Professor of Homiletics. I cannot understand why my letter to Charles Levi was in
any way considered disloyal by anyone. Before making it public I asked the
Cincinnati man whether a public statement on my part would be acceptable to
them, and they replied in the affirmative. After all, what was best to do? To sit
idly by and see violence done without moving a muscle?[39]

On January 4, 1908, Magnes informed Max Heller that he was
"interested in the formation of a Kehillah here [i.e., New York, where
he was rabbi at Temple Emanu-El], and a Vaad Ha-Chinuch."[40] On
March 2, 1911, he told Rabbi Heller,

As soon as you retire from the presidency of the Central Conference of Rabbis, it is my intention to send in my resignation. I shall, of course consider the
matter further until I decide definitely to take this step but, judging from the
way I look at matters now, I think that I shall be confirmed in my present
contention. . . . I rejoice to hear from you that there are younger men who
sympathize with our Jewish aspirations. . . . the fight must be made all along the
line. . . . I have had enough of protesting, . . . and the time has come for me to
achieve something positive.[41]

The continuing struggle over Zionism at the College is reflected in a
March 1915 incident involving Max Heller, his son James, and Kaufmann Kohler. Young Heller had complained to his father that Kohler
would not permit him to deliver a Zionist sermon in the College chapel, and Max Heller complained to Kohler. In his response to Heller,
Kohler said that he had told James that the sermon "was not in good
taste at this time," although this did not mean that he was refusing.
Moreover, said Kohler, the text James had chosen, "Nahamu ami"
("Comfort ye, my people"—Isaiah 40:1), "was not appropriate except for the Sabbath after the Ninth of Ab." By way of showing that
the anti-Zionist policy of his administration was backed by the board,
"which sought to define the measure of academic liberty which is to
obtain at the HUC with regard to the advocacy of Zionism," Kohler
included the following extract from the board's minutes:

Political Zionism may be championed at the HUC by competent speakers who have not been guilty of insulting hostility to the institution or its officers and who may be trusted to speak in a spirit consonant with genuine religious-ness. . . . a student who is to occupy the chapel pulpit as part of his homiletic training shall be permitted in his sermon to advocate political Zionism if the manner and temper of his advocacy are not in conflict with the sincerely religious note which is indispensable in the Jewish sermon.

Kohler concluded,

if you will re-read the resolutions passed by the Board as a result of the Conference on February 15, you will find that I acted in accordance with the tenor and spirit of the same. You will, I trust, recognize that those who have the welfare of the College and the students at heart, should endeavor to curb the spirit of defiance and disrespect toward the authorities of the College, rather than encourage the same.[42]

Many years later, during a defense of the College against charges that it was breeding Zionists, President Julian Morgenstern made the following corroborating observation:

I mention Dr. Kohler . . . because in his day . . . there was a definite, aggressive anti-Zionist policy governing the administration of the College and an attempt to control the students. I do not mention Dr. Wise's regime because there was not Zionism in that day.—(Louis Wolsey interjects, "That isn't so.") Zionism was just the beginning. . . . In Dr. Wise's day, toward the end, Levias began to find out that he was a Zionist. I was a student in those days, and I remember when Levias came and told us he was a Zionist. The issue came in Dr. Kohler's day, with Margolis.[43]

K'lal Yisroel (World Jewry)

Its antinationalism notwithstanding, the Reform movement was from the first committed to religious unity, and frequently sought to cooperate with other bodies in efforts in behalf of K'lal Yisroel. In his inaugural statement as president of the Central Conference, Isaac Mayer Wise cited various efforts in which he had been involved that had been made to create a united American Jewry. "In 1849 leading men . . . proposed—and did considerable work to realize the project—

to convene a meeting of delegates from the various congregations to devise means for concerted action, especially to erect hospitals, asylums, schools, etc. They failed." In 1855, he continued, there was another attempt to unite Reform and non-Reform Jews who agreed "to establish a permanent synod on strictly democratic principles, to establish and govern all necessary public institutions, and to direct all synagogal reforms. . . . By the most violent opposition of Rabbis who had not appeared in that Conference . . . the whole piece of work proved a sad failure." In 1867–68, another effort was made, but again the "projected union" was frustrated.[44]

Following these aborted efforts, the CCAR pursued a solitary course on the American scene. Nevertheless, in his President's Message of 1917, William Rosenau appealed for the support of a national fund for Jewish war relief. The convention delegates "heartily concurred . . . and urged that the Executive Board request the members of the Conference to speak on this theme during the High Holy Day season, and that they organize their communities for effective work along relief lines."[45]

In 1917, the Central Conference was giving serious consideration to joining the call for participation in the creation of the American Jewish Congress, which was then envisioned by Stephen Wise as an umbrella organization for American Jewry. A committee of four had already been designated to represent the Conference. However, a quarrel erupted between the CCAR and the Congress leadership over the inclusion of the issue of Zionism on the agenda. CCAR members felt that an agreement had been reached to delete it and that the agreement had been broken. Nevertheless, Max Heller presented a resolution urging that the CCAR's participation go forward, since "the Conference took part in the organization of the Congress by having representatives on the administrative and other committees." Samuel Schulman argued that "if the pact has been broken the place to say it is not here, but before the Congress." A motion to unconditionally stay out of the AJC won by a vote of 40 to 36.[46]

With the onset of World War I, the CCAR's attitude toward Zionism began to relent. At the 1921 convention, Max and James Heller together with Horace J. Wolf introduced the following resolution:

Inasmuch as our Conference has, at several conventions, declared its willingness to aid in building Palestine . . . ,

Inasmuch as the British mandate for Palestine (as published in the press and officially acknowledged in answer to an interpellation in Parliament), recognizes the Zionist organization as the representative of the Jewish effort for Palestinian reconstruction,

Inasmuch as Jewish leaders in the Western World, who, like the large majority of our Conference, do not approve of the nationalist aims of the Zionist organization, have felt it their duty to co-operate with that organization for such Palestinian work as has no connection with political aspirations or nationalist propaganda,

Be it Resolved, that this Conference, through its Committee on Cooperation with National Organizations, endeavor to arrive at some practical and expedient method of co-operation with the Zionist organization towards the rebuilding of Palestine.[47]

The Zionist reaction to the resolution is indicated by the denouement:

> The Resolutions Committee referred this to the Executive Board "for such favorable action as is in keeping with the declaration of its attitude on Palestinian reconstruction which the Conference made in Rochester, in 1920." During the brief discussion, Leo Franklin, President, commented that during the prior year he had been instructed by the Executive Board to write to the Zionist Organization and to offer the cooperation of the Conference "for work of reconstruction in Palestine." The only response which Franklin received was, "I beg to acknowledge receipt of your letter to the Zionist Organization of America." Franklin then informed the Convention that when his letter had been read at the Zionist gathering in Buffalo it "was greeted with silence; no action was taken upon said letter, although a definite offer of cooperation was made."[48]

The CCAR attempted, not always consistently, to differentiate between anti-Zionism and concern for the well-being of the Jewish people in Palestine and elsewhere. Sometimes this took on the form of supporting Jewish nationalism, as long as it was not concentrated in the land of Israel. Thus the 1906 convention passed a resolution endorsing the work of the Jewish Territorial Association,[49] and the 1921 convention, having agreed that the CCAR would unite with the Palestinian Development Council for the economic rehabilitation of Palestine, resolved to "invite all other Jewish organizations of national scope to associate themselves with the Conference and the Council in this work, to the end that an organization of united Jewry may be developed for the upbuilding of Palestine and cooperation with a Mandatory Power."[50] Moreover, in 1924, the convention resolved to heartily endorse the United Jewish Campaign "for $14,000,000 under the Joint Distribution Committee and calls upon the members of the Conference to aid the Campaign in their respective communities."[51]

In 1924, the president of the CCAR, Abram Simon, declared that "the official statement of our Conference remains as its repudiation of nationalistic Zionism. The march of events, however, often leaves finely woven theories behind. . . . Whatever we may say to the contrary, Palestine is a more impressive responsibility, and calls us as insistently as the condemnation of political Zionism."[52] He urged the delegates, and they concurred, to work toward the creation of "a Jewish Agency of equal Zionist and non-Zionist representations to carry into effect the expectation of the Balfour Declaration."[53] In 1928, the following resolution was passed without debate: "The Central Conference of American Rabbis views with satisfaction the productive labors of the Jewish Agency Commissioners, and felicitates them upon the program projected. We recommend that the members of this Conference give their sympathetic cooperation toward the realization of the aims which this program encompasses."[54] Serving on the committee which presented the resolution were non-Zionists Abram Simon and Solomon Freehof, and Zionists Morris Lazaron and Abba Hillel Silver.

In 1927, however, the CCAR rejected a resolution calling for "the formation of a Jewish Assembly democratically elected that will speak for American Jewry when and as occasion demands."[55] Similarly, when the American Jewish Congress , in 1939, invited the CCAR to appoint two delegates to serve on its Governing Body, the Executive Board declined on the ground that it had "no authority to appoint such representatives."[56]

The foregoing would indicate that early trends within Reform gravitated toward a more comprehensive, people-oriented view of Judaism rather than a purely theological one. The transition began to occur before the promulgation of the Pittsburgh Platform.

The Columbus Platform of 1937 has been regarded as being greatly influenced by Mordecai Kaplan's conception of Judaism as a civilization. Without minimizing the great impact of the founder of Reconstructionism on all branches of Jewish life in America, it is highly significant that on the first page of his *Judaism as a Civilization* (1934), he cites a questionnaire submitted to the members of the Central Conference in 1925, and a quotation by Bernhard Felsenthal. Among the questions asked was, "Is the trend toward placing less emphasis on Judaism as a cult and more emphasis on Judaism as a civilization, i.e., identifying it with all the activities and relations of life?" Those who replied "cult" number fifteen, while fifty responded "civilization."[57] This was well before the full impact of Kaplan on Jewish thought had been felt. The quotation from Bernhard Felsenthal reads,

> "Judaism" and "Jewish Religion" are not synonymous terms. "Judaism" is more comprehensive than "Jewish religion," for "Jewish religion" is only a part of "Judaism." Judaism is the composite of the collected thoughts, sentiments and efforts of the Jewish people. In other words, Judaism is the sum total of all the manifestations of the distinctively Jewish national spirit.
>
> The Jewish religion is, then, only a part of Judaism, though by far its most important part. Among no other people on earth has religion occupied so large, so significant a place in the spiritual life as it has among the Jews. But besides religion there were, and still are, other elements in Judaism.[58]

The placing of both of these items at the very beginning of *Judaism as a Civilization* indicates quite convincingly that Kaplan recognized early strains in Reform Judaism (in the case of Felsenthal, a very early strain indeed) which were compatible with the idea of a Judaism that transcends religion alone.

In 1972, after a period of "observing" executive sessions of the World Jewish Congress, and after tabling a recommendation to seek affiliation, the CCAR voted to apply for membership, and was accepted. In 1971 and 1972, members of the CCAR, American and Israeli, met in Oranim and at the Leo Baeck School in Haifa with representatives of the kibbutz movement, and out of the discussions, conducted in Hebrew, arrived at the conclusion that the time had come to create a Reform kibbutz. In 1972, the CCAR initiated a series of conversations (under the auspices of the Synagogue Council of America) with the National Council of Jewish Federations seeking to define areas of possible conflict and accord.

The most significant development involving the rabbinate and the Hebrew Union College–Jewish Institute of Religion was the decision, in 1970, to require rabbinical candidates to spend their first year of study at the Jerusalem School, founded in 1963. The primary objective was to enable students to acquire proficiency in the Hebrew language and rabbinic texts, but this has been accompanied by immersion in the life of Israelis and the Jewish people. It was Judah Magnes, of the class of 1900, who best defined the objectives of the program when he presciently proposed, from the Chancellor's Office at the Hebrew University,

> that the College helps [sic] the students of the graduating class to spend an extra year at the Hebrew University. There are all facilities for advanced instruction in Hebrew and other Semitic subjects. Jerusalem is an inspiration to all who look upon it. A year in Palestine will give you something of the rhythm and color and depths of the biblical background you would otherwise not acquire. It will deepen your Jewish consciousness and help formulate the problem of Jewish religion. The personalities of the Hebrew Prophets will become clear and will live for you.[59]

The total immersion in K'lal Yisroel came with the efforts by Reform rabbis, together with their Jewish colleagues of other denominations, to rescue victims of the Holocaust. Ephraim Dekel, one of the officials directing the Jewish exodus from Europe, writes concerning Chaplain Abraham Klausner, who served under General George S. Patton:

> The Holocaust and the condition of the survivors affected him deeply and he devoted himself wholeheartedly to aid and rescue. There was nothing in which the activity of the "Bricha" was not helped by his organizational ability. He provided documents for the transfer of refugees. . . . He appeared among them . . . encouraged them. . . . More than once he arranged transports . . . not heeding formal procedures. . . . His official vehicle was used . . . as a "transit visa" for many refugees. . . . Many devout refugees whom we cared for, referred to Rabbis Klausner, [Eugene] Lipman, and others . . . as "Lamed Vovniks," tzadikim garbed in American uniforms, through whose merit the Messiah will come.[60]

The American Council for Judaism

The American Council for Judaism[61] emerged out of the resistance of non-Zionist and anti-Zionist members of the CCAR to what they perceived as the growing and steady expansion of Zionist ideology within

Reform Judaism. Its effort to create a counterforce outside the Central Conference initially threatened a schism, but the organization went into an early decline. Nevertheless, the intensity of the struggle over the emergence of the Council represented a watershed in the record of the Reform rabbinate, for in its aftermath the diminishing anti-Zionist faction within the CCAR collapsed and Zionist thought as well as Zionist action dominated thereafter.

During the formation of the American Council for Judaism, the anti-Zionists themselves acknowledged two matters—first, that opposition to Jewish nationalism was indeed a central issue which consistently animated Reform and out of which the other issues proliferated; and second, that the Reform movement, especially the CCAR and the College, had lost its grip on the control of this issue.

On March 17, 1941, Stephen Wise, chairman of the American Emergency Committee for Zionist Affairs, sent a wire to American rabbis urging their support for the establishment of a "Jewish army under own insignia and allied command defending homeland as self respecting people."[62] When the Central Conference assembled in June 1942, a resolution calling for the endorsement of "a Jewish army, based in Palestine" was presented and passed after long and intense debate. It is significant that the fourteen-man resolutions committee, bringing in the army resolution, contained a minority of Zionists, and only one who was actively involved in Zionist affairs, Max Nussbaum.

The resolution read:

> Your committee recommends that this resolution be reworded as follows:
> Whereas, the free peoples of the world are now engaged in a war for decency, justice and good faith in international relations, and for the defense of their homes and their freedoms against oppression and slavery,
> And whereas, the Jewish population of Palestine is eager to defend its soil and its home to the last man,
> Therefore, be it resolved, that the Central Conference of American Rabbis is in complete sympathy with the demand of the Jews of Palestine that they be given the opportunity to fight in defense of their homeland on the side of the democracies under allied command to the end that the victory of democracy may be hastened everywhere.[63]

It passed by a vote of 64 for and 38 against, despite the argument by the opposition that the very discussion of the issue represented a violation of a 1935 resolution declaring that the issue of Zionism was a matter of personal conscience for CCAR members and not to be the subject of further debate. Known as the neutrality resolution it read: "We are persuaded that the acceptance or rejection of the Zionist program should be left to the determination of the individual members of the Conference themselves. Therefore, be it resolved, that the CCAR takes no official stand on the subject of Zionism."[64]

With this issue as the immediate rallying point, and under the leadership of Louis Wolsey, meetings were held for the purpose of organizing a body of "non-Zionist" rabbis who would attempt to counteract the influence of the Zionist movement and of Zionism, especially in the Central Conference. As Wolsey later noted, "The American Council for Judaism was born in Cincinnati in February, 1942, following the passage of the Jewish army resolution."[65] The leadership of the Central Conference, alarmed at the early growth of the anti-Zionist body, began to fear the possibility of a split within the CCAR. Rabbi James Heller attempted to head off this development by offering to make a statement of regret over the passage of the army resolution, inasmuch as he had been accused of violating the 1935 agreement and had neglected to call the resolution out of order when it was first called to the floor. In addition he was prepared to reaffirm the 1935 resolution. He also undertook a special session of the CCAR at which, in executive session, all the vexing issues leading to the confrontation would be aired. Morris Lazaron was eager that such a solution of the problem should be arrived at, and in a letter to James Heller, he expressed the hope that "you will be able to keep the extremists in hand."[66] Lazaron had assumed that Heller wanted the army resolution expunged, but in fact he was only prepared to say that "the passing of the resolution on a Jewish army was a mistake."[67] On the strength of this, he hoped to persuade the opposition to call off the impending meeting. Solomon Freehof was most supportive of Heller's conciliatory gesture and may even have stimulated it. Writing to Wolsey, he said, "We four [Wolsey, Goldenson, Freehof, Heller] represent the great preponderance of Conference members and we want to reestablish the Conference on solid foundations of brotherhood and friendship."[68] The sticking point, however, was whether the army resolution should be "regretted" or "expunged." An initial vote of the anti-Zionists favored calling off the meeting temporarily by a vote of 17 to 2 (one of the two was Elmer Berger, who seemed to be spoiling for a fight), but this was quickly reversed, and plans for the meeting, scheduled for Atlantic City in June, went forward. Heller was reminded that Zionist Reform rabbis were not being called upon to leave the Zionist Organization of America. A call was issued for a meeting in Atlantic City for June 1 and 2, 1942. It was addressed to 160 men, one-half of whom "responded one way or another."[69]

Early on, it became evident that the Jewish army issue was only the triggering device, not the central problem. The confrontation had been gestating since 1890. At a meeting of fourteen rabbis, presided over by Louis Wolsey, Dr. Jonah Wise said, "we ought not to discuss the Jewish army question at all, because it was only a symptom rather than a basic cause for our problems."[70]

On Monday, March 30, 1942 (four weeks after the CCAR convention in Cincinnati), a meeting was held at the Hotel Warwick in Philadelphia. The issue of the Jewish army was disposed of at the outset of the deliberations. William Fineshriber indicated that the "immediate cause" for the meeting was the Jewish army resolution and asked "whether or not we should call a meeting of Reform Rabbis opposed to Jewish Nationalism, to organize in opposition to this Jewish army." Norman Gerstenfeld called for a meeting to discuss the deeper implications of the issue, which involved "Nationalism versus Jewish Religion." Goldenson also argued that the question was not the Jewish army but nationalism and secularism, of which the army was the most recent expression. In other words, the issue was Judaism as a universal religion.[71]

The issue, as Philipson had put it long before, was the incompatibility, as asserted from the beginning, of Reform and Zionism. This explains the curious and clumsy phrasing of the debate in June 1942, which was entitled "Are Zionism and Reform Incompatible?" suggesting, correctly, that the burden of proof was on the Zionists. The anti-Zionists were arguing ideologically. The Zionists, while presenting ideological and theological arguments, were essentially applying them to the realities of the Nazi period, in which the Holocaust was becoming increasingly and terrifyingly evident. The anti-Zionists were playing by the rules of a game that had already, not to their satisfaction, been trampled into the mud of a chaotic world—universalism, the inevitable advance of reason and goodwill. Men like La-

zaron and Goldenson, who were doing all they could to restrain the
determination of others to have a showdown, and who pressed for the
Heller formula, were true believers. Others in their camp affirmed
their support of Palestine as a nonpolitical haven for persecuted Jews
whom Jewish philanthropy would sustain. Their arguments, framed
within the realities of the forties, were not evil but out of context.

The ground which the anti-Zionists were defending was nevertheless, for better or worse, authentic Reform ground, and they realized
that they were about to lose it. Reform, as they had inherited it, did not
(at least until the Columbus Platform of 1937) reconcile universalism
with particularism, but proclaimed the unambiguous victory of the
former over the latter. Thus they were fighting against what they considered the usurpation of Reform by the particularists. The Jewish
army issue was the last straw, and they saw quite accurately that Reform stood "in danger" of becoming transformed into something altogether different from what it had been called into being to represent.
Yet this process had been going on for a long time. The theoretical
groundwork for it had been laid by Caspar Levias and Bernhard
Felsenthal in 1899, and the foundations had been solidly established
in 1935 by Abba Hillel Silver in his enduring paper "Israel," in which
he attacked the opposition as Paulinists.[72] Thus, Silver and others did
not attempt to convince their opponents that the radical formulation
of the Zionists was authentically Reform, but rather that classical
Reform was not compatible with the spirit of Judaism. The anti-
Zionists understood the issue: It was Reform versus transform.

In the early, preparatory stages there was considerable anguish
among the anti-Zionists over whether or not to form a separate organization. Jonah Wise expressed the fear that "a minority group . . .
would achieve nothing but discord and embittered feeling."[73] Goldenson still entertained doubts as to the wisdom of holding the Atlantic
City meeting—first, because it could be assumed that no more than
seventy rabbis would attend, and second, because he was fearful of
creating a schism in the Reform rabbinate. Both men stressed the importance of emphasizing Reform universalism rather than an attack
on Zionism.

On April 6 in Philadelphia, Jonah Wise urged that a "modus vivendi" be worked out with the CCAR leadership and indicated that he
was not ready to issue a call for the creation of a "non-Zionist" body.

The existence of the Central Conference was at stake, and the UAHC was facing enormous problems of its own. On the other hand, Rosenau, who had at first feared a cleavage within Reform, felt that a definite organized stand must be taken against Jewish nationalism. Wolsey declared that if an organization was not brought into being, "we may just as well say Kaddish for Reform Judaism. The moment has come for fighting."[74]

In a letter dated April 30, 1942, James Heller urged the members of the CCAR "not to go through with this action, to envisage before it is too late what will result from their persistence in it."[75] None of this served to reduce tensions, and instead increased them. "I do not believe that ever, in the history of Judaism in America has there been such a campaign of vilification and abuse as has been hurled against the so-called minority."[76] The issue was Zionism, but it brought to a head many other latent resentments among the non-Zionists. "There has been a tendency to revive, in the Reform Temple, the Orthodox modes which had once been abandoned—more Hebrew than less, more of the old rituals and not fewer, more of the European importations rather than the usages uniquely American. Some of our colleagues are even proposing a restoration of the *Talith* and the *Yarmulke*."[77]

The Atlantic City meeting, attended by thirty-six men, dealt in large measure with the alleged dilution of the Reform nature of the Hebrew Union College by students from Zionist backgrounds. The delegates readily acknowledged the persistent suspicion that the College, which as a matter of policy had formerly repressed Zionist ideology, had at last lost control of the situation. Thus, at an organizational meeting of the yet unnamed American Council for Judaism, the role of the HUC in the problem was placed on the agenda: "The problem of the Hebrew Union College as an agency for education for Reform, was brought up by Dr. Wolsey."[78] While not categorically stated, the conjectures about the dismissal of Caspar Levias and later of Max Margolis from the College faculty because of their Zionism were treated as a given. Criticism of the College for letting the situation get out of hand and a proposal to cut off the source of the trouble by limiting the enrollment of students from suspect backgrounds were broached.

In defense of the College, Julian Morgenstern, its president, told the gathering: "The source of the trouble is the JIR (Jewish Institute of Religion) [which] has graduated 120. . . . at least 110 are very ardent

Zionists."⁷⁹ It was moved that "a committee be appointed to draw up resolutions expressing the sentiments expressed here tonight, with regard to the merger of the College [with Stephen Wise's Jewish Institute of Religion in New York], and such other matters as have been mentioned here tonight, which may be pertinent to that old problem, reference to the educational department of the Union."⁸⁰ The motion carried.

On November 23, the group unanimously adopted the name proposed by Lazaron: "The Council for American Judaism"; it was later changed to "American Council for Judaism." At the closing session, when a proposed Statement of Principles prepared by the Baltimore delegation was to be read, a debate broke out as to whether the statement could be conceived as signifying the formal creation of a separate rabbinical body. Since some of those present were also members of the CCAR Executive Board, which was to meet the next day, there was considerable anxiety as to how the statement would be construed, especially since the air was already charged with speculation about a possible schism. Morgenstern, Goldenson, and Wice pleaded for caution. The stenographic report quotes Goldenson:

> Among the first things that I read this morning was a headline in this morning's *Tribune* reciting the fact that 200,000 Jews have been killed in various parts of Central Europe. That has been in my mind ever since, and that sort of chastens me a little bit. It makes me more careful now than I would have been if I hadn't seen that article. For that reason any utterance about Jewish problems and Jewish troubles and Jewish hopes, I think we ought to take extra time and pause about any statement that we now make. It is not an academic matter. We are not dealing with abstract propositions.
>
> I read the original statement. I have listened very carefully to the reading of the Revised Statement, and I want to say that my general impression is—particularly since hearing the Revised Statement—that we are taking an all-out attitude of war, an all-out war attitude. I think that our Statement is a little too belligerent, too unrestrained, and we ought to be more careful about what we are saying and the way we are saying it. Another point is that to me it appears as though we are duplicating the entire conference program with the exception of some practical matters.
>
> I cannot feel that if we do all we are attempting to do that we are, in fact, becoming another conference, which was not in my mind certainly when I joined the men in discussing the program of our group in Philadelphia.⁸¹

The issue within the Council was whether it should be an anti-Zionist organization or a religious body stressing the universalistic theology of Reform Judaism. How it could have done the latter without ignoring the former is problematical, but the former could certainly be pressed without engaging the latter. The election of Elmer Berger as the Council's professional head guaranteed the prosecution of the anti-Zionist policy.

The debate became increasingly chaotic and resulted in the drafting of a less aggressive statement which was to be circulated by mail for additional comments before being adopted. The defeat of those who wanted a confrontational resolution that could have irreparably widened the rift with the CCAR effectively canceled secessionist possibilities, even if that may not have been perceived at the time. With a membership of ninety-five adherents, the Council had attained its greatest strength, and although the road toward the showdown in June 1943 was to be alive with hostility, the caution of Goldenson and Morgenstern had ensured the unity of the CCAR. Had the minutes of the meeting then been available, the internal ambivalence of the newly founded group would have been apparent. Significantly, the minutes state: "Dr. Wolsey raised the question of the publication of the Atlantic City Proceedings. Requests have been received for these minutes. It was moved and seconded that only the papers read at the Atlantic City meeting be mimeographed."[82] In what might have been a telephone conversation, perhaps in August 1942, Goldenson told Lazaron: "Jonah Wise talked with two laymen—one of whom was Paul Baerwald. Mr. Baerwald said definitely this is no time for us to publish any statement which would involve us in internal controversy."[83] This did not prevent Baerwald from telling the lay-rabbinical session of the ACJ on December 7, 1943, that "we must do our part in making America safe for our Jewish boys when they return from the war. Contrary to Wolsey's pessimism we have accomplished much. We have stirred up Zionists to realization of opposition."[84]

By June 1942, Elmer Berger was coming more and more into the picture. Lazaron thought highly of Berger's leadership, as shown by his assertion that "you are contributing something rare and splendid and we older men are grateful,"[85] as well as by his promise: "I expect . . . to see Lewis Strauss after lunching with [Sumner] Welles. It is important that we get him with us. I shall keep you in intimate touch."[86]

The restraint of Goldenson and Jonah Wise, and the hesitancy of others, is reflected in another letter from Lazaron to Berger,

> I received a telegram midnight yesterday as follows: "Owing to recent devel-
> opments in the war and the grave threat to Palestine especially to our own
> people there, the publication of our statement now would be a sad mistake. We
> urge you most earnestly to withhold it for the present. Jonah Wise and Samuel
> Goldenson." I also have a letter from Fineberg who raises the same issue. Ger-
> stenfeld, who suggested that we tie up our statement with a Jewish Army, is
> weakening.[87]

Several days later Berger responded to Lazaron,

> I do not know what we can do if Goldenson and Wise . . . if those men feel
> that the whole fabric of Zionism is a detriment to Jewish life then they ought to
> realize that in every crisis the Zionists capitalize upon panic, they fasten their
> grip tighter upon the victims. I somehow do not like their high and mighty
> concern . . . Goldenson has been halting from the first meeting in Wolsey's
> office last winter. . . . I am just a bit afraid that Wise does not know whether he
> ought to be a-foot or a-horseback because of the UJA.[88]

Lazaron was completely enamored of Berger. "It is a grand experience to have as comrade and collaborator a man like yourself."[89]

From September 1942 to January 1943, Lazaron tried to involve
Judah Magnes in the Council's program without specifically saying
so. He wrote, "We are trying to get across to the American Jewish
community that one can work for Palestine without indulging in . . .
political activity. . . . If there is any way you feel you can cooperate in
your efforts from this end, please let me know."[90] In his response,
Magnes enclosed material about Ihud ("Unity," a group he had helped
found which supported the idea of a binational Jewish-Arab state in
an undivided Palestine) and, referring to the statement of principles of
the American Council for Judaism, said, "I also have a universalistic
interpretation of Jewish history. But this for me is not in opposition to
the national elements and hopes of the Jewish people."[91] The correspondence resulted in public controversy when Lazaron quoted a
statement by Magnes that internal issues in Palestine could result in
civil war. This caused Magnes much embarrassment, and Lazaron
subsequently apologized: "I hope I have made you feel how unhappy I
have been at a thoughtless act. . . . Please forgive me if I have caused
any harm or hurt."[92] He attempted to link the ideology of Ihud with
that of the American Council for Judaism, and at the same time en-

couraged Berger to carry on his antinationalist program.

From January 1943, in anticipation of the CCAR convention, to be held in New York on June 22–27, strenuous efforts were being made to head off a collision. A meeting between representatives of the ACJ and the CCAR, held in the study of Morris Lazaron on January 5, sought ways of arriving at a conciliatory position. Heller stated that in return for the dissolution of the Council, he would recommend that the Conference reaffirm the neutrality resolution and adopt it as a by-law. The meeting adjourned inconclusively, but early the next month Rabbi Wolsey, provisional chairman of the Council, wrote to Heller, "This is to inform you that a mail vote of the Rabbinical members of the American Council for Judaism quite overwhelmingly declares it-self against liquidation of the Organization."[93] Thus, efforts to head off a confrontation and a possible break came to naught. The resolu-tion by the executive board of the CCAR calling upon "dissident groups to desist from organizing outside of the Conference" found-ered. As a result, the decision of the program committee, at the Octo-ber meeting of the board, to devote two executive sessions of the con-vention to a discussion of the ideas and issues bound up with the controversy became fully operative. A third step was also recommend-ed by Rabbi Heller—that conversations be initiated between repre-sentatives of the Zionist organization and the "erstwhile American Council for Judaism, looking toward the finding of a common ground in regard to Palestine, and the attempt to discover methods of cooper-ation."[94]

As the date of the convention drew nearer, the opposing forces ma-neuvered for advantage. A letter from Samuel Wohl, calling a caucus for June 21, was inadvertently sent to a Council member, prompting a similar call to "our 95" by five council leaders.[95] Defections from the Council began to take place even as early as the middle of January 1943. As Morris Lazaron recorded: "A few of our men are not stal-wart enough to stand the strain of . . . misrepresentation and are with-drawing."[96] Three more members withdrew due to what Elmer Berger called "brow-beating."[97]

Despite the intense efforts to head off a clash, the executive board of the CCAR had already determined, in the fall of 1942, to schedule a formal debate for the June 1943 meeting. The participants were to be Felix Levy, William Fineshriber, Hyman Schachtel, and David Polish.

At its preconvention meeting on June 22, 1943, the executive board resolved that "when the Committee which is to prepare a resolution summing up the opinion of the Conference as a result of the discussion on Zionism and Reform Judaism shall present its report, the discussion should be held in executive session; that no stenographic report of the Executive session be made; that no report of the discussion appear in the Year Book, but that the final resolution adopted shall appear in the Year Book."[98]

Following the debate and the floor discussion, which continued till after 2:00 A.M., the convention passed the following resolutions:

I

Of late, some of our members have renewed the assertion that Zionism is not compatible with Reform Judaism. The attempt has been made to set in irreconcilable opposition "universalism" and "particularism." To the members of the Conference, this appears unreal and misleading. Without impugning the right of members of the Conference to be opposed to Zionism, for whatever reason they may choose, the Conference declares that it discerns no essential incompatibility between Reform Judaism and Zionism, no reason why those of its members who give allegiance to Zionism should not have the right to regard themselves as fully within the spirit and purpose of Reform Judaism.[99]

II

The American Council for Judaism was founded by members of the CCAR for the purpose of combatting Zionism. The Zionist Movement and masses of Jews everywhere, shocked by the rise of this organization at a time when Zionists and others are laboring hard to have the gates of Palestine reopened for the harassed Jews of Europe, could not avoid judging this event in the light of past controversies, or seeing in it an example of what they had come to consider the constant opposition of Reform Judaism to Zionist aspirations. This impression does grave injustice to the many devoted Zionists in the CCAR and to the Conference itself.

Therefore, without impugning the right of Zionists or non-Zionists to express and to disseminate their convictions within and without the Conference, we, in the spirit of amity, urge our colleagues of the American Council for Judaism to terminate this organization.[100]

Louis Wolsey

According to Rabbi Malcolm H. Stern, the American Council for Judaism, "at its greatest," had "only about 60–70 colleagues." Even some of those who attended the Atlantic City conference in 1942 did not join.[101] Moreover, there was something of an inverse ratio between age and support for the Council. The greatest number of Council members and sympathizers was found among the older members of the CCAR. Thus, an anti-Zionist statement that was circulated among graduates of HUC in the early stages of the Council was signed by 70 percent of the members of the classes from 1883 to 1893 and 50 percent of the graduates from 1894 to 1903, but only 28 percent from 1904 to 1914, 23 percent from 1915 to 1924, 18 percent from 1925 to 1934, and 17 percent from 1935 to 1942.[102]

Disillusion with the Council was not long in coming even within its highest rabbinic echelons. By the end of 1945 Louis Wolsey resigned as vice-president of the Council, and in a letter to the *American Israelite* he said in part, "I feel in justice to myself I have not become responsible for pronouncements and declarations of the American Council for Judaism and I am not privileged to participate in formulating them."[103] On April 2, 1946, he wrote to Lessing Rosenwald, the Council's key lay leader, "The American Council for Judaism has performed a good and necessary task in that it recalls to thinking people the fact that there are two sides to the controversy. . . . I favor very much the dissolution of the organization, and to that end I herewith hand you my resignation as a member of the ACJ."[104]

A few months later, in a letter he wrote to Hyman Schachtel, also sending a copy to Bernard Heller, Wolsey provided a deeper understanding of the reasons for his resignation. Condemning Lessing Rosenwald's "departures from the principles of the founders of the American Council for Judaism, and the alienation of the Rabbis from its activity and even some of its principles," he says that Rosenwald "made the organization a refuge for atheistic and unJewish Jews who joined because they looked upon the ACJ as an instrument for assimilation—meanwhile proclaiming that we were Americans of the Jewish faith. That phrase 'Jewish faith' . . . has been nothing short of hypocrisy. The Chairman of the Philadelphia chapter is a blatant anti-religionist, and the President's home is a gathering place for Jewish anti-Judaism—the policy of the triumvirate has been to snub Rabbis and religion."[105] Wolsey does not name the members of the triumvirate, but we know that he felt equally strongly against Elmer Berger and Wallach. In another letter to Hyman Schachtel, Wolsey adds, "Our leaders have—entered into strife and controversy, and have emphasized the political note as much as those we condemn on the opposition."[106]

By October 13, 1947, Wolsey records that "only four or five especially selected Rabbis remain in the fold, most of them are inactive in the Council."[107] On May 3, 1948 Wolsey repeated his resignation, this time to the American Council for Judaism.[108] It was followed by a flood of congratulatory mail to Wolsey by laymen and rabbis, including former members of the Council. Among the rabbis who wrote was James Heller, who stated, "On behalf of those who feel that the new State of Israel deserves a chance of life and freedom, who are sure that our brothers there are filled with a genuine determination to take in the helpless Jews of Europe, I want to thank you."[109]

The rapid defections from the American Council for Judaism, climaxed by that of Louis Wolsey, represented both an acknowledgment of the realities of Jewish history and a recognition that the essential, unarticulated, but immanent premise of Pittsburgh that Judaism can be sustained by the power of an abstraction could not be supported. Wolsey's resignation, six years after the conception of the Council, sent shock waves through the organization and exultation among its opponents, since he was one of its founders and greatest ideological champions.

Morris Lazaron

The struggle to reconcile Zionism with universalism is embodied in the odyssey of Morris Lazaron, who oscillated from non-Zionism to political Zionism to radical anti-Zionism. Although Stephen Wise complimented Lazaron on April 15, 1915, for viewing "the question of Zionism admirably," and felt "so glad you feel as you do,"[110] Lazaron wrote to the Federation of American Zionists on October 13, 1916, as follows:

> I am not a Zionist because I am not a political nationalist Jew. If the Zionists would come out with a four square statement defining exactly what their claims and hopes are and repudiating the establishment of the Jewish political entity in Palestine or politico-nationalistic interpretation of Jewish history, and if they would declare that their sole intention is to encourage settlement in Palestine and further Jewish life there, they would probably have the cooperation of great numbers of American Jews who are at present their opponents.[111]

Despite this disclaimer, Lazaron soon changed his mind about Zionism, as is shown by another letter from Wise, less than a year later, expressing his surprise and joy "that you have recently come to see and feel the power of Zionism."[112] From that point on, and for many years to come, Lazaron was a devoted and enthusiastic Zionist and member of the Zionist Organization of America. His correspondence with Stephen Wise became very cordial, and he saluted him as "cousin Stephen"; Wise signed his letters in the same way. In October 1923, when Lazaron was selected as chairman of the Education Committee of the Baltimore Zionist District, Henrietta Szold congratulated him for "your devotion to the Cause,"[113] and in June of 1924, when he began a series of extensive trips in the South in behalf of the Zionist movement and the Keren Hayesod, Simon J. Levin, director of the Palestine Foundation Fund, wrote him, "Be assured that the Jewry of Richmond [Virginia] as well as the Keren Hayesod Committee will always remain indebted to you for the nobel [sic] services which you have rendered."[114] Toward the end of the year Lazaron wrote that he was "giving up about two weeks of my time from my work and I would not do this if I did not believe in this cause with all my heart and soul."[115] In another letter written around the same time, he said, "No effort is too great to put this thing across successfully and to warrant the effort I will make in the trip," adding that Louis Lipsky was scheduled to address his congregation.[116] Emanuel Neumann, secretary of the Keren Hayesod, thanked Lazaron for the "sacrifices you have made on behalf of the cause for the upbuilding of Palestine."[117]

When Louis Lipsky, chairman of the Zionist Organization of America, asked Lazaron for the names and addresses of the parents of the confirmants of the Baltimore Hebrew Congregation in behalf of the Hebrew University, Lazaron agreed.[118] During April of 1928 Lazaron strongly defended Chaim Weizmann, the president of the World Zionist Organization, against criticism by Stephen Wise, who "objects to Weizmann's policy in regard to Great Britain, is opposed to asking a loan from the League of Nations, and does not favor the establishment of the Jewish Agency as at present constituted."[119] Having failed in arranging for an arbitration between both Zionist sides of the dispute, Lazaron decided to stay away from the forthcoming Zionist convention in Pittsburgh "because I continue to maintain the position that I have held up to the present time—disassociation from the politics of the fight."[120] This was in response to a stinging rebuke that he had received from Wise a week earlier. On May 29 he was rebuked again, this time by Lipsky, who criticized his "caustic references . . . [and] your reference to the controversy in terms of the schism between east and west. This feeling . . . can do our cause tremendous harm. . . . we must do nothing that will build up resentment."[121] Still later, on November 29, 1934, Lazaron strongly criticized Wise for accusing German Jews of "lying down disgracefully."[122]

Despite these unpleasant exchanges Lazaron was elected to the National Committee of the Zionist Organization of America and accepted, "with pleasure."[123] Yet in a November 1935 memorandum, Lazaron sharply differed with certain Zionist policies, indicating himself to be "wholly out of sympathy with most of the personalities that have assumed the leadership of the Movement." His turn away from Zionism began at approximately this time. He strenuously objected to the passage of a resolution by the World Zionist Organization endorsing the proposed World Jewish Congress. "We Zionists of America will have to determine whether we desire the ZOA to become an instrument of the American Jewish Congress." He also objected to the reduction of the non-Zionist representatives at the Jewish Agency from five, standing in an equal ratio to the Zionist representatives, to two, making for a Zionist/non-Zionist ratio of eight to two.

> The Zionists may be within their rights in desiring to control the Agency but the action was significant of the determination to accept non-Zionist participation in Palestine reconstruction only on Zionist terms. It was apparently forgotten or ignored that tremendous non-Zionist funds went into the Palestine Economic Corporation, the Rutenberg concession, the Jordan project, and are now going into the Huleh project. . . . In the face of these facts it is easily understandable that men who were altogether sympathetic with the practical constructive work in Palestine, who had testified to their interest in maintaining a united front through years of effort and despite much personal unpleasantness should feel the time had come to part company. . . . The issue is shall the ZOA membership permit the organization created for the purpose of upbuilding the land of our fathers . . . to become an instrument in the hands of certain American Jews to be used for the promotion of their own ends.[124]

It should therefore not be surprising that in a letter to Morris Rothenberg of the Zionist Organization of America he wrote, "I am not interested in Zionist politics."[125] And on May 18, 1939, he submitted his resignation to the ZOA "with profound regret but believing as I do, there is no other course open to me."[126]

Now follows an episode with his brother-in-law, Abba Hillel Silver, over a projected visit to the United States by Weizmann. Lazaron objected to his coming because it will be "invested with political significance . . . the effects of which can only be harmful at this time. I know whereof I speak."[127] Silver responded that he himself had extended the invitation to Weizmann, and therefore he was declining Lazaron's invitation to speak at Lazaron's anniversary celebration. "You have made it quite impossible for me to accept it."[128]

Lazaron's alienation reached full bloom in 1940, when he wrote,

> There are two groups among us. One is represented by the Zionist Organization and the World Jewish Congress. This group . . . looks to the establishment in Palestine of an independent Jewish State. . . . They believe the Jews to be a people like any other people. . . . The second group is not interested in the political program of the Zionist-Congress group. It fears such a program as a departure from the Jewish culturo-religious tradition. . . . Responsible American Jewish leadership agrees today with Mr. Neville Laski when he says, "The idea of a Jewish state is no less distasteful now than it was 20 years ago."

Lazaron advocated that immigration to Palestine be "on the basis of the capacity and ability of the country to absorb it . . . to free such immigration from political implications and to allay the fears of the Arabs," and expressed the hope "that the ultimate constitution will establish a Palestine State in which Palestine Jews will *individually* possess the full rights of citizenship and at the same time have full *communal*, cultural and religious autonomy." He concluded his thesis with words clearly foreshadowing the yet unarticulated philosophy of the yet-to-be-created American Council for Judaism:

> American Jews must not elevate a political program to first place in Jewish concern. . . . American Jews must not introduce the Jewish people at this time into the maelstrom of international politics. American Jews must not . . . reduce in importance other places where the stricken may find homes. . . . American Jews must not isolate the Jewish situation from the problems of the world and attempt to solve it by Jewish effort alone.[129]

The debate on Zionism spurred the CCAR into intensified involvement in Jewish life. The call for an American Jewish Conference (also called the American Jewish Assembly) was issued for January 23–24, 1943, to be held in Pittsburgh on February 5. Its executive committee proposed to "consider and recommend action on problems relating to the rights and status of Jews in the post-war world; to consider and recommend action upon all matters looking to the implementation of the rights of the Jewish people in respect to Palestine; to elect a delegation to carry out the program of the American Jewish Conference."[130] Among the thirty-two participating organizations was the CCAR, with Solomon Freehof sitting on the committee on guidance, and James Heller on the committee on proposals.[131] On August 29, the Jewish Conference convened in New York. Among the five hundred delegates, and in addition to Heller and Freehof as official representatives of the CCAR, were twenty-six Reform rabbis, including three former members of the American Council for Judaism, among them Louis Wolsey. Members of the executive committee were Heller and Silver. Addressing the conference were Heller, Silver, Max Nussbaum, Stephen Wise, Philip Bernstein, and Freehof. Serving on various committees were Barnett Brickner (general committee), Jerome Folkman, Leon Fram, Max Nussbaum, and Abraham Shaw (committee on rescue of European Jewry), Freehof, Julius Gordon, and David Pearlman (committee on Palestine), Solomon Basel, Bernstein, Benedict Glazer, Ira Sanders, and Louis Wolsey (committee on postwar problems of European Jewry), David Wice (organization committee), and Joshua Liebman, Max Macoby, and Joshua Trachtenberg (resolutions committee).[132]

On Tuesday, August 31, while the conference was in session, the American Council for Judaism issued in the *New York Times* a statement signed by thirty-two rabbis and eighty-two laymen, "Americans of Jewish Faith," on issues affecting American and world Jewish life. Heller rose to respond and stated in the course of his remarks, "The American Council for Judaism represents a comparatively small minority of the Reform Rabbinate. . . . I as a Reform Rabbi, as a Zionist and as an American Jew, denounce and describe it here as treachery to that cause . . . which our country and its allies are pledged to save and serve."[133] The American Jewish Conference demanded the collective and official as well as individual commitment of the Reform rabbinate to the totality of Jewish life. After June and August of 1943, the CCAR was not again to be challenged on that issue.

Social Justice

The Reform rabbinate has always regarded a commitment to social justice as the one unvarying constant in Reform Judaism. Thus, in

1918, the CCAR's committee on synagogue and industrial relations, under the chairmanship of Horace J. Wolf, stated that "the ideal of social justice has always been an integral part of Judaism,"[134] while in 1956 the Joint Commission on Social Action of the CCAR and the UAHC reaffirmed that "programs of social justice are at the heart of Judaism and particularly Reform Judaism. . . . Judaism is a way of life which was never intended to be easy. . . . [social justice] is the ingredient which preserves the prophetic character of our faith . . . and which entitles us to wear the proud and ancient badge of 'Jew.' "[135]

Activism of Reform rabbis on behalf of social justice actually predates the formal establishment of the Reform movement. In 1861, for instance, Rabbi David Einhorn, who later exercised a decisive influence at the Philadelphia Rabbinical Conference in 1869, was forced to flee from Baltimore when his life was endangered because of his denunciations of slavery.

The classic formulation of Reform's concern with social justice is found in Article VIII of the Pittsburgh Platform of 1885: "In full accordance with the spirit of Mosaic legislation, which strives to regulate the relations between rich and poor, we deem it our duty to participate in the great task of modern times, to solve, on the basis of justice and righteousness, the problems presented by the contrasts and evils of the present organization of society."

Article VIII is important on the following counts: It appeals to "the spirit of Mosaic legislation" rather than to prophetic preachment; it unambiguously points to the "evils of the present organization of society," clearly confronting the prevailing economic system; it recognizes the need, rooted in "Mosaic legislation," to "regulate" economic and social relations; it undertakes for the first time in the history of a rabbinic body, to cope with injustices outside the Jewish community.

It is also noteworthy that while much of early American Reform has its origins in Germany, involvement in the socioeconomic issues of the host nation is distinctively American. This is underscored in item 5, whose first sentence reads, "We recognize in the modern era of universal culture . . . the approaching of the realization of Israel's great Messianic hope for the establishment of the Kingdom of truth, justice and peace among all men." This is immediately followed by a renunciation of Jewish statehood and laws related to it. Justice and peace thus become surrogates for statehood and cult. Moreover, the renunciation of

Jewish law in Article IV follows logically with the universalist message of justice and the proclamation of a messianic "realization." This is in keeping with a rabbinic allusion to the dissipation of legal requirements in the messianic age.

Despite the ethical affirmations of the Pittsburgh Platform, it was not until 1910 that the CCAR approved its first socially conscious resolution, endorsing international action to halt "white slave" traffic.[136] Two years later, the CCAR endorsed the principle of "Woman's equal suffrage," but added that "this is a matter for the individual Rabbi and [that it is] inadvisable for the Conference as a body to take action."[137] In 1914, this resolution was reaffirmed almost word for word. In 1915, the CCAR wished "God speed" to the Federal Council of Churches of Christ in its fund-raising in behalf of European war victims.[138] It also endorsed the principle of arbitration and accused the Ladies' Cloak and Suit Manufacturers of New York of disregarding that principle.[139] Concerning conscientious objection, it stated that "while the mission of Israel is peace . . . the individual Jew who claims this hope of Judaism as a ground of exemption from military service does so only as an individual, inasmuch as historic Judaism emphasizes patriotism as a duty, as well as the ideal of peace."[140] Among the opponents of this resolution was Professor Jacob Lauterbach of the Hebrew Union College. At the same convention, unambiguous endorsement of women's suffrage was finally adopted.[141] In 1918, the CCAR gave "fullest support" to "the establishment of a League of Nations" and proposed that it guarantee full religious and political freedom to "racial and religious minorities in all countries."[142] (Nothing was said specifically about Jewish minorities.)

The post–World War I America was beset by government-sanctioned attacks on suspected subversives. Attorney General A. Mitchell Palmer arrested "suspected persons wholesale, permitting the use of provocative agents to stir up 'seditious meetings,' insisting on the deportation of aliens rounded up by detectives from the Department of Justice."[143] During this period the CCAR made its first turn toward confronting major social issues, with varying degrees of assertiveness. In 1919, for instance, it made an appeal to the American government to release all political prisoners who "did not commit or counsel violence against the government."[144] It repeated this appeal in 1921 and also issued a call for the repeal of wartime alien and sedition acts. A landmark position was taken by the conference in 1918 when it passed the following social justice program: endorsement of a minimum wage, an eight-hour day, safe working environments, especially for women, abolition of child labor, workman's compensation for accidents, health insurance, unemployment insurance, the right to organize and bargain collectively, proper housing for workers, mothers' pensions, "constructive care of dependants, defectives and criminals."[145]

In 1920, the CCAR wished "God speed" to the "New State of Lithuania . . . in its present struggle for peace and independence."[146] In 1922, it called for American support of the Permanent Court of International Justice.[147] In 1924, the CCAR issued a call for the protection of monarchies![148] In 1926, it respectfully commended Governor Fuller of Massachusetts for his inquiry into the Sacco-Vanzetti case and expressed its full confidence that he would pursue "a full investigation." It also protested against the "militarization of our schools."[149] In 1927 "a forward looking" social justice program was adopted and commended for general distribution.[150]

In 1927, the CCAR called upon the American government to remove its troops from Nicaragua.[151] It also urged support of a fund for China famine relief. In 1928, it opposed peacetime military registration. It also opposed denying citizenship to applicants refusing to bear arms for the United States.[152]

The Great Depression accelerated the CCAR's involvement in social issues and produced an effort toward systematically assessing America's socioeconomic condition. The positions of the Reform rabbinate became more assertive, more extensive, more responsive to the liberal currents of the time, more secure in the deepening the American roots of the rabbis.

The CCAR was often embroiled in intense debate over social issues, with liberal positions prevailing by small margins. Individual members often maintained conservative and rightist positions. Samuel Schulman, president of the Synagogue Council, elicited from Edward Israel, chairman of its Commission on Social Justice, a commitment not to press for his own liberal agenda (December 26, 1935). Israel's assent was offset by a declaration of commitment to the New Deal in a letter to President Roosevelt.[153]

In the years since World War II and the Great Depression, perhaps the most important instance of the concern for social justice among Reform rabbis was seen in the area of racial equality. In the 1960's, as the postwar civil rights movement developed, courageous southern rabbis like Emmett Frank of Arlington, Virginia, Perry Nussbaum of Jackson, Mississippi, Jacob Rothschild of Atlanta, and Charles Mantinband of Alabama, Mississippi, and Texas, were ardent moral spokesmen for an end to segregation, undeterred by subtle pressures from other whites, sometimes including their own congregants, as well as personal threats against themselves and acts of violence against Jewish centers and synagogue buildings. Numerous other Reform rabbis from the North participated in freedom rides, mass demonstrations like the March on Washington in 1963, and other civil rights efforts. Standing together with liberal clergymen of many Christian denominations, they lent their stature as spiritual and moral leaders to the outstanding moral cause of the period.

Leonard Mervis offers a valid caution against overestimating the influence of Reform social action on the American scene. "The Central Conference was one of many working for a better American life, but it is to be regarded as one of the weaker sections of the phalanx." At the same time, Mervis provides a proper balance by adding, "But the true significance of the Central Conference is not understood unless its educational imprint upon its own members is noted. [It] inspired several generations of rabbis to accept the challenge of social justice. . . . A number of American communities are indebted to rabbis whose fearless words influenced thinking and action. . . . They have been forces of enlightenment in the land."[154]

We can also state that the Reform rabbinate, which was originally influenced in the direction of social *action* by one wing of American Protestantism, could have chosen (if it were merely the subject of outside influences) to follow the path of social and economic reaction, which was also rife within American religion toward the end of the nineteenth century and beyond. Although the course which the Reform rabbinate took, from its social justice pronouncement in the Pittsburgh Platform to this day, represented a novum in Jewish religious thought, the content of its position was authentically Jewish. (The novum was distinguished by the vigorous application of prophetic ethics to the non-Jewish society.) It stemmed from the prophets. Moreover, its advocates increasingly came from East European backgrounds, where social activism, social consciousness, and advocacy in behalf of labor and trade unionism were part of the Jewish ethos. The influx of seminarians from East European homes not only contributed to the stress on peoplehood but gave contemporary relevance to the prophetic ideology which helped launch American Reform Judaism.

Socioeconomic Issues

In 1929, with the depression "just around the corner," the CCAR passed a lengthy resolution on the rights of labor. In summary, it stated,

> We hold that the right of labor is one of the fundamental rights of man. . . . a large number of men and women are always out of work and this number is increasing today. . . . It is the duty of . . . employers and leaders of our economical life so to reorganize agriculture, industry, commerce, and our financial system that every man and woman will be assured continuous employment. . . . Each city government . . . [should] grant relief to the unemployed. . . . Congress [should] pass and the President approve unimpaired the three bills introduced by Senator Wagner designed to . . . establish nationwide state employment service and to develop a constructive Government program of work during industrial depression. . . . City, State, and Federal Governments [should] prepare at once plans for the construction of public works. . . . Measures [should] be passed limiting the hours of labor to not more than 40 hours a week. . . . Legislation [should] be passed raising the working age of children to sixteen years. . . . Unemployment insurance is necessary to care for the unemployed until the reorganization of their uneconomic life has removed the evil of unemployment from our social system.[155]

As the depression deepened, the CCAR declared, in 1931, that "the ravages of unemployment continue to take their terrible toll of millions in our land disrupting not only the economic but also the social and ethical stability of our country. . . . the voice of social protest must challenge . . . a society in which private business is either consciously heartless, indifferent, or impotent, while millions starve amid plenty, as results of the inequitable distribution and wasteful exploitation."[156] The government was called upon to launch a public works program to be secured from higher taxation "in the higher brackets and an increase in inheritance taxes." "We regard it as a distressing comment on our present civilization that people who want work must be kept from starving by charity."[157] "Business must bring to bear intelligence and decent forethought and consideration for the well being of the masses in the development of economic life by a searching modification of a profit motive which . . . exalts gain above all human consideration, or reckon in the not far distant future, with a more and more outraged social conscience."[158] The same report from the Commission on Social Justice called attention to discrimination against Jewish employees in large business.[159] This report was attacked by "some of our Conservative colleagues as well as some of our laymen."[160]

The 1933 convention of the CCAR praised the "courageous leadership and zeal for progressive ideals demonstrated by our President, Franklin Delano Roosevelt." It added the belief that a program "to secure adequate living wages, definite labor representation in the management of industry, and a proper social control of our present profit system places upon government a responsibility which cannot be delegated."[161]

The following year the Commission on Social Justice justified its position by stating that "our experience extends over a period of forty centuries and we have come into contact with every form of civilization, every system of law, and every scheme of salvation. In addition to this unique experience among the nations, it seems evident that Israel possesses a peculiar spiritual endowment that expresses itself in prophetic utterances and denunciations of social injustice."[162] The report referred to "the collapse of our economic system and the emergence of a new social order."[163] Among its recommendations was the "socialization of basic enterprises," which included "legislation that Congress has passed to create . . . a banking system to loan money to small industries that the bankers will not serve; . . . taking over of the transportation system by the Federal Government, as well as 'all power plants and sources of energy.' "[164] Once more, great admiration was expressed for the "socially minded leadership of Franklin D. Roosevelt."[165] The conference proclaimed that "an economic organization, governed by the principle of competition and production for profit, must be entirely re-motivated in the interest of a finer ethical ideal. . . . This form of economic organization must yield to a new system and . . . the economic life of America must be completely reorganized in accordance with the principles of cooperation and production for service and advancement of the common welfare."[166] It further declared that America could escape the dangers of both communism and fascism only by "establishing a thoroughly socialized democracy."[167]

In the 1960 report of the Commission on Justice and Peace, attention was called to the evils of poverty. "Two-thirds of the earth's population do not have adequate food, clothing and shelter. In an age when goods and food can be mass produced, we cannot accept such widespread poverty as inevitable . . . we believe that every willing worker is entitled to a minimum wage which bears some realistic relation to the cost of living. . . . individual states must provide more adequate unemployment compensation, to last through the full period of lay-off."[168] At the same convention, a resolution was passed calling for the abolition of the Committee on Un-American Activities.[169]

Peace

In 1931, the Central Conference of American Rabbis stated that "it is in accord with the highest interpretation of Judaism conscientiously to object to . . . personal participation [in warfare]."[170] In 1935, the committee on international peace, calling attention to the possibility of war as a result of "the persistent economic depression and brazen Nazi and Japanese ambitions," presented a resolution which had been approved in a mail ballot, 91–31, recommending to the members of the Conference "that they refuse to support any war in which this country or any country may engage on the ground that war is a denial of all for which religion stands."[171]

However, following America's entry into the war against Germany and Japan in December 1941, the CCAR convened from February 24 to March 1, 1942. In a lengthy statement on "The War and Our Peace Tradition," it stated, "If our country were engaged in a war of conquest . . . our faith would compel us to challenge its policies, but the cause of our country is a just one." In making proposals for a postwar world, this statement urged "the extension of democracy to all people, including those residing in colonial possessions; the creation of an international organization; . . . the establishment of an international police force to be used to restrain aggressor or outlaw nations; the recognition that the resources of the world belong to all the children of men." The statement concluded with a call for the creation of a peace commission "for the purpose of preparing studies and of reiterating such moral axioms as will eventuate in a peace based on the principles of our faith. We invite our brethren in the Conservative and Orthodox branches to join with us in the formation of the work of such a peace commission."[172] Nowhere in the ensuing discussion nor in the statement is any reference made to the dangers confronting European Jewry.

In 1962 the CCAR voiced its opposition to nuclear testing by the United States and the Soviet Union.[173] This time the committee on justice and peace included the question of peace in the Middle East as an integral part of its social justice concerns:

> We are appalled by the unanimous vote of the Security Council of the U.N. condemning Israel for her military action against Syrian guns which had been firing on Israeli ships in the Sea of Galilee. . . . The Arab refugee problem cannot be resolved until the United Nations presses the Arab States to declare a cessation of hostilities and to indicate a willingness to sit down with the State of Israel at the Conference Table for peaceful negotiations.[174]

Likewise, in 1964 the committee on justice and peace issued a strong statement on the Middle East, calling upon the West German government to recall its scientists who were working in the Egyptian military apparatus. It also called attention to the CCAR's participation in a national gathering in behalf of Soviet Jewry.[175] In a section on "The Rabbi and the Political Process," the report reaffirmed the "Rabbi's right and obligation to exercise political responsibility as a citizen and as a moral teacher. . . . the Rabbi derives his authority to speak and act on public issues not from his Congregation but from the heritage of Judaism, the dictates of his conscience, and the conviction that religion must ever maintain a critical perspective of society."[176]

Race

At its 1933 Convention, the CCAR urged the abolition of economic and civil injustice against "the Negro" and called upon "Congregations of all faiths" to support their leaders "in their activities in behalf of a persecuted race."[177] At the same time the Conference reaffirmed freedom of the pulpit, which "must not be made an echo of the comfortable prejudices and conventional bigotries of the day."[178]

In 1956, the Joint Commission on Social Action of the Central Conference and the Union of American Hebrew Congregations strongly supported the need for developing a civil rights program within the Reform movement and countered those who claimed that segregation is not a moral and religious issue by stating, "this illustrates as nothing else can the over-riding need for our Social Action Program to bring home to every Reform Jew that our religious faith is related to life."[179] In reaffirming its antisegregationist position, the CCAR noted that "for the first time, segregationists struck violently and directly at Jewish communities with attempts to blow up synagogues and community centers," and issued a call against submitting to intimidation.[180] A similar expression was repeated in 1959.[181] A year later the Conference added the warning, "If racial inequalities are not removed voluntarily, the retribution may be violence."[182]

During the period of the Great Depression and into the early stages of World War II, the Reform rabbinate manifested three characteristics in its approach to social issues. First, it pursued a classical liberal ideology which was consistently expressed in matters of unemployment, war and peace, race relations, and the reordering of the social structure. Second, while the Reform rabbinate addressed itself on occasion to the issues of anti-Semitism, particularly its manifestation in Father Coughlin and others, there was an implicit assumption that the improvement of society would also redound to the benefit of the Jewish people. Third, the social justice platform of the Central Conference, while invoking prophetic Judaism and Jewish social consciousness, was devoid of a systematic identification and ratification of its position in authoritative Jewish sources. The Pittsburgh Platform's reference to "the spirit of Mosaic legislation" deliberately avoided anything more specific than that. Yet the need for something more than a liberal philosophy tinged with prophetic precedent began to be expressed. At the 1935 convention, Professor Zvi Diesendruck of the Hebrew Union College, during a debate on the floor, stated:

> I do not believe that we are justified in the somewhat blunt statements made in this resolution about the historical attitude of Judaism to war and peace. If we go on record with statements about the Jewish attitude in the past, they should be made on the basis of a scholarly study of the subject. . . .

I do not believe sending out the resolution will be enough. I think a scholarly committee ought to clarify the standpoint of Judaism on the question of war and peace and this should serve as a basis for historical statements and may also be helpful in our arriving at an opinion.[183]

Nevertheless, the invocation of rabbinic authority was applied by the Reform rabbinate more consistently in areas of Jewish observance than of social concerns.

One notes a departure from early cautiousness to greater assertiveness in the pronouncements by the CCAR. The post–World War I period is marked by more outspoken positions. These become even more pronounced during the depression and after the Second World War. This was due not only to the growing sense of rootedness in America among the Reform rabbinate but to a rapidly changing perception about the nature of American society, reflected in both secular and Christian thought, to which the rabbinate was sensitive. There were not only changes, there were contradictions. In 1892, in his *Triumphant Democracy*, Andrew Carnegie wrote that "the blazing sun right over head casts no shadow. . . . One man's right is every man's right." Yet a year before, the Populist program had declared "that the fruits of the toil of millions are boldly stolen to build up colossal fortunes for a few."[184] The immanentist theology of the late nineteenth and early twentieth century placed God in the midst of society. Liberal religion applied this to validate the goodness of man and the possibilities of religious redemption within history. The social gospel emerged from this, together with belief in progress and social perfectibility. From the 1890's, the social gospel permeated liberal Christian thought and also typified the thought of Reform rabbis like Morris Newfield of Birmingham, Alabama, but "its leaders were not so much activists as they were preachers, proclaimers, educators."[185] In 1917, Walter Rauschenbusch was writing, "No social group or organization can claim to be clearly within the Kingdom of God which drains others for its own cause. . . . This involves the redemption of society in the natural resources of the earth, and from any condition in industry which makes monopoly profits possible."[186] In a similar spirit, the second volume of the *Union Prayer Book for the High Holy Days* (1922) included a long socioeconomic exhortation.

Individual rabbis were understandably more militant and activist than the CCAR. Two illustrations follow. Judah Leon Magnes was a fervent supporter of Scott Nearing, the radical theorist and activist of the far left during World War I. Dismissed as "a fanatic" by Max Eastman, and making Roger Baldwin uneasy with his "intransigence," Nearing was urged by the Jewish labor leader Morris Hillquit and Magnes to assume the chairmanship of the radically pacifist People's Council. The civil rights lawyer Louis Marshall "warned his brother-in-law, Magnes, to avoid associating with Nearing, Hillquit and the 'half-baked political economists and sociologists' of the People's Council. But Magnes and Hillquit remained Nearing's closest collaborators within the executive committee. Were the government to 'put Lochner and me in the coup [*sic*],' he wrote to them, 'we are counting on you' to prevent moderates from trying to 'wreck the whole machine.'"[187] In February 1918, when the People's Council sponsored a National Conference of Labor, Socialist and Radical Movements, Magnes, together with Hillquit and Amos Pinchot, was one of the chief speakers.[188] When Nearing was on trial for violation of the Espionage Act, of which he was acquitted, among those at his counsel table was Magnes.[189]

In Edward Israel, a product of Philipson's congregation, Bene Israel in Cincinnati, there is a polarity between personal militancy and organizational discipline. During the 1931 encampment of World War I veterans who had converged on Washington to protest against the government's disregard of their plight, he hired a taxi which he filled with food supplies and instructed the driver to enter the camp. Finding it guarded by army personnel, the driver refused to go on, but Israel took over and drove through the line.

Until they were drawn to the Zionist movement, men who had in no way been involved with it, or had only been marginally involved, had been deeply immersed in American social-economic issues. While rabbis like Stephen Wise and Abba Hillel Silver had been virtually born into Zionism, their Jewish outlook impelled them likewise to take their places in the great social causes of their times. For others, however, Zionism and the plight of Jewry, which evoked Zionism, increasingly became a dominant social issue of their lives. When Maurice Eisendrath and Edward Israel, two of the four Reform rabbis at the first World Zionist Congress gathering in Geneva in 1936, encountered Wise and Nahum Goldmann in their intercession for a desperate East European Jewry, their way toward Jewish particularity was assured.

During the forties, fifties, and sixties, Reform rabbis found their social concerns and their devotion to the State of Israel to be compatible. They participated in civil rights demonstrations, in some cases went to jail, marched to Selma and Montgomery, Alabama, were active in integrating public schools and housing. At the same time, their participation in Israel-oriented affairs was intense. They raised money, sold Israel Bonds, interceded politically in Israel's behalf, opened their congregations to Zionist exhortations and activities, and during the Six-Day War and the Yom Kippur War, rallied their congregations and their communities behind Israel. The union of universalism and particularism was pronounced. During the Vietnam War many rabbis actively opposed the American government's prosecution of the war, counseled young men who were opposed to the draft, and in one case, six rabbis were prosecuted for trespassing on federal property in their opposition to the war. The apparent discrepancy between this posture and support for Israel was pointed out by President Lyndon Johnson, who cited a strong anti-Vietnam statement by a leading Reform rabbi when a Zionist delegation came to him in behalf of Israel. In another instance, Prime Minister Yitzchak Rabin denounced Reform rabbis for jeopardizing Israel's position by their active opposition to the Vietnam War.

Toward the end of the sixties, the balance between universalism and particularism began to tilt, with growing pressures and disaffections resulting from the civil rights struggle. At the same time, increasing numbers of Reform rabbis became disenchanted with liberal activism. They had marched and demonstrated in behalf of numerous liberal causes, but in many cases, their non-Jewish liberal allies and the beneficiaries of their efforts had failed to rally in Israel's time of need before the Six-Day War. The increasing emergence of ethnicity as a new form of secular religion in America, and even more, the aftershock of the Holocaust, also contributed toward the increasing tilt in the direction of Jewish particularism. This became apparent in the CCAR, where Zionist and pro-Israel concerns occupied a growing share of rabbinic attention, while social action, although not disavowed, occupied a less prominent place. There was a drastic shift of position from periphery to center, and vice versa.

With the final identification of Zionism with Reform Judaism, vast changes took place. First, issues affecting Jewish welfare as well as Israel began to take precedence over social issues. During the period from 1950 to 1970, there were about three times as many references to Israel and related issues in rabbinic resolutions as there were to social issues. Second, social action ceased to be identified exclusively with the universal impulses in Reform Judaism, and incorporated Jewish matters as legitimate areas of social concern. The assumption that the improvement of society will likewise improve the lot of the Jewish people ceased to be tenable.

HUC-JIR

Even after the Hebrew Union College ceased to be a Zionist battle-ground, it continued to reflect the ferment of approaching change within the Reform rabbinate. When the issue of the possible merger with the newly created Jewish Institute of Religion began to assert itself, Stephen Wise wrote to Morris Lazaron that

> I learned the other evening from Rosenau that you said you had made the proposition to tour the country with Morgenstern appealing for funds 80% of which were to go to the Hebrew Union College and 20% to the [Jewish Institute of Religion], and it was turned down flat. Did he understand you correctly? And may I ask who turned down the proposition? Was it brought up at an Executive Committee Meeting of the Union? I think the matter should be thoroughly understood.
>
> I still am greatly desirous to be of whatever service I can in bringing the two institutions together. As I told your brother-in-law, Mr. Davis, last summer, I do not see why some common basis of agreement cannot be reached whereby a part of the time can be spent by the student in Cincinnati and the concluding years in New York using the great Jewish Community there as a laboratory.[190]

In the twenties and thirties, the battle between theism and humanism was being joined in the College chapel. During the same time concern was being directed to the academic program of the College. In the early thirties faculty-student relations committees met to discuss the possible modification of the curriculum.

In 1968, the president of the CCAR, Levi Olan, appointed a committee on rabbinical training, later to be known as the committee on the future of the rabbinate. The committee set for its goal a "study of the realities of Synagogue life as the Rabbi confronts them, the realities of Jewish life outside the Synagogue for which the Rabbi has responsibility, and the function of the Seminary in preparing him intellectually and practically to cope with those realities." To this end it was proposed that "we should learn authoritatively how Congregations, Jewish communities, Seminaries and Rabbis view the Rabbinic calling. . . . We should learn how our existing Rabbinical training program which has faced the challenge of the pre- and post-war world can best equip itself for the uncertainties of the remainder of this century, and the next."[191] On November 12, Olan reported that the Board of Governors of the Hebrew Union College had "responded very favorably to the final request for a very early meeting between our Rabbinic Training Committee and Laymen's Committee of the Board. Dr. Nelson Glueck, president of HUC-JIR, enthusiastically supported the idea of a study."[192] In the same letter, Olan refers to "a statement prepared by [present chairman of the Board of Governors of HUC-JIR] Richard Scheuer last April which was a memorandum to the Executive Committee of the HUC-JIR Board of Governors." This refers to a proposed plan for a JIR building program in New York.

The committee engaged Theodore H. Lenn, who was asked to prepare a study that would address itself to the following questions, among others. "What equipment does a Rabbi need for such times from his pre-student recruitment days to his Seminary years to his Rabbinic experience? Is his role the same as it was a generation ago? Are Congregations the same and do they have the same expectations of us? . . . These and other questions could result in comprehensive self assessment within our Movement. . . . The most effective kind of study [should] be one in which the collaboration of the HUC-JIR with the Conference is enlisted."[193]

Since Lenn's findings have been published and are readily available,[194] we will not address ourselves to the contents of the study. One of the by-products of the committee on the future of the rabbinate was a recommendation that "subject to the approval of the Executive Board of the Conference [the committee] offer its cooperation to the HUC-JIR in helping to develop a program of third year studies in Israel."[195] In an undated memorandum it is recorded that HUC professor Dr. Fritz Bamberger told "of the deep interest of Dr. Glueck and the possibility of a required year of study in Jerusalem by our Rabbinical students."[196] The hope was also expressed "that the prospects for training Rabbis for service throughout the world at the Jerusalem School will soon reach fruition." The same report asks, "should our centers of learning be Seminaries or should they become Universities of Jewish Studies to accommodate the training not only of Rabbis but of the proliferating categories of Jewish civil servants, with theological training a part of the entire enterprise?"[197] In another report, the following appears,

> We have twenty-six students currently attending our Jerusalem school from the HUC-JIR in the United States. A year in Jerusalem *should be made compulsory with credit* as soon as possible—and *it is possible to do it immediately!* It is not as expensive as the administration of the HUC-JIR always argues. There are professors at the Hebrew University. The notion that this should remain voluntary and lengthen studies to a period of six years and sometimes even seven years, doesn't encourage recruits for the Rabbinate and doesn't improve the "emotional mood of future students. . . . " Dr. Glueck mentioned that the February Board of Governors' meeting [dealt with] building up the regular school in Jerusalem with ordination. This school would supply manpower for Congregations in other "liberal" programs and activities in Israel and in various countries around the world outside of the United States. It might also become the source of a positive "liberal" ideology for Eretz Israel. . . . the liberal ideology in the nineteenth century in Central Europe or the USA cannot be the foundation for the "liberal Judaism" in the State of Israel in the second half of the twentieth century.[198]

The issue of the building priorities of the College-Institute was also raised in the course of the deliberations of the committee on the future of the rabbinate in an undated memorandum after March 1968 and in all probability later in 1968. The following proposal was made to the Executive Board of the Central Conference of American Rabbis, that

> Before the Capital Fund Program for necessary work in New York and Cincinnati is made final, some basic questions about the future Rabbinic training which concerns the CCAR be the subject of a meeting between the proper representatives and the Board of Governors. Such a meeting should occur very soon so as not to delay whatever plans need immediate attention. This, we believe, will help the Board of Governors to plan the financial requirements and allocations in relationship to a changing American Jewry.[199]

On December 21, 1972, the committee adopted a resolution that "the Committee expresses its strong conviction that the New York

school should be considerably expanded—academically and physically—and there should be no further expansion of the Cincinnati campus."[200] This was partly an affirmation of the master plan presented by
Richard J. Scheur to the Board of Governors on May 8, 1968, recommending that the New York school "affiliate with a major university,
move to the university campus, conduct an expanded program including the award of the Ph.D."[201]

The issue of the scholarly qualifications of rabbis was an early
source of concern. Addressing the graduation exercises of the Jewish
Institute of Religion in New York on May 27, 1934, David Philipson
had said, "The Rabbi's first concern should be continuing study and
scholarship. Unless he build upon this as a foundation he builds upon
sand."[202]

When the committee on the future of the rabbinate undertook its
studies, the theme of the academic preparedness of the rabbi continued to be a source of concern. In a critical analysis of the Lenn Report,
Levi Olan made the following observation:

> The role of scholar is ranked lower by the Rabbis today than that of leader-
> ship in the Jewish community, Pastor, Priest, adult teacher and religious teacher.
> The younger men show this trend away from Jewish scholarship more than
> those rabbis who have been in the Rabbinate for ten years or more. The report
> says it is a "reflection of some rejection by the younger generation of intellec-
> tualism in terms of specific Jewish scholarship."[203]

Authority in Jewish Life

In 1871, at a conference of Reform rabbis in Cincinnati, the following
resolution was passed.

> The members of the conference take upon themselves the duty to bring prom-
> inently before the congregations, to advocate and to support by their influence,
> the following project of co-operation of the American Hebrew Congregations:
> The congregations to unite themselves into a Hebrew Congregational Union
> with the object to preserve and advance the union of Israel; to take proper care
> of the development and promulgation of Judaism; to establish and support a
> scholastic institute, and the library appertaining thereto, for the education of
> rabbis, preachers, and teachers of religion; to provide cheap editions of the
> English Bible and text books for the schools of religious instruction; to give
> support to weak congregations, and to provide such other institutions which

elevate, preserve, and promulgate Judaism.

Resolved, that whenever twenty congregations, with no less than two thousand contributing male members, shall have declared, in accordance with the preceding resolution, their resolution to enter the H. C. U., the said committee shall envoke the synod to meet at such time and place as may be most satisfactory to the co-operating congregations.[204]

The Central Conference of American Rabbis was yet to come into being, but under the long and persistent urging of Isaac Mayer Wise, the rabbis' body issued the call for the creation of a union of congregations. Two years later, the Union of American Hebrew Congregations came into being.

It is noteworthy that the first organized body of Reform Judaism in the United States was an assembly of congregations, and that the impetus for it came from a rabbinical group. Even more noteworthy is the reference to the request that the organizing committee "shall envoke the synod."

Today the Reform movement, as represented in this study by the Reform rabbinate, finds itself vastly and globally enlarged, and radically altered programmatically, ideologically, and in its very identity. It is an overstatement but, nevertheless, suggestive to say that the entire movement retains little of its origins except its name.

Change generates far-ranging problems, and for Reform one of them involves the encounter with the halakhic tradition, which has been renewed, in large measure, by the Holocaust and the axial shift toward Israel. Yet the issue is not new. The issue is more acute than ever before. Its roots extend to mid-nineteenth-century Germany, and from there to the resolution calling for the creation of a union of congregations. Nowhere else in the resolution is there reference to a "synod," and we can be sure that the term was not a casual one. It had been inserted with full awareness that it was a fighting word in the debates within the Reform movement, and the resolution's framers indicated by its use that for them, at least, the proposed union was to go beyond the stated objectives outlined in the second paragraph of the resolution.

The conflict over whether a Reform synod should be convened had its genesis in Germany, where, in the mid-1840's, some rabbis were urging that a synod be called for the purpose of issuing a declaration of faith by rabbis and laymen. The synod issue was a consequence, perhaps inevitable, of an ideological tension within the Reform movement in Germany. Although Reform had emerged, in part, as a revolt against the stringency of rabbinic authority, as well as a response to the promise of emancipation, a significant sector of the movement was not prepared to eradicate its traditional and rabbinic ties.

This ambivalence manifested itself in the radically different approaches of Abraham Geiger (1810–1874) and Samuel Holdheim (1806–1860). Geiger was concerned about the proliferation of impromptu reforms by a number of rabbis, and his primary concern, in his public and more guarded pronouncements, was the synthesis of the Jewish spirit with "a sound science." At the same time, he inveighed against "many overeducated and sensual ones that would willingly throw away all ancient treasures . . . and divest themselves of their own character and past as something useless."[205] Significantly, he scanned the horizon for "a new Hillel." Holdheim's extremism manifested itself in the position that, except for purely ecclesiastical matters, the autonomy of the rabbinate was superseded by that of the state in many Jewish areas, including marriage, which is a civil act. Jewish national identity had ended. "All laws and institutions which are based upon the election of a particular Jewish people . . . have lost all religious significance and obligation."[206]

As conceived within the Berlin Reform Society, the synod

> was to take into consideration the changes which had come upon Jewish life and thought in the new environment of the nineteenth century, re-interpret the truths of Judaism in the light of those changes and give authoritative expression to what constituted the fundamentals of Jewish thought and practice. . . . The individualism which followed in the train of breaking loose from the fetters of code observance threatened disaster in the view of many. In place of the fixed anchor—the ceremonial law—to which Jews had clung aforetime, there was now no support; reform went to greater or less lengths according to individual caprice. . . . The synod which was agitated for by the Berlin reformers . . . was to concern itself with determining the significance and the essence of Jewish belief and practice, to pronounce upon the relation of modern reform Judaism to the traditions, to interpret the present attitude upon all vital points, as the liturgy, marriage and divorce, the ceremonies, the position of woman, the dietary laws and the Sabbath.[207]

The intent of the synod was made unmistakable by the words of one of its protagonists, Ludwig Philippson, who declared in 1849 that it was as necessary for contemporary Judaism as was the Sanhedrin at

Tiberias after the destruction of Jerusalem.

The proposed synod did not come into being, but for the purposes of our discussion it is important to note the following: (a) The proposal recognized the danger of nihilism within Reform. (b) It addressed itself not only to Jewish ceremonies but to halakhic issues, such as marriage and divorce. (c) It contemplated procedures which would be binding upon its adherents. (d) Decisions would be made by joint action of rabbis and congregants. (e) It was a live issue which agitated the Reform community, and was not considered to be irrelevant to its concerns, or outside the scope of its deliberations. Two subsequent synods did take place in Leipzig and in Augsburg, but they "failed to realize the hopes of their projectors." The time was evidently not ripe for such a movement. There were too many differences among Jews.[208]

The issue was transplanted, however, from Germany to the United States. Evidently, the call for a synod in the Cincinnati resolution of 1871 was overlooked or side-stepped in the birth of the Union of American Hebrew Congregations, because in 1881 Isaac Mayer Wise was still agitating for it. In the debate at the CCAR conventions in 1904, 1905, and 1906, the critical point at issue was the authority of the synod. If it was able to coerce compliance, the opposition feared, it might eventually become an ecclesiastical court with power to enforce its decrees. In 1906, the CCAR voted down the advisability of a synod after having approved it by a small margin in 1904, but this did not end the discussion. In fact, David Philipson, in his book on the development of Reform Judaism, concludes his chapter on the Leipzig and Augsburg synods as follows: "There can be little doubt that in the present unsettled state of Jewish opinion on many vital points, owing to the transition from the old to the new, there is a great need for a central organization of this kind composed of rabbinical and lay delegates, whose power shall be not to loose or to bind, but to pronounce judgments on controverted points of doctrine and practice."[209]

We will discuss the American Reform rabbinate within the context of the synod issue not only because it is implicit in the creation of the Union of American Hebrew Congregations, but because the issue is as germane today as it was a century ago, and has manifested itself in such apparently disparate issues as Jewish law and Zionism. The unresolved issue implicit in the synod controversy continues to nag, and the Reform movement is more heavily engaged in it than ever before, and with the same ambivalence which agitated it in its origin, although there is the beginning of a shift of balance. There is no call today for a Reform synod, but the operative component of the synod approach, authority, is very much in evidence. We will momentarily forgo assessing the critical question of imposed versus internalized authority, but the source and the nature of authority are central to all discussions that are linked to halakhah. The intensity of the issue can be gauged by the mounting frequency of the very term "halakhah," as against former references to "ceremonies" and "customs." This is not to be construed as necessarily a general turn to halakhah but, rather, a recognition that the halakhah must be responsibly confronted even where it cannot be conscientiously accepted. If this does not differ substantively from the approach of the more traditional earlier reformers, there is a heightening of this sense of concern and responsibility in the Reform rabbinate.

Today it is not necessarily the merits of particularism that we should stress but, rather, the conditions out of which it is emerging in Reform. The catastrophic events of the twentieth century have compelled a reassessment not merely of the effectiveness of the emancipation but of its intrinsic motivation. If it was prompted by a desire to offer freedom to Jews, it was equally impelled to strip the collective identity of the Jewish people as its price.

About 1928, we note the beginnings of a new direction in the Reform rabbinate in which there is a conscious effort to uncover traditional elements for the enrichment of Jewish life. It is significant that the period in which this occurred coincides, roughly, with upheavals in our society and in Jewish life to which the Reform rabbinate responded in typical Toynbeean "challenge and response" fashion. Leaving aside the rising surge of Zionism, the growing despair over the unfulfilled promise of emancipation had a decisive effect on the attitude toward tradition within Reform (and from a Geigerian standpoint it could have been predicted). The Versailles Treaty, in which minority rights had been granted to Jews in Eastern Europe, was followed by a tidal wave of anti-Semitic excesses in the lands of greatest Jewish concentration. The rise of Nazism, even before its legalized triumph in Germany, shook the confidence of many Reform rabbis in the credibility of the emancipation, much less its durability. In America, the alarm over the dissemination of the *Protocols of the Elders of*

Zion by Henry Ford, the archetype of everything that was intriguing to middle-class Jews in industrialized America, undercut their confidence in the nation's immunity to anti-Semitism, as did the Father Coughlin era. All this was exacerbated by the depression, which shattered any lingering illusions about the deterministic messianic mystique of the American system. It is not coincidental that the Columbus Platform of 1937, affirming the need for intensified Jewish observance, was promulgated while the depression was at its nadir. In the realm of intellectual history, Freud had created a psychological revolution, shaking the dogmas of the liberal religious world, whose scientific rationalistic suppositions were overwhelmed by the eruption of the unconscious. For the Reform rabbinate this compelled a reexamination of the Jewish experience as an ideational construct alone, and required a confrontation with the irrepressible, nonrational, primordial components in Judaism.

It is legitimate to ask how these events resulted specifically in the turn by the Reform rabbinate toward a stronger encounter with Jewish tradition and with Jewish law. Why did they not produce a heightened commitment to pure universalism and total antinomianism as an act of defiance against historical aberrations which must be resisted in order to preserve the fruits of emancipation? This did, in fact, occur among a segment of the Reform community. But the overwhelming weight of conviction leaned toward heightened stress on particularism, and articulated it in Zionism and greater adherence to tradition. This is borne out by the Lenn study on the future of the rabbinate, published by the Central Conference in 1972. Thus, in one statistical table, 49 percent of strong or moderate particularists, as against 8 percent of strong universalists, insisted on the use of a *huppah* (canopy) at weddings, 49 percent of strong or moderate particularists, as against 6 percent of strong universalists, disapproved of rabbis officiating at intermarriages.[210]

When the Reform rabbinate began its turn toward greater stress on tradition, it did so largely in the context of customs and ceremonies. The Columbus Platform stated that Judaism, instead of being a religion only, was "a way of life" which "requires in addition to its moral and spiritual demands the preservation of the Sabbath, festivals and Holy Days, the retention and development of such customs, symbols and ceremonies as possess inspirational value."

The practical application of this view was increased stress on Hebrew in the services, Bar and Bat Mitzvah, and the cultivation of various rituals. The CCAR instituted a committee on ceremonies in 1938, and much of its work dealt with ritual in the narrower context of the term. Confrontation with issues of day-to-day mizvot and with the halakhah was yet to come, and it is doubtful whether it could have occurred as drastically without the rebirth of the State of Israel. Israel accentuated the sense of peoplehood, but peoplehood also compelled a confrontation with those halakhic issues which made peoplehood compelling. Toward the end of the 1950's, terms like "mizvah" and "halakhah" became increasingly normative, and this development is more significant than might appear, because the issue in Reform is no longer ceremonies but whether we are addressing ourselves to mizvot or to the halakhah, or perhaps in some cases to the former, and in others to the latter. In certain respects, Reform is experiencing a déjà vu in which the issues of Shabbat observance and authority are being resurrected after their earliest vitality about seventy years ago, when the CCAR had a Commission on the Sabbath.

At the heart of the issue is whether observance in Reform is to be required by fiat or by personal and collective internalization. Is a synodal approach to be decisive or persuasive? Antecedent to this, is Jewish observance to be the product of an official body or of individuals? In 1942, the committee on a code of practice, under the chairmanship of Professor Israel Bettan, referring to an earlier paper by Solomon Freehof on "A Code of Ceremonial and Ritual Practice," proposed that "in the field of marriage divorce and conversion, we must draw up a clear-cut code which shall have the effect of law for us . . . while the dietary laws may be ignored altogether." This was followed by a recommendation "that a Special Committee of the Conference be charged with the task of preparing a Manual of Jewish Religious Practices."[211] This was not pursued. In an effort to cope with both of these issues, the late Rabbi Frederic Doppelt and the author produced our *Guide for Reform Jews* in 1957. Note that we used the word "guide" in the title, not "code." This book was prompted by our conviction that Reform Judaism required sturdier observance of rituals, that this should be systematic rather than impromptu, that it could come about (at that juncture) through the efforts of individuals, that it was a hortatory not a mandatory device, and that it could not be presented without a rationale. Basic to the entire effort was the desire to differentiate between mizvot and minhagim, and, as a consequence, each section of the *Guide* began with "It is a mizvah to . . . "

From its inception, Reform has been mindful of the claims of halakhah to its attention, if not to its obedience. As recently as 1982, plans were launched to include a mikvah ceremony in a new proposed *Rabbis' Manual (Netivot)* and also to include in it a document acknowledging the dissolution of a marriage with rabbinical involvement. The continuing work of the responsa committee of the CCAR reflects not merely a concern with issues of observance but a commitment to searching out halakhic precedent, employing halakhic dialectic and, where unable to submit to the halakhah, not to reject it capriciously. It is true that this approach has its shortcomings as an instrument of seeking affirmation when it is available and going on a deviant path when it is not, but even this procedure is not altogether alien to rabbinic law-making. In the latter case, the predilection is to find precedent suitable to a generally rigorous construction. In the former instance, the predilection is to find a more permissive precedent. In 1921, by a vote of 56 to 11, the CCAR declared that "women cannot justly be denied the privilege of ordination."[212] This followed a long debate during which women participated and during which Jacob Lauterbach argued that the "law that women cannot be Rabbis was always taken for granted in the Talmud." David Neumark refuted Lauterbach's talmudic references point by point, and then concluded, "You cannot treat the Reform Rabbinate from the Orthodox point of view. Our good relations with our Orthodox brethren may still be improved upon by a clear and decided stand on this question. They want us either to be Reform or to return to the fold of real genuine Orthodox Judaism, whence we came."[213]

Solomon Freehof has contributed several volumes of responsa under the imprimatur of the Reform movement. Most recently, the CCAR, through its Shabbat committee under the chairmanship of its current president, Gunther Plaut, has produced a *Shabbat Manual (Tadrikh l'Shabbat)* in which the mizvot, the customs, the music, and the folkways of Shabbat are set forth.

In the more volatile public sector, the Reform rabbinate has come to grips with the issue of intermarriage, which crosses two highly sensitive boundaries—our relationship with Israel, and the autonomy of the rabbi. The second issue, of necessity, deals with the problem of authority—is there an authority higher than the individual?

The autonomy of the rabbi and the congregation has been, in theory, a paramount principle of Reform, and has been invoked whenever critical issues have arisen. In the debates concerning a proposed synod, the issue of personal freedom and immunity from any form of coercion became central.

In 1905, the president of the CCAR made the following appeal: "It is in this wherein lies the strength of the Central Conference of American Rabbis, and the promise of its future. It is and will continue to be merely a deliberative and advisory assembly, not an ecumenical council, convened for the purpose of establishing creeds and dogmas, of fixing forms and ceremonies, and making compliance with them obligatory and difference from them heretical."[214]

The same argument was employed by Stephen Wise in 1917 during a debate on Zionism.

> If you pass this resolution, no matter how you water it or mitigate it, the moment you say that we who are Zionists are anti-religionists, that we are enemies of religious Judaism, that moment we must regretfully yet with absolute conviction say, "We can stay no longer within the Conference." I stand here today not as a Zionist, but as a reform rabbi. I would not have you say that a reform teacher or rabbi has forfeited the right to be a teacher of reform Judaism because he has subscribed to the Zionist platform. I appeal not for Zionism, but for the inclusiveness and comprehensiveness of liberal Judaism.[215]

The CCAR has adhered to the principle of personal sovereignty, although at times it has been charged with flouting it.

No issue, however, has placed the encounter of personal freedom and authority in greater tension than the intermarriage question. In 1909, the Central Conference issued the following resolution: "The CCAR declares that mixed marriages are contrary to the tradition of the Jewish religion and should, therefore, be discouraged by the American Rabbinate."[216] It has subsequently been suggested that the reason for not calling upon Reform rabbis to desist from officiating was that so few rabbis indulged in the practice at the time. It is more plausible to believe that the intense synod debates prior to 1909 had hardened the resistance to any kind of authoritarian statement—to such an extent, in fact, that the call to "discourage" intermarriage was issued not to

members of the Central Conference but to "the American Rabbinate."
On a number of occasions, efforts were made to strengthen the resolution, but they failed by narrow margins. In 1962, at Minneapolis,
there was an abortive effort to approve officiating at intermarriages.
When the issue was joined in 1971 and resolved in June 1973, the
following resolution was passed by a vote of 321 to 196.

> *Section I*
> The Central Conference of American Rabbis, recalling its stand adopted in
> 1909 "that mixed marriage is contrary to the Jewish tradition and should be
> discouraged" now declares its opposition to participation by its members in any
> ceremony which solemnizes a mixed marriage.
> *Section II*
> The Central Conference of American Rabbis recognizes that historically its
> members have held and continue to hold divergent interpretations of Jewish
> tradition.
> In order to keep open every channel to Judaism and K'lal Yisrael for those
> who have already entered into mixed marriage, the CCAR calls upon its mem-
> bers:
> 1. To assist fully in educating children of such mixed marriage as Jews;
> 2. To provide the opportunity for conversion of the non-Jewish spouse;
> and
> 3. To encourage a creative and consistent cultivation of involvement in the
> Jewish Community and the Synagogue.[217]

The resolution issues a request that Reform rabbis do a specified
thing—i.e., not officiate at intermarriages,—something the Central
Conference had never done in this specific context, although it did so
in another setting, the request to leave the American Council for Judaism. It deliberately stops short of enforcement procedures, although it
takes note of the fact that some rabbis will disregard the call to desist.
At the same time, certain matters were referred to various committees
for further inquiry. One is the ethics committee, which has enforcement capacity in matters of rabbinical violation. Nevertheless, the
individual rabbi is urged, but not compelled, to abstain. The expectation is that the collective voice of the Conference will exert moral
deterrence for many. The resolution is illustrative of an effort to reconcile various contradictions—disapproval without coercion, personal
rights in encounter with the needs of K'lal Yisroel, inner direction in
encounter with outer direction. It is not suggested that the reconciling
process is altogether satisfactory in this case. It is indicated only that
within the context of a movement which had been torn, from the very

beginning, in two directions—between antinomianism and receptivity to halakhah, between synodism and antisynodism—the Conference took a positive step toward voluntaristic responsiveness to the demands of Jewish law and the needs of the entire Jewish people.

It is significant that the major reconsiderations of the issue of intermarriage took place in the wake of the Holocaust/Shoah and the struggle for the State of Israel. It is questionable whether the acute sensitivity to K'lal Yisroel would have been so sharply manifested without the State of Israel. We are not here concerned with justifying the noncoercive policy of the CCAR but, rather, in pointing out that, in taking its new position on intermarriage, it has taken a stand on a critical halakhic issue in Jewish life and has also defined (not for the first time) the role of the individual in the setting of authority. It demonstrated that the individual cannot claim authority for himself in defining what is required of him as a Jew and as a rabbi. His freedom to differ and to deviate is not affected, but his claim to personal authority is. Thus, while the issue of the ultimate source of authority will continue to agitate all within Jewry to whom this is a problem, the ultimacy of the individual has certainly been dismissed. There is a higher (though not necessarily highest) authority, and that is the consensus of the accredited rabbinic leadership within the Reform community. There is also the implicit authority of the world Jewish community, which cannot be excluded. This authority deliberately is not administrative, but from a moral standpoint it is not thereby diminished. It may be asked how this authority differs from that of the 1909 resolution, which states that intermarriage should be discouraged. By altering the "discouraging" from an abstract judgment which declares its "opposition" and appeals to "the American Rabbinate" to a specific call directed to every individual Reform rabbi, the resolution takes on concreteness and personal relevance.

Certain aspects of Jewish life, primarily in the public sector of marriage, conversion, and divorce, will require confrontation with halakhah, whether affirmatively or negatively. The halakhic problems of divorce and conversion are now on the agenda of Reform, and some individual rabbis require mikvah and tevilah for conversion. The CCAR recently advised its colleagues that candidates for Reform conversion should be made aware of the option of mikvah and tevilah so that they can make a choice. In 1891, an intense debate on whether male converts should be circumcised was fought by both sides with recourse to talmudic and responsa literature. There was great concern on the part of members of the opposition that they be supported by rabbinic authority. Thus, Dr. Sonneschein cited the Maharil in his *Nitzachon,* saying, "The faith is not dependent on milah . . . whoever believes properly is a Jew, even if uncircumcised."[218] Some Reform rabbis also advise divorced couples of the possibility of a get (rabbinic divorce), so that they will be aware of possible complications in the event of remarriage. As a body, the Reform rabbinate defends its right to perform its own conversions in its own way, and standards for conversion stress study of Judaism.

Unlike the public sector, the private sector (within Reform, at any rate) will not be governed by halakhah but by what can be referred to as a mizvah-system. One lives under the halakhah. One performs mizvot. From a Reform perspective, individual mizvot can be performed, altered, suspended, or created, but if the halakhah is dealt with similarly, it ceases to be The Halakhah. If it is retained substantially, Reform ceases to be. One does not accept halakhah selectively, any more than one picks and chooses in the civil law of his community. Mizvot (in the context in which they are here presented, not in the traditional context) are specific responses to existential situations in which the Jew answers to history, to his current situation, to the sacred, to the life-cycle, to the calendar, to the rites of passage. Through mizvot, the individual is capable of reliving the central elements of his people's history and of bringing history into the circumstances in which he and his people presently find themselves. The mizvah becomes an immediate response to a given moment. It is not bound to an absoluteness to which few can submit. In this setting, Reform is becoming increasingly mizvah-aware, and receptive to guidance in a mizvah-system in which the demands of the human spirit are more enforceable than any coercive device, human or divine.

In 1971 and 1972, the Reform rabbinate was engaged in an attempt to fulfill the hopes of some of the early synodists. Whether or not it will succeed is yet to be determined, but for a time an effort was made at defining the basic principles of Reform. Following, perhaps unconsciously, the lead of the German synodists, a group of rabbis, scholar-specialists, and laymen, under the leadership of the late Rabbi Dudley Weinberg, long deliberated on a series of theological and philosophical issues. Unlike the Pittsburgh and Columbus Platforms, this was an attempt to speak in behalf of the entire movement, not rabbis alone. Among the issues dealt with are: who is a Jew; marriage and divorce; the covenant; personal and social ethics; the synagogue; plural models within the halakhah; Israel, diaspora, and mission; Judaism and world religions.

Unlike the Pittsburgh and Columbus Platforms, which are cryptic and almost catechistic, the proposed guiding principles attempted to be more expository. In addition, the very effort was a recognition that, de jure as well as de facto, the Pittsburgh Platform had been supplanted and the Columbus Platform required extensive restructuring. For lack of consensus on any issue among the rabbis, however, the enterprise foundered and was abandoned. In place of this failed enterprise, the Central Conference, in June 1976, adopted the "Centenary Perspective," which frankly recognizes the difficulty at this time of adopting a platform and stresses, instead, the pluralism within Reform, as well as its achievements.

In at least two critical issues, the American Council for Judaism and intermarriage, the Central Conference chose not to interpret personal freedom as implying the inherent right to unlimited freedom of action. It is clear that, short of ethical or administrative (not halakhic) violations, the Conference has deliberately chosen not to impose discipline. It has placed its confidence in the slower, but far less catastrophic, processes of debate and suasion, always accompanied by the omnipresent guest of the Jewish people, history.

One can note, with some justification, that while formal structures are being worked out, there seems to be a de facto receptivity by Reform rabbis to the concept of, if not adherence to, a higher measure of a mizvah-system, both in their personal and their collective lives. To have attained to the degree of receptivity is itself a mizvah which points further. Thus, the development of a new prayerbook (*Shaaray Tefillah*) and a new mahzor (*Shaaray Teshuvah*), to be opened, in most cases, from right to left, is indicative. So is the publication of the *Shabbat Guide*. The growing number of Reform congregations which conduct *Slihot* services in an idiom which is open to both the traditional liturgy and new creativity is a clue. The declaration by the Central Conference that Yom Ha-Azmaut and Yom Ha-Shoah are official days on our calendar, to be observed with appropriate liturgies; the decision by some rabbis to observe the second day of Rosh Ha-Shanah as a sign of our religious link with the Jews in Israel; above all, the affirmative response to the call for a mizvah-system, reflect a new perception of Reform in which the tradition-based impulse appears to assert itself over the antinomian impulse.

This does not mean simplistically that Reform is becoming Conservative, as one segment of folk-wisdom would have it. It means that an identity struggle is at work in which the full outcome is yet to be determined, and the intermarriage issue is the most volatile manifestation of that struggle. While one wing of the Reform rabbinate is turning toward the tradition, another is also deeply committed not to be undifferentiatingly subservient to it, and it is equally committed to creating its own way which would become part of the traditional continuum.

Retrospect and Prospect

One cannot assess the Reform rabbinate without considering its possible effectiveness. What has been its influence within the Reform movement? What has been the nature of its leadership—initiating or responding to outer initiatives? As with all rabbis and all movements in contemporary Judaism, the dual impact of the Holocaust/Shoah and Israel in radically transforming Jewish life is a given. Only within these parameters can we fairly judge the Reform rabbinate's influence. There are ample illustrations confirming the lead which the Central Conference of American Rabbis has provided to Reform. In June 1937, the Columbus Platform paved the way for the emergence of a similar ideology within the Union of American Hebrew Congregations at its biennial later that year in New Orleans. The CCAR has largely determined the liturgical forms and renewed practices of the movement. It has provided strong leadership in behalf of Israel. Where it has questioned Israeli policies, it has been more assertive than others, yet often circumspectly. It has set the pace in issues of social concern, including civil rights and the issues of peace.

Most recently, however, although the CCAR has asserted its traditional theological leadership, this time on the issue of patrilineal descent, it has done so only by responding to a prior initiative from the Union of American Hebrew Congregations. This is partly due to the fact that the Conference stands in a triune relationship with the Union and the HUC-JIR. Subtle controls and correctives have been exerted by each upon the others, resulting in self-restricting autonomy. Sometimes, shifts in balance or occasional institutional grid-locks are determined by charismatic leadership in one body or another. Despite this, it is to the credit of the movement that its physically weakest segment, the CCAR, has enjoyed as much freedom as it alone chooses to exercise. Ultimately, its freedom or the self-imposed limitation thereof is based on nothing more substantial than its moral strength or weakness. Ultimately, its influence and its leadership depend not only on its capacity but on its will to persuade and to take stands.

As Reform and American Judaism enter upon yet undefined transformations, the role of other Jewish religious movements in the development of the Reform rabbinate takes on significance. One of them is Reconstructionism. It is generally assumed that it was Mordecai Kaplan's thought which redirected Reform ideology, but this is too simplistic. It is more accurate to say that there have been mutually involved influences. As has already been indicated in this study, the influence of Felsenthal on Kaplan is acknowledged in *Judaism as a Civilization*, where Felsenthal offers a concise "Reconstructionist" definition of Judaism. In the same book, a 1925 survey of the Central Conference clearly indicates a turn toward "Judaism as a Civilization" at a time when Kaplan's philosophy had not yet made a strong impact. Reform students and rabbis were reaching their own "Reconstructionist" conclusions through the writings of Achad Ha-Am and the pages of *He-Atid*, containing a seminal symposium which paralleled Kaplan's philosophy. Equally important was the singular example of Reform, which "ran interference" for the rest of American Judaism in challenging old perceptions and practices, and charting new paths of belief and practice. No movement more assiduously built its own program on these bold principles than did Reconstructionism. At the same time, nevertheless, Kaplanism made obvious inroads into Reform thought by presenting a compelling critique of classical Reform as primarily a theology, and by stressing the principle of peoplehood. This made its way into the Columbus Platform. In addition, some of the leading early figures in the Reconstructionist camp were Reform rabbis who acknowledged an abiding debt to Kaplan for shaping their Jewish outlooks. Thus, each movement has exerted a telling influence on the other.

The transformation of the Reform rabbinate may be traced in its garb and style—from Prince Albert cutaway, to striped trousers, to academic robe, often with narrow stole, to kipah and expansive tallit, at times covering a dress.

Are there constants in the highly transitional Reform rabbinate? There is a greatly developed sense of individualism, of personal autonomy, of deference but not unconditional obedience to Jewish law. Ultimately, changes seen as desirable are considered legitimate, even if they are not compatible with Jewish law. This represents a radical deviation from other rabbinical bodies.

In assessing the Reform rabbinate over an entire century, we realize that it has been less the product of ideology than of history. No more convincing testimony to this exists than the Pittsburgh principles themselves. Their repeated appeal is to historical forces which are referred to as modernism. Accordingly, Jewish religion developed "in accordance with . . . progress of . . . respective ages." Jewish observance must conform to ""modern civilization." Jewish nationalism is incompatible with "the modern era." The Jewish mission responds to "the broad humanity of our age." Judaism must address itself to "the present organization of society." This observation acknowledges that ideology is constantly interacting with history. Any ideology which is impervious to history becomes a Samaritan or Karaitic sect and suffers the consequences. Reform underwent cataclysmic changes of thought because it believed that events justified the changes. The massive transformation of the Reform rabbinate cannot be explained in terms of Reform definitions, except in the broadest possible sense. Today's Reform is neither universalist nor particularistic but Jewishly ecumenical. The rabbinate is the greatest embodiment of change. A number of primary factors account for this: the Jewish ecumenicity of Jewish chaplains during World War II; a similar phenomenon in Hillel Foundations; the Holocaust/Shoah with its shattering of Jewish denominational distinctions; and most recently and perhaps most compellingly, the first-year-in-Israel experience, by now encompassing about one-third of the active Reform rabbinate.

The foundations of this radical shift were laid by the Classical Reformers themselves, who proclaimed the legitimacy of change under the compulsion of changing times. The very emergence of Zionism, which had been anathema to early Reform rabbis, and which changed Reform almost beyond recognition, was by their own definition a normal development. Reform has changed so substantively that it might, except organizationally, be seen as another entity, just as the second Mrs. Sherman Stein is a different person from the first Mrs. Sherman Stein. The early Reform rabbis established the basis for a serious current predicament. If the spirit of the times is to be taken as a dominant factor in the shaping of Reform, then the revolutionary and dazzlingly rapid transformation of our world makes change and adaptation not only difficult but often premature and unfeasible. The process of adaptation becomes subject not to the inner demands of ancient tradition but to the compulsion of an external environment alone. Salvation is contingent on the age as much as on the past, but the founders of Reform could not have conceived how the age would betray both the Jews and universal humanity. The segment of Reform Judaism which was conceived on the premise, among others, that "the times" warranted radical departures from tradition misread history. It continued, even into the First World War, to see the world in messianic terms. Thus, in the year of America's entry into the war, the Central Conference declared, in justifying its opposition to joining the American Jewish Congress, "the Russian Revolution has radically altered the condition of our co-religionists in Russia, promising to secure the civil and religious rights of the Jews all the world over."[219] History itself should have persuaded us that the appeal to the age's validation alone is a weak reed. The abiding issue is whether, fully recognizing the adaptational demands of history, we can abide as Jews in conformity to a higher mandate than modernity.

Most recently, the Centennial Perspective (1976) of the Central Conference attempts to disengage itself from tribute to the "progress of the ages" by speaking of "our uncertain historical situation." Unlike the Pittsburgh Platform, which offers a religious monolith, the Perspective "does more than tolerate diversity; it engenders it. . . . we must expect to have far greater diversity than previous generations knew."[220] While Pittsburgh uses such terms as "reject," "foreign to," "no longer," the Perspective speaks of "tolerate," "stand open," "accept differences," "unity," "precious differences." Where Pittsburgh is triumphal, the Perspective is reserved; where Pittsburgh is dogmatic, the Perspective is moderate; where Pittsburgh is confident, the Perspective is cautious; where Pittsburgh discards, the Perspective conserves. One of the conserving elements in contemporary Reform is the renewed concern with Jewish law. Yet this too has plunged Reform Judaism into a web of contradictions. A movement which is clearly returning to traditional values and practices while incapable of stemming the erosion of those values and practices, is torn indeed.

What can be more contradictory than a rabbinate which has taken an explosively mizvah-oriented direction while the number of rabbis who perform intermarriages increases? (David Philipson considered intermarriage a major danger for American Jewry.) Members of the CCAR overwhelmingly scorn the performance of "ecumenical marriages" with Christian clergy but will not legislate against it. Another, more constructive contradiction is the growing difference in style, content, and discipline between the Israeli Reform rabbinate, represented organizationally by MARAM (Mo'ezet ha-Rabbanim ha-Mitkaddenim—the Council of Progressive Rabbis), and the American Reform rabbinate. The former is committed to the full observance of the halakhah in matters concerning marriage, divorce, and conversion. The ultimate source of contradiction is the hitherto inviolate principle of freedom of individual conscience which, unlike in any other rabbinate, leaves rabbis virtually immune to any discipline except the opinion of their colleagues. This exacts a high collective price, but also safeguards against collective repression. It fosters both freedom and license. No proposals for resolving this dilemma have been advanced. If a request were to be made that gross violations should be subject to sanctions, it would be defeated.

Yet it should be recognized that the Reform rabbinate, like others, finds itself in a time of such Jewish upheaval that neat and orderly denominational structures are neither feasible nor desirable. The dislocations of the post-Holocaust/Shoah explosions still await rearranging. One of the dislocations is the imbalance between Jewish religion and Jewish ethnicity. Whenever that balance is disturbed, Jewish life is disturbed. When Reform arbitrarily excluded ethnicity, and when political Zionism excluded religion (except in a political context), a serious Jewish schism erupted. Taking into account the great religious contributions Reform has made in Israel—the Jerusalem School of

HUC-JIR, the Reform Kibbutz Yahel, and MARAM—the dominant perception is still that of a movement where ethnicity rivals religion. Reform is now challenged to exert its prophetic-religious influence in an increasingly politicized Jewish world. The synthesis of both is difficult to attain, but this must be a primary task of the Reform rabbinate.

David Polish is the founding rabbi of Beth Emet—The Free Synagogue in Evanston, Illinois. He is the author of, among other works, *Renew Our Days: The Zionist Issue in Reform Judaism*.

Notes

1. *CCAR Yearbook* 2 (1891): 4.
2. Ibid., pp. 7–22.
3. Ibid., p. 4.
4. Ibid., p. 31.
5. Ibid., p. 5.
6. Ibid., p. 23.
7. Ibid., p. 80.
8. Ibid., p. 82.
9. Ibid., p. 31.
10. July 15 proceedings, ibid., p. 31.
11. Ibid., p. 23.
12. *Hebrew Observer*, October 16, 1891, cited by Lloyd P. Gartner, *History of the Jews of Cleveland* (Cleveland: Western Reserve Historical Society, 1978), p. 151.
13. *Jewish Review*, November 8, 1895, cited by Gartner, p. 152.
14. *Jewish Review and Observer*, March 22, 1912, cited by Gartner, p. 152.
15. From an address by Philipson, undated, text in *CCAR Yearbook*.
16. *CCAR Yearbook* 1 (1890): 87–88.
17. Ibid., pp. 109–110.
18. Ibid. 3 (1892): 93.
19. Ibid. 2 (1891): 25–26.
20. Ibid., p. 26.
21. *American Israelite*, July 24, 1890, p. 7.
22. *CCAR Yearbook* 2 (1891): 54.
23. Ibid., p. 62.
24. Ibid. 1 (1890): 118.
25. Undated address in American Jewish Archives.
26. For further data, see David Polish, *Renew Our Days: The Zionist Issue in Reform Judaism* (Jerusalem: World Zionist Organization, 1976).
27. Wise to Herzl, November 28, 1899, in ibid., p. 121.
28. Ibid.
29. Ibid.

30. Ibid., in Morris Lazaron Papers, American Jewish Archives, Cincinnati (hereafter cited as MLP).

31. Stephen Wise to Lazaron, January 25, 1915, MLP.

32. Ibid.

33. Max Margolis to Max Heller (?), January 18, 1916. Max Heller Papers, American Jewish Archives (hereafter cited as MHP).

34. M. Margolis to M. Heller (?), April 26, 1907, MHP.

35. M. Margolis to M. Heller, April 19, 1907, MHP.

36. M. Margolis to M. Heller, May 4, 1907, MHP.

37. M. Margolis to M. Heller, July 24, 1907, MHP.

38. Michael Meyer, *Hebrew Union College–Jewish Institute of Religion at One Hundred Years* (Cincinnati: HUC Press, 1976), p. 66.

39. Judah Magnes to M. Heller, April 30, 1907, MHP.

40. J. Magnes to M. Heller, January 4, 1908, MHP.

41. J. Magnes to M. Heller, March 2, 1911, MHP.

42. Kaufmann Kohler to M. Heller, March 16, 1915, MHP.

43. Stenographic record of American Council for Judaism meeting, Atlantic City, N. J., June 1–2, 1942, American Council for Judaism Papers, American Jewish Archives (hereafter cited as ACJP).

44. *CCAR Yearbook* 1 (1890): 14–15.

45. Ibid. 27 (1917): 201–202.

46. Ibid. 27 (1917): 22, 29, 78, 133 ff., 195.

47. Polish, *Renew Our Days*, pp. 61–62.

48. Ibid. See also Howard R. Greenstein, *Turning Point: Zionism and Reform Judaism* (Chico, Calif. Scholars Press, 1981).

49. *CCAR Yearbook* 16 (1906).

50. Ibid. 31 (1921).

51. Ibid. 34 (1924).

52. Ibid., p. 136.

53. Ibid., p. 54. *CCAR Yearbook* 38 (1928): 140.

54. *CCAR Yearbook* 38 (1928): 140.

55. Ibid., p. 37 (1927). Cited in *CCAR Yearbook* Index, 1, p. 159.

56. Ibid. 49 (1939): 32.

57. Ibid. 36 (1926): 320.

58. Emma Felsenthal, *Teacher in Israel* (New York, 1924), p. 212.

59. *HUC Monthly*, June 1931, p. 5.

60. *B'Netivay ha-Bricha*, vol. 2 ([n.p.]: Tzva Haganah l'Yisrael, 1958), pp. 456–457. See also Thomas Liebschutz, "Rabbi Philip S. Bernstein and the Jewish Displaced Persons" (rabbinic thesis, Hebrew Union College–Jewish Institute of Religion, Cincinnati, 1965).

61. The American Jewish Archives possesses a good collection on the activities of the American Council for Judaism, as does the Wisconsin Jewish Archives in Madison.

62. *CCAR Yearbook* 5 (1941).

63. Ibid. 52 (1942).

64. Ibid.

65. Address by Rabbi Louis Wolsey to the American Council for Judaism, Cincinnati, May 18, 1944, ACJP.

66. Morris Lazaron to Max Heller, May 13, 1942, MLP.

67. Lazaron to Solomon Freehof, May 14, 1942, MLP.

68. Solomon Freehof to Louis Wolsey, May 14, 1942, MLP.

69. The date of the meeting is unknown; it probably took place in March 1942, ACJP.

70. From minutes of the meeting, undated, probably March, ACJP.

71. Ibid.

72. Abba Hillel Silver, "Israel," files of American Jewish Archives.

73. (?) 1942 Minutes, ACJP.

74. April 6, 1942 Minutes, ACJP.

75. April 30, 1942 Minutes, ACJP.

76. Isaac E. Marcuson, Executive Secretary of the CCAR, to (?), May 24, 1942.

77. Abraham Cronbach, May 4, 1942 Minutes, ACJP.

78. Minutes of Atlantic City meeting, ACJP.

79. Julian Morgenstern, Minutes, Atlantic City meeting, ACJP.

80. Minutes, Atlantic City meeting, ACJP.

81. Stenographic report, ACJP, pp. 172–173. See also the forthcoming dissertation on the American Council for Judaism by Thomas Kolsky of George Washington University.

82. Minutes, November 2, 1942, p. 4, ACJP.

83. (Undated), ACJP.

84. Minutes, December 7, 1943 meeting, ACJP.

85. Morris Lazaron to Elmer Berger, June 11, 1942, MLP.

86. M. Lazaron to E. Berger, June 24, 1942, MLP.

87. M. Lazaron to E. Berger, June 26, 1942, MLP.

88. E. Berger to M. Lazaron, June 30, 1942, MLP.

89. M. Lazaron to E. Berger, July 7, 1942, MLP.

90. M. Lazaron to J. Magnes, September 7, 1942, MLP.

91. J. Magnes to M. Lazaron, October 6, 1942, MLP.

92. M. Lazaron to J. Magnes, January 15, 1943, MLP.

93. Louis Wolsey to M. Heller, February 4, 1943, ACJP.

94. James Heller to the members of the CCAR, January 11, 1943, ACJP.

95. Samuel Wohl to CCAR membership, ACJP.

96. M. Lazaron to J. Magnes, January 15, 1943, MLP.

97. Report by Elmer Berger, January 18, 1943, ACJP.

98. *CCAR Yearbook* 53 (1943): 36.

99. Ibid., p. 92.

100. Ibid., pp. 93–94.

101. Malcolm H. Stern to David Polish, May 19, 1982, in possession of author.

102. *Congress Weekly*, March 19, 1943.

103. *American Israelite*, January 7, 1946.

104. Louis Wolsey to Lessing Rosenwald, April 2, 1946, Louis Wolsey Papers, American Jewish Archives (hereafter referred to as LWP).

105. L. Wolsey to Hyman Schachtel, December 16, 1946, LWP.

106. L. Wolsey to H. Schachtel, January 6, 1947, LWP.

107. Louis Wolsey to (?), October 13, 1947, LWP.

108. Louis Wolsey to American Council for Judaism, May 3, 1948, LWP.

109. James Heller to Louis Wolsey, June 8, 1948, LWP.

110. S. Wise to M. Lazaron, April 15, 1915, MLP.

111. M. Lazaron to Federation of American Zionists, October 13, 1916, MLP.

112. S. Wise to M. Lazaron, April 3, 1917, MLP.

113. Henrietta Szold to M. Lazaron, undated, MLP.

114. Simon J. Levin to M. Lazaron, June 12, 1924, MLP.

115. M. Lazaron to Gustav Lichtenfels, Asheville, N. C., December 18, 1924, MLP.

116. M. Lazaron to Simon J. Levin, Baltimore, December 24, 1924, MLP.

117. Emanuel Neumann to M. Lazaron, February 4, 1925, MLP.

118. M. Lazaron to Louis Lipsky, May 27–28, 1925, MLP.

119. James Heller to M. Lazaron, April 13, 1928, MLP.

120. M. Lazaron to Stephen Wise, May 15, 1928, MLP.

121. L. Lipsky to M. Lazaron, May 29, 1928, MLP.

122. M. Lazaron to S. Wise, November 29, 1934, MLP.

123. M. Lazaron to Robert Szold, November 16 and 20, 1921, MLP.

124. Memorandum by M. Lazaron, November 1935, MLP.

125. M. Lazaron to Morris Rothenberg, June 18, 1936, MLP.

126. M. Lazaron to Dr. Louis L. Kaplan, May 18, 1939, MLP.

127. M. Lazaron to Abba Hillel Silver, November 30, 1939, MLP.

128. A. H. Silver to M. Lazaron, undated, MLP.

129. M. Lazaron memo (?) 1940, MLP. For a comprehensive view of Lazaron's rabbinic and political activities, see the forthcoming senior rabbinic thesis by Scott Shpeen at the Hebrew Union College–Jewish Institute of Religion, Cincinnati.

130. *The American Jewish Conference* (New York, 1944), p. 45.

131. Ibid., p. 322.

132. Ibid., pp. 345–370.

133. Ibid., p. 287.

134. *CCAR Yearbook* 28 (1918): 101–102.

135. Ibid. 66 (1956): 117.

136. Ibid. 19 (1909): 164, 210.

137. Ibid. 23 (1913): 120, 133.

138. Ibid. 26 (1915–16): 157.

139. Ibid.

140. Ibid.

141. Ibid.

142. Ibid. 28 (1918).

143. Charles Beard, *The Rise of American Civilization* (New York, 1930), vol. 2, p. 670.

144. *CCAR Yearbook* 30 (1920): 101.

145. Ibid. 28 (1918): 102.

146. Ibid. 30 (1920).

147. Ibid. 32 (1922).

148. Ibid. 34 (1924).

149. Ibid. 37 (1927), cited in *CCAR Yearbook* Index, 1, 153.

150. Ibid. 37 (1927).

151. Ibid.

152. Ibid. 38 (1928).

153. Rabbi Samuel Schulman to Rabbi Edward Israel, in Edward Israel Papers, American Jewish Archives.

154. Leonard Mervis, "The Social Justice Movement and the American Reform Rabbi," *American Jewish Archives* (June 1955): 222–223.

155. *CCAR Yearbook* 39 (1929).

156. Ibid. 41 (1931): 88.

157. Ibid.

158. Ibid., p. 89.

159. Ibid.

160. Ibid. 43 (1933): 58.

161. Ibid., p. 61.

162. Ibid. 34 (1924): 97–98.

163. Ibid., p. 99.

164. Ibid., p. 102

165. Ibid.

166. Ibid., pp. 103–104.

167. Ibid., p. 105.

168. Ibid. 70 (1960): 67.

169. Ibid., p. 122.

170. Ibid. 41 (1931): 76.

171. Ibid. 45 (1935): 57–76

172. Ibid. 42 (1932): 106–111.

173. Ibid. 72 (1962): 78.

174. Ibid., p. 77.

175. Ibid. 74 (1964): 83–85.

176. Ibid., p. 85.

177. Ibid. 43 (1933): 60.

178. Ibid.

179. Ibid. 66 (1956): 117.

180. Ibid. 68 (1958): 99.

181. Ibid. 69 (1959): 93.

182. Ibid. 70 (1960): 67.

183. Ibid. 45 (1935): 73, 76.

184. Beard, pp. 209–210.

185. Robert T. Handy, *The Social Gospel in America, 1870–1920* (Oxford University Press, 1966), p. 11. See also Mark Cowett, "Rabbi Morris Newfield and the Social Gospel: Theology and Societal Reform in the South," *American Jewish Archives* 34 (1982): 52–74.

186. Walter Rauschenbusch, *A Theology for the Social Gospel* (New York, 1917), pp. 131–145.

187. Stephen J. Whitfield, *Scott Nearing: Apostle of American Radicalism* (New York: Columbia University Press, 1974), pp. 82, 87.

188. Ibid., p. 92.

189. Ibid., p. 116.

190. S. Wise to M. Lazaron, March 10, 1924, MLP.

191. Preliminary work draft for the Rabbinic Training Committee.

192. Levi Olan to Louis H. Silberman, November 12, 1968, CCAR Papers at the American Jewish Archives (hereafter cited as CCARP).

193. Report of the Committee on Rabbinic Training, CCARP.

194. See Theodore I. Lenn and associates, *Rabbi and Synagogue in Reform Judaism* (New York: Central Conference of American Rabbis, 1972).

195. Report of the Committee on Rabbinic Training, November 1968, CCARP.

196. Ibid.

197. Report of Committee Chairman to the Executive Board of the CCAR, CCARP.

198. Undated memorandum in CCARP.

199. Undated memorandum in CCARP.

200. Committee resolution of December 21, 1972, CCARP.

201. Report of Richard H. Scheuer to Hebrew Union College–Jewish Institute of Religion Board of Governors, May 8, 1968, Board of Governors Minutes, Hebrew Union College–Jewish Institute of Religion Papers, American Jewish Archives, Cincinnati.

202. David Philipson address, May 27, 1934, in David Philipson Papers, American Jewish Archives, Cincinnati.

203. Memorandum by Rabbi Levi Olan (1972), CCARP.

204. Cited in David Philipson, *The Reform Movement in Judaism* (New York, 1967), p. 510.

205. Ibid., pp. 389–392.

206. Ibid.

207. Ibid., pp. 333–334.

208. Ibid., p. 458.

209. Ibid., p. 459.

210. Lenn et al., *Rabbi and Synagogue in Reform Judaism,* passim.

211. CCAR Yearbook 52 (1942): 123–124.

212. Ibid. 32 (1922): 50–51.

213. Ibid., pp. 156–157.

214. Ibid. 15 (1905): 176.

215. Ibid. 27 (1917): 139.

216. Ibid. 19 (1909), as cited in CCAR Yearbook Index, 1, p. 115.

217. Ibid. 83 (1973): 97.

218. Ibid. 2 (1891): 99.

219. Ibid. 27 (1917): 134.

220. *Centennial Perspective of the Central Conference of American Rabbis* (New York, 1976), pp. 2 ff.

Index